The New Guardians

The New Guardians

POLICING IN AMERICA'S COMMUNITIES FOR THE 21st CENTURY

Dr. Cedric L. Alexander

With a Foreword by
Charles H. Ramsey
Former Commissioner, Philadelphia Police Department
Co-Chair, President's Task Force on 21st Century Policing

ISBN: 1532797451
ISBN 13: 9781532797453

Table of Contents

Foreword

I first saw Dr. Cedric Alexander on CNN discussing the aftermath of the shooting death of Michael Brown in Ferguson Missouri. I was immediately impressed with his grasp of the growing discontent toward police in many African-American communities and by the depth and breadth of his expertise in policing. Unlike many of the commentators and "subject-matter experts" who appear on cable news programs, he brought necessary and badly needed balance to the discussion.

In late 2014, the White House called me to ask if I would co-chair the President's Task Force on 21st Century Policing. I immediately asked Cedric to become a member of the team we were assembling. As I expected he would, Cedric brought to our deliberations the same level of insight and perspective I had seen in his CNN commentaries.

As I see it, *Dr.* Alexander enriches the discussion concerning the myriad challenges facing policing today because he possesses a depth of knowledge in both law enforcement and clinical psychology. I happen to be married to a psychologist, and I have come to appreciate her viewpoint when we discuss a variety of contemporary issues.

Now Dr. Cedric Alexander brings his unique depth of knowledge to this book, *The New Guardians*. He takes the reader inside his own journey through law enforcement, a journey that has taken him to the top of his profession. His odyssey was fraught with obstacles he had to overcome, and that experience has turned him into the leader we see today. His perspective on the current challenges facing policing is a reflection of his entire career—in policing, in psychology, and in policing again. It is an experience that uniquely qualifies him to lead both the police and the communities we serve toward ways of working productively together to solve the many problems our society—our nation, our world—faces today.

I am proud to be associated with Dr. Alexander, and I am honored to introduce his book to you. It is a must-read for us all, in law enforcement and in the communities served by law enforcement.

Charles H. Ramsey

Former Commissioner, Philadelphia Police Department

Co-Chair President's Task Force on 21st Century Policing

Immediate Past President, Major Cities Chiefs Association

Immediate Past President, Police Executive Research Forum

PREFACE

Invaders or Guardians?

L eading the DeKalb County Police Department in the Atlanta metro area is a full-time job and then some, but when I was asked to join The President's Task Force on 21st Century Policing early in 2015—amid a nationwide series of officer-involved shootings, brutality charges, in-custody deaths, and the sometimes violent protests that followed—I knew it was something I needed to do and wanted to do.

I entered law enforcement during the last century, in 1977, as a sworn deputy sheriff in Leon County, Florida, just as American policing was on the brink of many changes. The 1960s and 1970s were an era of profound social transformation, progress, and discontent. Too often and in too many places, America's communities saw the police as a reason for discontent rather than a source of progress. As part of what President Lyndon Johnson called a "War on Crime" in 1965 and President Richard Nixon in 1971called a "War on Drugs," the police in our cities became increasingly militarized. They were equipped and armed with surplus federal military gear. Their policies, attitudes, and tactical training were influenced by Defense Department manuals and mentors. Even the traditional cop-on-the-beat uniforms were often swapped for BDU (battle dress uniform) fatigues all but indistinguishable from those worn by members of the armed forces.

To the extent that the "war" metaphor permeated policing in America, many of our communities—typically, those most challenged—increasingly came to see themselves not as served and protected by the police but held by them under hostile occupation. The police began to look and sometimes behave like invaders rather than guardians, let alone members, of the communities in which they operated. Too often, fear and antagonism gripped both the public and the police. Wars, after all, are about fighting, taking sides, and winning victory by inflicting defeat. Wars are not about achieving common goals for the common good. Armies break things and kill people. The police are supposed to help to heal and build.

There was never a time in which we as police or we as communities could afford to be at war with one another. A state of perpetual combat was a corrosively dysfunctional model of police-community/community-police relations in the 20th century. In the 21st, its effects are even more devastating and dangerous. Far more.

If *war* was once a metaphor to describe life for police officers and citizens in all too many of our neighborhoods, *war* is today a literal reality. War, very real war, has in fact come to our most challenged communities. The terrorist onslaught of September 11, 2001, was the Pearl Harbor of this war. Since then—for the most part—our enemies have largely shifted from the weapons and tactics of highly and horrifically visible mass destruction to those of internal desolation, aimed at capturing the hearts and minds of disaffected, marginalized individuals. It is a war terrorist groups such as al-Qaeda and ISIS wage one person at a time, one after the other. Disaffected, marginalized, hopeless, these are our fellow citizens, our neighbors, typically young, our children, youth who no longer feel a connection with—much less a stake in and allegiance to—their community and nation.

Until the December 2, 2015 attack on a San Bernardino (California) public health facility, in which fourteen were killed and 24 injured (including two police officers), the outward, violently lethal effects of this hearts-and-minds war was felt mainly in Europe. The January 7, 2015 assault on the offices of the Paris-based satirical magazine *Charlie Hebdo* (twelve killed, eleven injured) and the attack on a kosher market in that city and the attacks in that city during November 13 and 14, 2015 (in which 130 were killed and 368 injured) were, for example, the work of "radicalized" youth living in Paris but never embraced by the community, let alone integrated into it. It was this spiritual and intellectual vacuum that "foreign" terrorists rushed to invade and fill. Using the premier technology of our time, the Internet, and the most pervasive application of that technology, social media, ISIS and its ilk reach far beyond their geographical conquests in the Middle East and North Africa to court and conquer the allegiance of those whose proximate communities—whose very nations and neighborhoods—have offered them only alienation in the form of neglect or outright abuse.

What happened in Paris, France, Europe, can happen in (for instance) Garland, Texas, United States of America, where, on May 3, 2015, two ISIS-inspired young men, Elton Simpson and Nadir Soofi, were killed during their heavily armed assault against an arena and conference center hosting an exhibition of cartoon images of Muhammad. Thirty-year-old Simpson was a native of Illinois and grew up in suburban Chicago. Soofi, age thirty-four, was born in Dallas and grew up in Plano, Texas. They, like Syed Rizwan Farook in San Bernardino, were American citizens by birth and upbringing. They are not exceptional. As CNN reported shortly after the Garland attack, FBI director James Comey told a group of police officials from around the country that his agency urgently needed their help.

"It's an extraordinarily difficult challenge task to find—that's the first challenge—and then assess those who may be on a journey from talking to doing," Comey said. "We're working on it every single day, but I can't stand here with any high confidence when I confront the world that is increasingly dark to me and tell you that I've got it all covered. We are working very, very hard on it but it is an enormous task."[1]

Since at least the early 1950s, membership in what were commonly called "youth gangs" has been a subject of great concern, especially in urban America. Hundreds of books and movies as well as academic studies have been devoted to the subject. Most of these have recognized that people, especially young people, have a basic need to belong and to be part of something bigger than themselves. If their community fails to embrace them, to offer them a stake, a compelling motive for identification and allegiance, they *will* seek alternative communities. Today, the aberrant form of Islam we see in ISIS is one such alternative, but, as another Texas outbreak of group violence recently demonstrated, it is hardly the

only alternative. The biker gang shootout at the Twin Peaks restaurant in Waco on May 17, 2015, in which nine died and eighteen were wounded, was a bloody demonstration of the powerful bonds *any* outlaw community can create.

I am director of public safety in a great and diverse metropolitan community that, like every other community in our country, faces formidable economic, social, and political challenges. I want to help my community—and, with it, my country—in the way I am best equipped and positioned to help, by creating and implementing a new dynamic for policing our neighborhoods. I want to help us all to productively reimagine our "wars" on crime, on drugs, and, too often, on one another. I want to create and implement an alternative to post-9/11 paramilitary policing that will build, heal, and advance our diverse democracy in this 21st century, not make it even more vulnerable to corrosive violence from within and without.

I have a degree in sociology and a doctorate in psychology, and I have been a clinician and a university professor. But this is decidedly not a clinical or academic book. I have also been a deputy sheriff, a street cop, a law enforcement executive. This book, therefore, is a vision of 21st century policing from the perspective of a public safety director in the urban South tasked with helping to lead the national conversation on the role of law enforcement in American communities that are at risk from threats both local and—have no doubt—global. In presenting this vision, I must focus first and foremost on what I know best: policing.

My hope and my intention are to move law enforcement beyond its present perceived pervasive military and adversarial model, in which officers are compelled to operate in our communities—and to be perceived by those communities—as agents of a hostile invasion and occupation. The "new" alternative I offer is, in fact, as old as Plato and his *Republic.* As that Greek philosopher envisioned them, "the Guardians" were not just defenders and protectors of the Republic, they were also its guides and leaders. The training Plato prescribed for the Guardians would enable this combination of roles. They were to be physically conditioned, made swift and strong. They were to be mentally cultivated, exposed to the best education the community could give them.

The ancient Platonic concept offers a model of the police officer not as a soldier locked in perpetual combat with the community, but as a

Guardian, endowed by the community with the power and authority to heal, protect, build, and generally steward it. A leader and mentor, the Guardian is not a dictator or tyrant, but a servant of his or her neighborhood, city, and nation. I present this old/new model of policing in the awareness that its implementation will require profound cultural shifts not only within law enforcement, but within each of us.

Police as Guardians? In the end, if we are to nurture, improve, strengthen, and, finally, save the nation in which we all live, we must all, police officer and civilian alike, become Guardians.

PART I
A Chief's Story

CHAPTER 1

The Door Opens

Three minutes of a Saturday afternoon, August 9, 2014, in the predominantly black town of Ferguson, St. Louis County, Missouri. At one minute past noon, Ferguson officer Darren Wilson drove his Chevrolet Tahoe police SUV toward Michael Brown and Dorian Johnson, who were walking down the middle of Canfield Drive.

That was the first of the three critical minutes. Leading up to them was a short span of busy time for Wilson. At 11:47, he had driven to Glenark Drive, just east of Canfield, in response to a call that a baby was having problems breathing. While Wilson rendered aid, some blocks away, at the Ferguson Market, a security camera recorded Brown—six-foot-four, nearly 300 pounds—stealing a box of Swisher cigars and then shoving aside a clerk. At 11:53, a police dispatcher put out the call of a "stealing in progress" at the market. At almost precisely this moment, Brown and Johnson left the market. At 11:58, police dispatch broadcast a description of the "suspect": black male, red Cardinals cap, white T-shirt, yellow socks, khaki shorts, accompanied by another black male. Two minutes after this broadcast, at noon sharp, Wilson radioed that he was back in service after the Glenark Drive call and asked if units 25 and 22 needed assistance in searching for the shoplifting suspects. A minute later, 12:01, he was driving up on Brown and Johnson. At 12:02, he radioed for backup: "21. Put me on Canfield with two. And send me another car."[2]

What happened in the last of the three minutes, 12:03, depends on who tells the story. There are more than a few stories. They all end the

3

same way, however. Michael Brown was shot dead by Darren Wilson, one of 50 white officers in a force of 53 sworn members.

The narrative pieced together from various witness statements and Wilson's own account[3] is that the SUV drove up to the young men, Wilson ordered them off the street and onto the sidewalk, and then drove on a short way before backing up and stopping close to the pair, who were still in the street. A struggle ensued between Brown and Wilson. Wilson was seated in his SUV, and Brown, standing outside, reached through the driver's window. During this interaction, the officer's gun discharged twice from inside the vehicle. Officer Wilson later said that Brown was trying to wrest his gun from him.

One bullet struck Brown's right hand. At this point, he backed off and, with Dorian Johnson, fled. Wilson got out of his SUV and pursued them on foot. In the course of the pursuit, Wilson fired repeatedly, hitting Brown, who was unarmed, six times.

As Michael Brown lay dead in the middle of the street, another Ferguson officer arrived, a supervisor was requested, additional units were dispatched, and the Ferguson dispatcher also asked the St. Louis County police for aid. By 1 p.m., twelve units were gathered at the scene. County detectives arrived by 1:30, and, an hour later, a forensic investigator showed up. Shortly after 2 p.m., gunshots were reported, and additional units were summoned. Soon, there were twenty in all, from eight different local forces.

As a crowd gathered and rapidly grew in size, the police ordered investigative personnel to take cover, and canine units were brought in for crowd control. A SWAT team arrived at 3:20. Ten minutes later, supervisors on scene decided that the dogs and SWAT provided sufficient crowd control for the medical examiner to begin an examination of Brown's body at the scene. By 4 p.m., the ME cleared the body for transportation to the morgue. The remains of the eighteen-year-old had lain in the street for four hours.

By evening, some residents had transformed the site of Brown's death into an impromptu shrine with candles and flowers. It was reported that a canine officer allowed his dog to urinate on this memorial. Later, police vehicles ran it over.

Police-community tensions increased, and although August 10 began with peaceful demonstrations, some of those present became increasingly loud and unruly. Police responded by mustering about 150 officers—well over twice the strength of the entire Ferguson PD—in full riot gear. A riot followed their arrival: looting, vandalizing of cars, arson, hostile and sometimes violent confrontations with officers. This carried over to the next day and night, August 11, as police used tear gas and fired rubber bullets at protestors. They, in turn, hurled rocks at the police. The officers added bean bag rounds to their arsenal, but the unrest continued through August 12 and 13. The police now deployed smoke bombs, flash grenades, rubber bullets, and tear gas. Protestors threw rocks and other projectiles, Molotov cocktails among them.

Despite a heavy-handed attempt to curb coverage by arresting journalists, video was broadcast throughout the 24-hour news cycle. In April 2013, I was hired as chief of police of metro Atlanta DeKalb County and, since December of that year, served as public safety director. Like so many other Americans, I watched the chaotic events unfold on television, a flat screen flickering on my office wall. Amid the video blur, what stood out sharply for me was CNN footage of an officer in riot gear calling to the crowd: "Bring it, you fucking animals, bring it."[4]

I recognized the line. It was the all-too-familiar script of a police force and a community at war with one another.

A month before the shooting of Michael Brown, I had been elected president of NOBLE—the National Organization of Black Law Enforcement Executives—and, in August, I was still early in the process of defining myself in this new role. Headquartered in Washington, DC, NOBLE is the preeminent membership group of black law enforcement CEOs and command-level officials, with fifty-seven chapters throughout the United States in addition to one in St. Kitts and Nevis and one in the UK. It was founded in 1976 during a symposium that discussed crime in black urban communities, the socioeconomic background of crime and violence, fairness in the administration of justice, issues in police/community relations, fairness in the hiring and promotion of black police officers and administrators, and many of the unique problems faced by black police executives and officers alike.

As I watched from my desk in Georgia the sad and searing events in Ferguson, I thought about NOBLE's stated mission: to "ensure EQUITY IN THE ADMINISTRATION OF JUSTICE in the provision of public service to all communities, and to serve as the conscience of law enforcement by being committed to JUSTICE BY ACTION."[5]

Justice by action. What action could I possibly take, sitting some 550 miles to the southeast of the troubled St. Louis suburb?

I knew that nobody, not in DeKalb County, not in Ferguson, not in the rest of the country, would benefit from a southern black police executive grandstanding in a distant jurisdiction. Nor did I want to go up there, as a representative of NOBLE, merely to criticize or condemn. My professional background combines policing (I had been a deputy sheriff, an urban police officer, and a police chief) with psychology (I hold a doctorate and have practiced clinically). My special passion in law enforcement has long been community policing, creating positive collaborative relationships between communities and law enforcement. My years in community-oriented policing and my training and practice in psychology taught me to join with others, to help rather than raise hell and rain down condemnation. It taught me to solve problems by providing support that builds relationships and trust.

So, with the television images flashing on the wall in front of me, I muted the audio, picked up the phone, and called one of my colleagues at NOBLE, who put me in touch with the president of our organization's St. Louis chapter. I asked him to arrange a call between me and Tom Jackson, the now-beleaguered chief of the small Ferguson PD. To my surprise, Chief Jackson was eager to talk. I introduced myself and explained that what was happening in Ferguson was a national issue that NOBLE needed to get involved in.

"I'd like to come up to meet with you, Chief, to see what NOBLE as an organization can do to help you."

At that hour, at that moment, it was what he most needed to hear: the voice of someone who wanted to help him. I flew up to Missouri. News crews from Atlanta's ABC and Fox affiliates followed me to Ferguson, and CNN was already on the ground there. The local media tracked me all weekend, but my main objective was to meet with Chief Jackson. After I did, I asked him to arrange for us, together, to meet with members of the

Ferguson community—clergy, community organizers, African American business people. He acted swiftly, and we assembled in a local church. Chief Jackson was highly receptive to the people we met with, but I believe it was the very first time he had gotten together in this way with leaders and representatives of the community he served.

Over that weekend, I did what I had been trained to do and what I always tried to do. I built and brokered relationships. When I returned to my desk at DeKalb County, I was changed. I was no longer only a local police administrator. I had now entered the national conversation on police, community, justice—and on justice by action. There would be no turning back.

. . .

My entrance onto the national stage may have been sparked by the events of just three terrible minutes in a St. Louis suburb, but, for me, Ferguson was also a stopover in a long journey, which began thirty-eight years earlier at a sheriff's office in the panhandle of Florida.

The Leon County Court House in Tallahassee was a two-story building with a central doorway flanked by four flat fake Doric columns and topped by a clock just below a big hurricane siren. The building shone dazzling white in the Florida sun. I walked through that doorway to see Sheriff Raymond Hamlin. It was 1976, but "Sheriff Raymond" had a reputation for policing like it was 1956. Folks called him a "good ol' boy" and a lot worse. None of it seemed to bother him, and he did nothing to deflect the epithets. Matter of fact, he was a self-styled "redneck," locally famous (as I vividly recall) for once proclaiming to a reporter, "I like my women the same way I like my coffee. White and hot."

I had dropped out of FAMU, Florida Agricultural & Mechanical University, because my wife was pregnant and I was determined to support her and our baby and make sure at least one of us—namely, she—finished college. My ambition was to get into law enforcement on the federal level, maybe the FBI, but I had no idea how to even apply. I mean, it was not like you could go online in the mid-1970s and email an application. I knew the FBI had a local office in Tallahassee, and, one day, I worked up the courage to drop in. It was an ordinary office in a bank building. A couple of men in suits and ties met—"intercepted" is the better word—me as I opened the door and walked in. Maybe they were agents. I never knew, because they didn't introduce themselves.

"Can we help you?"

Not knowing what else to say, I just blurted out what came into my head: "How do you apply for this gig?"

"Do you have police experience?" one of them asked politely. "The Director is looking for candidates with police experience—and you do also need four years of college."

As for meeting requirements, that put me at exactly 0 for 2, so I thanked them for their time (which was less than a minute) and left. Some days later, I walked into Florida Highway Patrol headquarters, also in Tallahassee. I followed a sign that said the headquarters was up some stairs. As I was landing on the second floor, two big white guys approached me. They looked sharp, shirts pressed, ties crisply tied, uniforms immaculate.

"Can we help you, son?"

"I wanna sign up to be a state trooper."

The response was more direct than that of the FBI guy. "Son," one of the troopers said, "whyn't you find yourself somethin' else to do?"

I was twenty, scrawny, and a college dropout in off the street. Plenty of reason for both the FBI and the state not to give me the time of day. I was also black at a time when the FBI was, let's just say, not actively recruiting agents of color. As for the Florida Highway Patrol, it had only one or two black troopers throughout the entire state at the time.

After these initial assaults on the outer perimeter of law enforcement, I did some poking around and found that you didn't need four years of college to join a local force in Florida—just a hundred bucks to pay the police academy fee and the signature of a chief law enforcement officer from anywhere in the state. I'd gotten married in December 1975. My wife became pregnant early the following year, and my daughter was born in January 1977. My father in law, a preacher, owned a little house he let us live in, and I put together one odd job after another, scrambling to make ends meet. I woke up one morning contemplating another day flipping burgers at Burger King when it suddenly occurred to me to just try to become a deputy sheriff.

Scraping together a spare $100 from the sorry money I was pulling down would be hard enough, but getting the needed signature seemed downright daunting. I could have gone to the chief of the Tallahassee PD, but word was that he "had his quota" of black officers at present. Another option was the chief of the FAMU campus police department. FAMU was a historically black university, and its small PD was staffed and led by African Americans exclusively. I made an appointment with him, he saw me, and I asked him for his signature.

"No, Alexander. You see, I remember you, and you ain't been the most stellar student around here in your freshman year."

Truthfully, I couldn't argue with that. Back when I was seventeen, I was a very immature seventeen, and I often acted out of my immaturity. I wasn't exactly John Dillinger, either, and, as I saw it and still see it, that FAMU chief was just being a jerk, a mean-spirited jerk. Apparently, I wasn't the only one who thought so. The chief never rose from behind his desk. As I looked down at him, I caught a glimpse of his lieutenant rolling his eyes and shaking his head. Clearly, he knew his boss had no good reason not to sign for me, except pure orneriness, I guess. All I could do was say "Okay," write him off in my mind, and go out the same door by which I had entered.

Now I had just two options left, neither of them remotely promising. Because the Tallahassee city department had its African American quota, I was sure I wouldn't get hired there. But I didn't need a job, at least not directly. I just needed a signature. The problem was that the city chief had the reputation of being an even bigger bigot than the Leon County sheriff was. He certainly would not feel that he owed me any favors. So I decided to try the man I judged to be at least marginally the lesser of two evils, Sheriff Raymond Hamlin. I would give *him* the honor of turning me down before I presented myself to the city chief for rejection. Such was the fairly hopeless state of my mind as I walked through the doors between the phony columns and beneath the real clock.

I had called ahead, talked to the sheriff's secretary, and made an appointment. The day came, and I found myself waiting in the man's outer office, dressed like the typical college kid of the era, jean jacket, jeans, skull cap. I meant no disrespect, but I didn't have the faintest idea of how to dress for an interview. It was, in fact, the same set of clothes that had gotten me nowhere with both the FBI and the highway patrol, and so I should have known better. After what seemed a long, long time, Hamlin's secretary came out.

"The sheriff will see you now," she said without a trace of emotion, let alone sympathy.

From the office doorway in which I stood, "Sheriff Raymond" looked just the way I'd seen him in the papers: clad in a shapeless suit, thin lips clamped down on a short, small, cheap cigar, natty Dobbs straw hat on the hat rack in the corner, his trademark banded candy cane-style cane slung below it.

With maybe three black detectives and two black deputies already in the department, I knew that he, like the city chief, had already "met his quota." So I didn't dare *hope* for a job. But all I *needed* was a signature. What I *expected* from him was I don't know what manner of abuse, but I did not expect a real interview, let alone that signature. Still, I had nothing to lose.

Nothing to lose was in fact what I had told myself over and over just to work up the courage to walk into that white court house—the whitest building I had ever seen, painted white, and then bleached white by the Florida sun. *Nothing to lose*, I had said to myself as I passed through that door between the columns and under the clock, and I kept on saying it until I found myself in the doorway of the sheriff's inner office. Standing there, I was not so much looking at him as looking through him, to the knotty-pine paneled wall behind the big brown schoolteacher desk at which he sat.

"Come on in," he said, looking up from the desk, eyeing me, "and have a seat."

He did not get up. I had not expected him to—not because he was white and I was black, but because he was the sheriff and I was a kid. And as I lowered myself into that old, hard seat, it crossed my mind whether sitting down was even worth the effort. After all, how long could it possibly take for him to say no?

But for the next two maybe three hours, the sheriff never got up from behind his desk, and I never moved from the seat in front of it. The two of us—twenty-one-year-old kid in a skull cap, middle-aged white southern lawman in an old suit—talked about, well, I don't remember what exactly, but I do recall it was pretty much everything under the sun. I mean, it was a genuine conversation, if you define "conversation" as two people actually interested enough in each other to talk on and on.

There was a time—it was a few years before I came to see Sheriff Hamlin, but it was a time under his watch—when white and black deputies did not eat together in the Leon County department. And now, probably more than an hour into our conversation, the sheriff said to me, "Cedric, I can talk to *anybody* about *anything*."

Even then, it struck me as an odd remark, but it also seemed to me a really important one. Thinking back on it today, I don't believe it was a boast or some random declaration. True, Raymond Hamlin was not an educated man—and yet he was sheriff in the state capital, home of FAMU as well as FSU, Florida State University. Maybe he just intended to let me know that he wasn't intimidated by his surroundings, that he could hold his own in a conversation with anybody, from a FAMU dropout to an FSU professor. But I think that "I can talk to *anybody about* anything" was an expression of pure discovery. I don't know whether he had decided to sign or not to sign for me when I first sat down in his office, but I doubt he ever expected to talk with me for two, maybe even three hours.

But that's what he did. We just kept going, and while the details of the conversation have vanished with time, I do remember that, for all the embarrassing and outrageous things he had said in public and out loud over the years, what I heard now was the conversation of a man of tremendous common sense, honest, real, and respectful. Did he sound better educated than he was? Far from it. But there was a life of experience in every word he uttered. He wasn't mouthing off to a faceless public about women "white and hot." He was speaking *with* me, one-on-one and face-to-face. We had something to say to one another.

I admit that I recall *feeling* that I should *not* be impressed by this guy. He might not have been the enemy, exactly, but he was far from being a friend. And yet I was impressed, very, and my feeling remains the same today.

At last, both he and I were talked out. Sheriff Hamlin patted his chest a couple of time with his palms.

"Cedric," he wrapped up, "I am not going to hire you ... but I *am* going to sign for you—get you into the academy."

"Well, that's all I ask, Sheriff." The fact is that I had been so engrossed in the conversation that I'd very nearly forgotten what I had come for.

He held out his right hand and motioned for my papers. Next, he opened the middle drawer of his desk and fished out from it a Bic pen. Through its clear plastic shaft I could clearly see that the ink was green. In the state of Florida, I believe that green is the official color of all county sheriff's offices, and in that official green ink, he signed my application to the academy. With that, he pushed the signed papers back toward me, stood up, clamped down harder on his stubby cigar, and extended his hand across the desk. I rose, took his hand, we shook, I left, and I never saw him again.

So, no, we did not become best buddies, he and I. But I'm a top police administrator today—after nearly four decades in law enforcement, an earned doctorate in psychology, presidency of NOBLE (National Organization of Black Law Enforcement Executives), member of the International Association of Chiefs of Police, and an appointee to President Obama's 21st Century Policing Task Force—because of Sheriff Raymond Hamlin. He opened the door, not just onto a career, but onto the revelation at the very heart of this book: How someone can appear to be everything you deplore and resent, how he can even present himself as that stereotype, the very caricature of a bigot, and *still* make a connection, both human and professional, and *still* do the right thing, person to person, one individual to another.

Whatever else he did for me that day—and just by signing his name in green ink, he did everything—Sheriff Raymond Hamlin taught me that people are just people, and most people have a surprisingly powerful and resilient need to do the right thing, especially if you give them a good reason to.

■ ■ ■

My father and mother were both educators, my father a high school teacher and a college instructor who lived in Mobile, Alabama, after my parents divorced in 1960, my mother a schoolteacher. They had met about 1952 in Montgomery, at Alabama State University, where they were both students. My father, one in a family of six children from Mobile, had started there in

1948 and stayed two years until he was drafted into the army during the Korean War. When he got home in 1952, he returned to college and met my mother, who was a freshman from Pensacola. They got married right away, very young, I was born in 1954, and their marriage ended in divorce when *I* was still a baby. In Mobile, I spent a lot of time early in life with my dad's grandparents, who showed me all the love in the world. My mother remarried not long after her divorce. My stepdad was from Chicago, an Air Force guy based out of Eglin AFB, near Fort Walton, Florida. Mom, who had graduated from college, taught school in Pensacola. Except for a year or so in Chicago, my mother, stepfather, and I lived in Pensacola. That is where I did most of the rest of my growing up—though I also went back and forth to my father in Mobile. There he had also remarried and, with his second wife, had two more children.

I admired my mother's intellect and her dedication to teaching, but I was in positive awe of my father's facility with the most abstruse mathematics and physics. He was a very popular teacher, charismatic, brilliant. My mother used to flatter me by saying I was *just like* my dad, but I knew I wasn't half as smart. He had a Master's degree from Tuskegee in math and physics, and in the mid-1960s, he began working on a PhD. His studies took him to various colleges and universities during the summer months, when he wasn't teaching in Mobile. All his credits accrued at the graduate school of the University of Texas, Austin, where his mentor, who was funded by the National Science Foundation, was based. It was hard work, which I deeply admired, and a great life for him until his mentor died, my father's access to funding dried up, and his health began to decline. He struggled valiantly to complete his doctorate, but was never able to, and he succumbed to pancreatic cancer in 1999. My mother and stepdad mostly raised me. Like her, he was loving and supportive while also being a strong disciplinarian. I also became very close to my father back in Mobile, especially as the end approached.

My high school education, in Pensacola, spanned 1969 to 1972 and included Navy ROTC—Pensacola having earned the title of "Cradle of Naval Aviation" as the home of the first naval air station commissioned in the U.S., back in 1914, and, to this day, the home base of the celebrated Blue Angels flight exhibition team. The military life appealed to me, especially the prospect of action and the climate of crisis. These really got my blood moving. Still does, I have to admit. But faced with the decision of whether to enlist directly in the Marines straight out of high school in 1972 or go on to college, I chose more education.

Florida A&M—universally known as FAMU—offered Navy ROTC when I enrolled there in 1972, but all my friends, high school classmates who had chosen FAMU, joined the Army ROTC. Maybe it's a measure of my immaturity at seventeen that I followed my homeboys and signed up with the Army, not the Navy, ROTC. In any event, I didn't stay with it very long. Away from home for the first time in my seventeen years, I was feeling my oats, going to parties, pledging fraternities, and generally being what even I thought of as a bad boy while attending class more or less on the side. I was in no mood be told what to do and where to go. If I wasn't serious about ROTC, well, I wasn't really all that serious about life. Acquiring that degree of maturity would take a few years—not to mention getting married young, very young, just like my parents.

And then becoming a father. *That* was the dose of reality that really kick-started my adulthood. The rewards were great but the responsibilities awesome and sometimes even painful. I didn't want to drop out of FAMU. Three years into it, I was just beginning to get serious about it. I had discovered sociology and that meant I was learning to ponder how people behaved in society, in groups, in neighborhoods. I hadn't thought it through at the time, but sociology was a logical major for somebody gravitating toward law enforcement. It was a mind opener. And now I had to give that up or at least put it on indefinite hold.

■ ■ ■

Getting my wife through college and making sure she and our coming baby would be fed, clothed, and housed gave me direction, but leaving FAMU for a string of menial catch-as-catch-can jobs also uprooted me. It was a hungry feeling, which, I suppose, made me desperate enough to work up the courage to go to Sheriff Raymond Hamlin that day. Wandering into the FBI and state troopers, I had no idea what I'd encounter. But Hamlin? He was a bigot. Everyone knew he was a bigot. The majority of the people of Leon County must have been just fine with that, since they elected him to office over and over again. The sheriff himself certainly did nothing to counter his redneck image.

But it was thanks to him and our long conversation about "everything under the sun," a talk that ended with an official green signature on a state form, that I went to the police academy. Back then, in 1976, the academy course covered basic state laws, street investigative techniques, vehicle stops, and the essentials of what we today call tactical survival. After eight weeks of this, I emerged from the academy, a freshly minted lawman.

I was excited when I was hired straight out of the academy by the Leon County sheriff's department, in Tallahassee, the town I lived in and really loved. By this time, Raymond Hamlin had been voted out. The community elected a young man who had lost to Sheriff Hamlin in the previous election, W. Ken Katsaris. On paper, he was about as far from Hamlin as you could get. Whereas Hamlin rose through the ranks of law enforcement, Katsaris was light on practical policing experience, but he had something almost unheard of in southern law enforcement at the time—and not all that common elsewhere: academic credentials. He held a Master's degree in criminology from Florida State. Also, where Hamlin had been for better or worse a good ol' boy, Katsaris was a northerner by birth, young, and full of new ideas. Among the most important of these was his eagerness to recruit more African Americans, including for the supervisory ranks. There was an element of politics in this, to be sure, but his primary motive came from his own philosophy of policing: he wanted his force to more closely reflect the demographics of a community that, at the time, was perhaps 20 or 30 percent black. Under Sheriff Hamlin, Leon County had, I recall, three black detectives and two deputies out of a department of maybe 100. Sheriff Katsaris's motive in recruiting more blacks was to help align the values of the department with those of the community. It was an early hint of the emergence of community policing, which, at the time, was barely a blip on law enforcement radar. I should add as well that he also recruited women, who, after all, make up at least half, if not more, of any community!

The contrast with Raymond Hamlin was dramatic—and, for me, revelatory. Now, I'm here to tell you that, against all odds and even appearances,

Raymond Hamlin proved to me that he was a decent man who, given the right circumstances, was prepared to reach out. I'm not going to say that Ken Katsaris's intelligence and academic qualifications were of greater value than Hamlin's common sense and self-professed ability to "talk with *anybody* about *anything*." Both are valuable in law enforcement. But if there was any element of tragedy about Sheriff Hamlin, it was that his upbringing in the culture of the Deep South at mid-century had imposed on him a heavy set of limiting biases. None of us are born with biases. We acquire them—all of us do—some more, some fewer. Generally, the more successful among us learn to recognize our biases and either modify them or overcome them by working around them. The ability to do one, the other, or both of these is indispensable to modern law enforcement. Hamlin proved to me that he *could* overcome. I think, however, he finally failed to prove that to the community, which unmistakably sent a message when it voted for someone new and something fresh. Sheriff Hamlin was, in his way, a highly effective lawman. Unlikely as it may seem, his example has inspired me for nearly forty years now. In the end, however, he became a victim of those biases he could not somehow overcome.

While I bore no malice toward Sheriff Hamlin—on the contrary, I was deeply grateful to him—I was also impressed by the community's apparent elevation of education, of policing enlightened by sound academics, over the good ol' boy system. As impressed as I had been with Hamlin's common sense as well as the fact that he and his deputies were usually quite respectful in the discharge of their duties, under the leadership of Ken Katsaris I began to learn about the possibilities of truly systematic progressive change in law enforcement, including a recognition of the need for and value of diversity and a foretaste of the community policing concept.

Not that becoming a new deputy, especially a black deputy, was an easy ride. Most of the other deputies were men that most people—and by "most people," I don't just mean black people, but other whites *and,* most important, the deputies themselves—would have called "rednecks." They were, most of them, very different from me. What is more, they were of a cultural type or profile that I had been taught to distrust and even fear. Buried deep in the back of my consciousness somewhere were stories I had heard as a boy about one of my uncles getting murdered by

Klansmen, who pushed a load of lumber over on him in the Alabama lumberyard where he worked. A lot of southern black kids of my generation had stories like this, dim and fragmentary, in their background. As I worked side-by-side with these guys, their redneck ways didn't change—they looked the same and they talked the same—but we came to see each other less as racial and cultural stereotypes than as brother officers. In the beginning, many of these men feared and distrusted me as much as I feared and distrusted them. Now, this situation would have prevailed with the introduction of any newbie, regardless of race or ethnicity. Can you rely on him? Will he have your back? Or will he do something stupid that will get you hurt or killed or maybe just fired?

We had to prove ourselves to each other, both they and I. I was determined to do my part, and, given a chance, the great majority of my fellow deputies were down-to-earth decent guys. The first I encountered right after I was hired was Deputy Ary Miller. Sheriff Katsaris called him in and told him, "I want you to take Deputy Alexander around and show him where to buy a gun and gun belt." In those days, the county furnished your uniform and other equipment, but each deputy was responsible for buying—and personally funding!—his or her own gun and gun belt. The upside of this policy was that you could buy whatever kind of weapon you wanted, up to and including a cannon. Most deputies chose .357 magnums—Ary Miller carried a .41 magnum—big, powerful revolvers, which we were required to carry in cross-draw holsters, handle facing forward. I was a scrawny kid at the time, maybe 140, and that gun together with gun belt must have weighed more than I did. Now, the downside of the choose-your-weapon-and-buy-it policy—certainly in my case—was finding the money to pay for it. I had a wife and a baby and my previous employment had been flipping burgers. Ary understood. The first place he took me to, about nine in the morning, was not the gun store, but the local Beneficial Finance office. Ary knew a guy there, introduced me, and told his friend that I had just come to work for the department, had no credit history whatsoever, but was a good young man in need of $400 for a gun and gun belt. The guy behind the desk told us to come back about two o'clock. Ary and I did that, and, sure enough, he had cut me a check for $400, handed it to me, I cashed it, and Ary and I went to the gun store, where I bought my gun belt and a .357. I own the weapon to this day.

Now, my first training officer behaved very differently from Ary Miller. To put it politely, I would describe him as a real piece of … work. Unlike the academy course, there were no formally prescribed guidelines for how a training officer worked with you, and the training period was entirely open-ended. When your TO said you were ready, you were considered ready to go out on your own—but not a moment before he signed off on you. My TO—let's just call him Deputy Zero because, sorry to say, that's pretty much what he amounted to—started out innocuously enough, driving me around, familiarizing me with the patrol area, and then turned the driving over to me. Once that happened, he fell into a routine. I'd drive us around for the first half of the shift, and then he'd order me to "pull over there under that shade tree." He'd hand me a sheaf of papers and tell me to write up all the morning's police reports. So I'd start furiously scribbling while Deputy Zero lay back, closed his eyes, and took a siesta. This was repeated daily, a ritual capped off not with thanks, let alone praise, but a nit-picking critique of every report I wrote. It got old for me pretty quickly. Worst of all, he made no attempt to instruct. He just complained. And he gave me no acknowledgment that I had made any progress. Personally, I don't think he saw any progress in me. He didn't want to.

One evening, we were nearing the end of the three-to-eleven shift we were working. At this point, I hadn't even gotten my uniform yet. I had my gun and gun belt, but I was wearing a suit. At the end of your shift, you always gassed up the car for the next-shift. So we pull into the gas station, and Deputy Zero tells me, "I'm going inside. Just fill up the tank, and I'll be out."

He leaves, and I start filling up the car. The car radio is on, of course, and, all of a sudden, a deputy comes on the air.

"He's got a knife, he's got a knife!" crackles over the speaker. The voice was high-pitched with very real fear. "Officer needs help!"

I can't tell you what overcame me, but something sure kicked in. I jumped in the car and just took off. Didn't even take the gas pump nozzle out of the filler pipe. Just left that nozzle back on the ground—and Deputy Zero inside the gas station.

I was running blue lights and siren, and moving fast, but by the time I got to the call, it was all over and under control. That's when another call came over the radio—the sergeant summoning me to come back to the station.

Talk about a slow ride back. Waiting for me were all these redneck deputies, standing outside as I walked in, their arms folded, their eyes piercing me with distaste and disapproval as I passed by. The sergeant wrote me up, and I thought, Oh, shit. I'm fired. I'm damn sure fired. And before I even got into a uniform.

Well, I was right. They did try to fire me. Sheriff Katsaris called me into his office. Standing there were my lieutenant, a burly white guy named Jack Revell, my sergeant, Bob Smith, a little guy with a close-cut crewcut, tightly built, looking like a Marine drill instructor, and Deputy Zero. I believe that those three men all thought they had been called to participate in my dismissal.

Sheriff Katsaris asked me to tell him what happened. I told him. I made no excuses, but I told him the truth. Then I scanned the faces of the lieutenant, the sergeant, and Deputy Zero in an effort to gauge their sentiments. It wasn't difficult. They all had blood in their eyes, every one of them. They had come for one purpose and one purpose only: to witness an execution.

All Katsaris said was, "You know, one thing I have to say about you, Cedric—you don't mind working." Next, turning to his right-hand man, Chief Deputy Leonard J. Territo (an officer who would go on to write a number of distinguished textbooks on policing and law enforcement subjects) and then back to me, he continued: "We're gonna put you with somebody else."

And that's what the sheriff did. My new training officer, I happened to know, was Jewish. I have no idea if this item of background had entered into Ken Katsaris's mind when he chose him for the job of riding with me. But I can tell you that we clicked immediately, and it doesn't take much imagination to conclude that he was almost as much a stranger in a strange land when it came to serving in a Florida Panhandle sheriff's department as I was. After just two or three days together, he said to me, "Cedric, why are you not out there riding by yourself? You got this down already."

"I don't know," I answered. "Deputy Zero must've just told them I was not ready."

After two weeks riding together—two weeks that were nothing but fun—he told Sheriff Katsaris that I was ready, ready to go. The sheriff put me back on the squad commanded by Lieutenant Revell and Sergeant Smith. Unlike my second TO, who had been hired by Katsaris, Revell and Smith were Hamlin holdovers. They were not bad people. If anything, they were victims of their time, and the fact is that the more we worked together, the more fear turned into confidence and distrust evolved into trust. It was not a profound or complicated transformation. It was just that once we got to know each other, in action—once they knew I could do the job, and I knew they were no longer just out to get me—the fears and distrust evaporated on both sides. Those sentiments simply became unnecessary and therefore vanished.

So I was getting to be a seasoned deputy sheriff, a black deputy on a squad populated by good ol' boys. I was coming in off a shift one night, driving along Pensacola Street, when these three white boys drive up along next to me in a pickup truck. One of them points a shotgun out the window and straight at me. At least, that's what it looked like. On the other hand, I was well aware that just about everybody in Leon County who drove a pickup also had a shotgun or two or more on a rack across the rear window. Those boys might—*might*—have just been moving the shotgun. But I wasn't about to wait for the situation to develop one way or another, so I called it in.

"I'm on Pensacola Street. I've got three white males in a pickup truck with a shotgun," I said into the mike.

Next thing I know, there were blue lights approaching from every direction. Those good ol' boys, off-duty and on, responded to my call—from everywhere. But there was more. It wasn't just squad cars that pulled up. It was also guys in pickups with gun racks and shotguns and little rebel flags either flying from their radio antennas or emblazoned across their back windows. These civilians—who looked *exactly* like the "three white males" who had prompted my call—all had police scanners and spent a lot of time listening to them. They heard the call, and they knew who I was, by which I mean they knew I wasn't a white cop calling for help. And they answered the call of a police officer.

With everybody watching—some of those "rednecks" cradling their shotguns as they looked on—the traffic stop was made, and the "three white males" sheepishly emerged from their pickup, one after the other.

"We were just movin' the gun around is all!" one of them meekly protested.

"What do you want to do with them?" one of the deputies who answered my call asked me.

"Let 'em go," I said. From the looks of it, I could see that my fellow deputies were ready to eat these guys alive.

So there was my lesson in comradery and loyalty, the values of got-your-back solidarity that not only holds every really good police force together, but extends into the community, despite all superficial appearances. The Confederate battle flag was common as common could be throughout the South in the 1970s. Many people—people of color especially—knew what that banner ultimately signified, and that made it a hateful symbol. Although the rebel flag was probably not as deeply resented as it became in the days following the massacre, by a "young white male," of nine members of a Bible study class gathered in Charleston's Emanuel AME Church on the evening of June 17, 2015, a lot of us didn't like it. But on that night years ago in Tallahassee, we all were just people who valued law and order. At the sound of my radio call, all gathered to support one another. I was an officer in need of help—for all anybody knew, maybe in desperate need of getting my life saved—and fellow officers and citizens alike rallied to give me whatever I needed, even with rebel flags waving.

When I got back to the station, old Bob Smith was sitting there.

"I was gonna come," he assured me, "but it looked like everybody else already went!" He was exactly right.

■ ■ ■

What I went through in training and what happened that night of the shotgun were personal experiences. Everybody in law enforcement has them, I suppose. But one experience was more public, of a higher profile.

If the name Theodore Robert Bundy—Ted Bundy—doesn't mean much of anything to you, type it into Wikipedia. You'll find him described as "an American serial killer, kidnapper, rapist, and"—oh, yes—"necrophile." You'll learn that he "assaulted and murdered numerous young women and girls"—nobody knows exactly how many—"during the 1970s and possibly earlier." Nobody knows when the killings started, but, just before he was sent to the electric chair, he himself finally confessed to thirty murders in seven states between 1974 and 1978. Most authorities believe there were more.

He did not look like a serial killer. I saw him, close up, more than a few times. But, then, who "looks like" a serial killer? What I remember is a well-groomed young man, handsome, I guess, with a perpetual smirk, the right side of his mouth always slightly higher than the left. The few women who interacted with him and lived to tell about it called him "charismatic." I understand that he once described himself as "the most cold-hearted son of a bitch you'll ever meet." That seems about right to me. One of the attorneys who defended him at his final trial, in Orlando, later wrote that he "was the very definition of heartless evil."

As I was coming off my shift some time after 3 p.m. on January 14, 1978, I ran into Deputy Willie Reams, who happened to be maybe the last black deputy Raymond Hamlin had hired. I'd met Willie before I became a deputy. I was still working at Burger King plus holding down a job serving dinner at a senior citizen center and living with my wife and baby in a little house owned by my wife's parents. I had met Willie I forget where, but the two of us became friends, and he would stop by that little house from time to time to talk. He would pull that green and white squad car to the curb, keep the motor running, and step out with the radio cranked up loud enough to hear anything that might come in for him. I can't tell you how exciting it was to hear those police calls crackling over the radio. I'm like, *Wow! Wow! This is for me.*

So that afternoon I ran into Willie, he was in a big hurry.

"Willie," I asked him, "where're you goin'?"

"Man, we got a weird call over at Florida State—some guy runnin' around with a baseball bat."

That's the way it came through. It was the end of my shift, and I thought nothing of it, but the next day, it all blew up. I didn't witness any of it, but you can look it up. Read about it. How, in the Chi Omega sorority house, twenty-one-year-old Margaret Bowman was found, having been bludgeoned to death in her sleep not with a baseball bat but a large piece of oak firewood, and how a nylon stocking was used to strangle her; and how Lisa Levy, twenty, had been beaten unconscious and strangled, one nipple mutilated, her buttocks deeply bitten, and how she had been sexually assaulted with a bottle of hair mist. Three others, Kathy Kleiner, Karen Chandler, and (in a nearby apartment just off campus) Cheryl Thomas, survived—with, among them, concussion, broken jaws, severely lacerated shoulder, dislocated shoulder, knocked out teeth, crushed finger, fractured skull.

The sheriff's office concluded it was the work of Ted Bundy, who had escaped from a Colorado jail and was at large. On February 15, 1978, a police officer in my hometown of Pensacola stopped him near the Alabama line because he was driving a stolen VW Beetle. The officer, David Lee, placed him under arrest, there was a tussle, Bundy ran, Lee fired a warning, fired again, ran after him, and tackled him to the ground. Bundy grabbed for Lee's gun, but the police officer got the better of him.

He was brought back to Tallahassee—though, pursuant to a successful change of venue motion, he was ultimately tried in Miami. But while he was held in our county jail, I was assigned to drive Bundy back and forth from the jail to the courthouse. He was shackled hand and foot in the backseat behind a cage barrier, a K-9 unit trailed my car, and a chopper flew overhead.

Before we drove off, I leaned over Bundy to adjust his shackles. My captain, Gene Goodman, was watching, and he didn't like how my cross-draw holster nearly brushed up against Bundy. Once I had Bundy secured, Goodman took me aside.

"Cedric, let me tell you somethin'. Don't you ever get that close to him again. He'll kill you dead."

"Yes, sir."

"And don't you say nutthin' to him, either. Just drive. Don't say nutthin'."

"Yes, sir."

And I didn't say a single word. But I couldn't keep my eyes from flicking up to the rearview mirror. It was a reflex, like a moth to a flame. I saw his face in pieces, sort of: hair, eyes, smirk. He did not look like a man about to be tried for murders both attempted and accomplished. I have never forgotten those furtive, stolen, fleeting rearview mirror images.

And I have never forgotten the survivors, who some of the deputies, me included, took alternate shifts guarding while they lay in what was then called Tallahassee Memorial Hospital. What's the cliché? "Beaten within an inch of their lives." It was that—and then some.

The sights, sounds, smells, and witness and victim stories surrounding any violent crime go right to a police officer's gut. A lot of us try to pretend we're not disturbed by any of it. Some pretend more successfully than others. But always the reality is that the pain and fear and loss these acts inflict both disturb us and drive us. I had been on the job about a year when I met Ted Bundy. If I had any doubt about the necessity and the value of the work I had chosen to do, proximity to him and to his victims banished it from my mind forever. There *is* evil in the world. I had it two feet in back of me, sitting behind a cage in my car. Somebody had to stand between it and our communities. I was that guardian. Driving this serial killer, a man whose monstrous deeds and impenetrable motives I don't think any of us could ever understand, I understood, to its depths, my role in society with a clarity as stark as any I would ever experience. I was a lawman.

CHAPTER 2

Miami Vice, Miami Virtue

On December 17, 1979, Arthur Lee McDuffie was beaten to death at the intersection of 38th Street and North Miami Avenue, Miami.[6] Two days earlier, he appeared to be a man finally getting his life back. A top associate manager for Coastal States Life Insurance, he had nevertheless fallen on hard times, divorcing his wife of ten years, spending more than he made, bouncing checks—including one in 1975 for a $42 traffic fine, which resulted in a suspended license. Subsequently, he skipped a court date for driving with expired tags. Now, however, he had picked up odd jobs as a painter, car washer, and mechanic to supplement his regular income, and he was making amends to Frederica, his ex-wife, who had just agreed to marry him—again. Together, the couple attended the Coastal States office Christmas party and then, together, shopped for Christmas gifts to put under the tree for their daughters, eight-year-old Shedrica and two-year-old Dewana.

McDuffie and Frederica spent the night together, and then she drove him to his sister's house, where he was living. McDuffie had lent his car to someone, so he rode off to a friend's house on the 1973 black-and-orange Kawasaki motorcycle borrowed from his cousin. The friend, a coworker at the insurance company, later testified that she and McDuffie went riding in Miami Beach that night at "85 to 90 mph" before returning to her apartment. McDuffie left the apartment on the motorcycle about 1:30 on the morning of December 17.

Metro Miami had a population of some 2,600,000 in 1979, a big American city. Frederica, a nurse's aide at Jackson Memorial Hospital, had no way of knowing that her ex-husband, tenuously clinging to consciousness despite a skull (a witness later testified) "cracked like an egg," was slowly dying in an ICU four floors below her. For now, all that the world beyond the corner of 38th Street and North Miami Avenue would know about what happened to Arthur McDuffie came from a police report on Case No. 369-7432-Z, initially filed by Metro Sergeant Ira Diggs. It said that an unidentified black man "attained speeds in excess of 100 mph, running approximately 25 red lights and stop signs with his lights off" in an effort to evade arrest at NW 50th Street and 27th Avenue in the police department's predominantly black Central District. After a seven-minute chase, the "subject attempted to turn the motorcycle left, west, onto NW 38th Street. He lost control, wrecking same. As the subject hit the curb, his helmet came off and the motorcycle fell. Subject immediately got up and attempted to flee on foot at which time Sgt. Diggs attempted to apprehend the subject." Officially, he was charged with reckless driving, willful flight, leaving the scene of an accident, battery on a police officer, and resisting arrest with violence.

McDuffie was picked up by Miami Fire Rescue at 2:06 am, just four minutes after receiving the call from police, and he was admitted to the Jackson Memorial ICU at 2:25. Eleven pints of blood were transfused into his body, and as his brain began to swell uncontrollably, doctors drilled holes in his badly fractured skull in an effort to relieve the pressure. Nevertheless, his brain died days before he was pronounced dead at 2 p.m. on December 21.

From the moment he reviewed Diggs's report, Central District captain Dale Bowlin smelled a rat and turned everything over to Major Steve Bertucelli of internal affairs. Later, as the city was torn by rioting, *The Miami News* (May 19, 1980) recounted how the police version of December 17 disintegrated.[7] Officer John Gerald Gerant told Metro homicide chief, Captain Marshall Frank, that McDuffie had been beaten and that the beating sickened him. In an official statement, Gerant reported that, as more and more squad cars arrived at the scene of the arrest, one officer remarked, "Wait a minute, there are too many witnesses." One of those witnesses, Officer Richard Gotowala, reported that McDuffie, handcuffed behind his back, was beaten "in pure vengeance." It looked to him as if officers were trying to break his leg, and that, as officers piled on, their "sergeant was yelling, 'Wait a minute, one at a time.'"

Deputy Dade County Medical Examiner Ronald Wright received Case No. 369-7432-Z on Christmas Eve and drove to the yard of Barbon Towing to examine the motorcycle. "I thought it was a relatively minor accident faked up to look worse," he wrote in his report. On Christmas Day, investigators concluded that McDuffie's death was a homicide and that his killer was a police officer.

Metro Dade officer Charles Veverka Jr. testified to an assistant state attorney on December 26 that Sergeant Diggs had made up the story of the accident. What had really happened, Veverka said, is that he, Veverka, pulled McDuffie off the motorcycle, McDuffie swung at him and also hit or kicked another officer. In response, Veverka struck McDuffie and then the others joined in. Veverka claimed that he tried to rescue McDuffie from the melee, which lasted two or three minutes. The next day, Metro officers Frank Mungavin, Ubaldo delToro, Mark Meir, and Veverka were suspended, along with Officers Herbert Evans Jr. and William Hanlon. Florida State Attorney Janet Reno then announced that Arthur Lee McDuffie had been murdered.

Indictments came on December 28, 1979, and included manslaughter charges against Diggs, Hanlon, Marrero, and Officer Michael Watts; and evidence and accessory charges against Evans. The next day, McDuffie was mourned at Jordan Grove Baptist Church, and his funeral included a military honor guard to assist in the burial of the thirty-three-year-old former Marine. As the victim was laid to rest, the Dade County ME released the autopsy report. Death was caused by blows to the head "wielded with 90 times the force of gravity, cracking the skull cleanly between the eyes and in back of the head." The medical examiner speculated that the probable weapon was a "heavy-duty police Kel-lite flashlight, swung two-handed, like an ax." Homicide captain Marshall Frank told a reporter, "When all the facts are made known, it will make you hair stand on end. It's really a weird case, a frenzied killing."

Officer Hanlon told a polygraph examiner early in January that he had choked McDuffie with his nightstick while another officer handcuffed him. He admitted to trying to hurt him and to get "one last shot" at his legs, which he struck two or three times with his nightstick. He also said that he had jabbed McDuffie several times with the stick. The following month, on February 1, Officers Meir and Veverka resigned from the Public Safety Department after being granted immunity from prosecution in exchange for their testimony against fellow officers. On the same day, Public Safety Director Bobby L. Jones fired eight Metro Dade officers: Eric Seyman, who was an acting supervisor, and Francis Mungavin in addition to Diggs, Evans, Watts, Marrero, Hanlon, and delToro, who was also charged that day as an accessory after the fact. A month later, on March 1, Circuit Court Judge Lenore Nesbitt declared that the trial would be moved out of Miami, where the very "word 'McDuffie' has become a byword, a symbol of terror, of white police officers who beat up black citizens, of lying by police officers." She said that Miami was now a "time bomb," and on February 5 announced Tampa as the alternate venue.

Late in March, before jury selection began, Officer Hanlon was added to the list of prosecution witnesses when charges against him were dropped because his statements to Captain Frank and to the polygraph examiner were ruled inadmissible. The police officer had not been advised of his Miranda rights. On April 16, an all-white, all-male jury, middle-class and middle-aged, was impaneled to hear the manslaughter cases against five Metro officers. In advance of opening testimony, the defense revealed its intention to argue that the outcry from Miami's black community had prompted the Public Safety Department to offer up five of its officers as scapegoats.

The prosecution had 90 witnesses on its list. From April 25 to May 8, jurors and public heard testimony. Officer Meier said that McDuffie had hollered "I give up" before "four to seven" officers beat him. McDuffie, he said, did not resist, and it was Officer Marrero who outlined the story the officers would fabricate. Hanlon testified that he had not only choked McDuffie with his nightstick, but had stepped on his glasses, suggested to other officers that they break his legs, and shot at McDuffie's wristwatch but missed. Enraged, he smashed the watch against a building and threw the remains down a sewer. The day after the beating, he broke into the towing yard to remove the Kawasaki's oil pan cover, knowing that it typically comes off in an accident. Not only did he admit to lying to investigators, he announced to the jury, "Everyone lied." In eight hours of testimony, Officer Richard Gotowala, who quit the Metro force the day after the beating, testified that Officer Marrero had twice popped open the cylinder of his service revolver and complained, "I missed the m----rf----r twice!" Yet he also had to admit that he failed to pick Marrero out of a photo lineup. Later, a University of Miami professor of civil engineering testified that his examination of the motorcycle definitively revealed that it had not been involved in an accident," and Deputy Dade County Medical Examiner Ronald Wright called the blow that had killed McDuffie "equivalent to falling four stories and landing between your eyes." He said it caused an "incredibly massive" fracture, "as much fracturing as you can get."

Before the defense presented its case, it moved for acquittal of Ubaldo delToro, Marrero, Evans, Watts, and Diggs. Judge Nesbitt granted the motion in the case of DelToro, but rejected the others. In his defense, Sergeant Ira Diggs testified that McDuffie had violently resisted arrest and was himself kicked in the knee with sufficient force to knock him down. He denied striking McDuffie. Marrero admitted hitting McDuffie after he twice grabbed for his gun. He claimed to having seen Officer Veverka strike McDuffie with his flashlight. He testified that McDuffie was not handcuffed when he scuffled with him, and he remarked that while he felt bad about the man's death, if he had it to do again, he "would do it the same way." In fact, McDuffie resisted with such violence, he said, that he would have been justified in shooting him.

On May 17, after deliberating just three hours, the jury acquitted the four remaining defendants on all thirteen counts of the indictment. Some jurors told the press that they could not get past the reasonable doubt created by conflicting witness testimonies as to the weapon used—nightstick or flashlight?—and as to just who wielded it.

Miami's black community had no such doubt. The verdict came like a thunderbolt out of an angry South Florida sky. At first, it ignited protests in the streets. On the day of the verdict, some five thousand protested at the Downtown Miami Metro Justice Building. By six in the evening, the protest had become a riot. That night, three people were killed and at least twenty-three injured, some rushed to hospitals in critical condition.

Governor Bob Graham responded immediately by summoning five hundred National Guardsmen to the site of the rioting. As violence escalated, he called in an additional five hundred the next day. A thousand Guardsmen were not enough to prevent the deaths of another twelve people and the injury of 165 as rioting spread to the Black Grove, Overtown, Liberty City, and Brownsville neighborhoods of Miami. Besides shootings, arson, break-ins, burglaries, and looting became epidemic. Fearing snipers, police and fire personnel refused to answer calls in parts of the city.

That second day of rioting proved to be the worst. By day three, with Miami under an 8:00 p.m.-6:00 a.m. curfew and sales of both liquor and firearms temporarily suspended, outbreaks of violence and looting diminished. Hoping to secure the peace, the governor called in another 2,500 National Guard troops to supplement the thousand already in Miami. At the same time, local police cut off much of black Miami from the rest of the Metro area, erecting barricades across major streets. Despite the reduction in mass violence, reports of sniper fire closed down freeways for a time. All of the metro area was effectively paralyzed. Under intense media coverage, Miami became a kind of national urban nightmare, terrifying beyond even the grim toll of eighteen killed, 350 injured, 600 under arrest, and property losses well in excess of 100 million 1980 dollars. President Jimmy Carter issued an executive order customarily reserved for areas devastated by some natural disaster—earthquake or hurricane, He declared Miami a federal disaster area.

Even as the ruins of some Miami neighborhoods continued to smolder, the Miami Fraternal Order of Police threatened to call for a walkout of their officer members if the McDuffie defendants, duly acquitted, were not given their jobs back. Rather than face a strike in midst of crisis, all were reinstated. On July 28, however, a federal grand jury, convened at the behest of the United States Department of Justice, indicted Charles Veverka—who had been granted immunity on state charges—for having violated the civil rights of Arthur McDuffie. The media called it the "trial nobody wants." Federal courts in Atlanta and New Orleans, both tapped as venues, both with large black populations, petitioned for disqualification, and the trial ultimately took place in San Antonio, Texas. The week-long trial resulted, on December 17, 1980, in yet another acquittal. There were outbreaks in Miami—minor in comparison to what had followed the original verdict. Although the McDuffie family would eventually settle a $25 million lawsuit against Dade County for $1.1 million (of which the family's legal team received nearly half), the official police report, which called the death of Arthur McDuffie "accidental," remained unchanged.

• • •

In early in 1980, I left Tallahassee and the Leon County Sheriff's Department to serve in Miami as a state arson investigator. I was there just six months before I left—only a few weeks before the outbreak of the riots—to return to county-level policing, as a deputy with the Orange County Sheriff's Department in Orlando.

Miami in 1979-1980 did not just suffer from oppressive policing by a department with a reputation for brutality. It was afflicted by political corruption, social indifference, and poverty. Many of the Metro communities—white, Latino, and black alike—had lost hope of the possibility of improvement. In black communities particularly, residents had long felt that the police were their enemies—for all intents and purposes, a hostile force of occupation. The McDuffie case was the tipping point, and it set that city on fire.

Early in 1981, largely in response to the crisis in the Miami community, I applied for a position in the Miami-Dade Metro police. It was technically the sheriff's department for Dade County, but it called itself a police force and its members "officers" rather than "deputies." I by no means saw myself as embarking on a one-man crusade. I was simply answering a call for minority recruitment, a call that was intended to transform a predominantly white, male force—a force with few women, Latinos, and African Americans—into one that better reflected the highly diverse communities it served. In fact, many white officers joined the general "white flight" that followed the riots. Local police forces were, as a result, depleted of officers, regardless of race. Miami represented not only an opportunity for me—I was eager to get into policing in a more intense urban environment than Tallahassee and even Orlando—but it made me part of a movement that was good for the community and good for policing in the community.

Orlando, in Central Florida, is a different racial, political, and cultural environment from Tallahassee in the Panhandle of the far northern part of the state. Yet policing in Orlando had more similarities to Tallahassee than differences, especially in its rural outskirts, where good ol' boys abounded. There was one area, deep in the woods, that was a source of frequent calls—neighbors complaining of loud country honky-tonk music and partying. These calls were hard to reach. They were remote dwellings on lots that had been hacked out of the woods. The roads leading to them were not only unpaved, but often unimproved even with gravel. You could drive them with a wide-tired pick-up truck, but a police sedan was another matter altogether. I'd venture in on my own, alone, roll up on the boys. My approach was always respectful—but, then, it always was and always is.

"Guys," I'd say. "You gotta bring this down a little. Your neighbors are complaining about the noise."

I'd put it to them quietly and calmly. I never told them they were breaking the law, just that they were disturbing their neighbors. I made no threat. I just presented it as a problem they could help me solve.

We were alone together: one black deputy and I don't know how many backwoods white guys looking at the world—and me—through beer goggles. They could have chased me out. They could have beaten me up. They could have killed me. Instead, each time I came out on a disturbance call, they were as respectful as could be.

"All right. Sorry, deputy. We'll take care of it."

More than once, I had a hard time pulling out of their woodland paradise. If there had been rain or the road was rutted, my wheels would spin and spin, digging me deeper into the muck. Whenever this happened, one of those boys would call out.

"Need help, deputy?"

And he'd pull his pickup into position, hook up his chains, and pull me to dry road. I'm sure I don't need to tell you that that pickup was decked out with the same rebel flags that adorned the pickups of Leon County. It didn't matter. People are just people—when you show them enough respect to behave like people.

My six-month stint as an arson investigator in Miami had already shown me that this city, near the very tip of the Florida peninsula, was a world apart from both Tallahassee and Orlando. It is a metropolitan city of great diversity, with equal helpings of New York and the Caribbean, as well as a blend of older residents looking for nothing more than a warm, sunny, relaxing retirement; young people looking for action of every conceivable kind (licit and illicit alike); wealthy folks seeking an elegant refuge from northern winters; hard-working white, brown, and black families finding the economic rewards of the middle class; and poor people, plenty of those. Some were Miami natives, and many were immigrants, including refugees from Castro's Cuba. Some of these had arrived as recently as the Mariel boatlift. With Cuba in the throes of an exceptionally severe economic downturn, Fidel Castro announced early in 1980 that anyone who wanted to leave Cuba was free to do so. Between April 15 and October 31, some 125,000 Cubans made what was a perilous journey to Florida in a motley assortment of massively overcrowded vessels, most of which were barely seaworthy. About half of the Mariel newcomers—perhaps 60,000 people—moved directly into Miami. The economy was slow to absorb them, and the local unemployment rate rose from 5 percent at the start of the boatlift to just over 7 percent by midsummer. This provoked some resentment and unrest in the community, sentiments that were exacerbated by news that Castro had flipped a most undiplomatic bird at the United States by opening Cuba's prisons and cynically packing off a large number of violent criminals. In the end, U.S. immigration authorities determined that just 2 percent of the boatlift immigrants—2,746 persons in all—actually had violent criminal records. These individuals were subsequently denied citizenship. The public perception, however, inflated the miscreant trickle into a tsunami of criminality. This, in turn, led to a clamor for "law and order" essentially by any means necessary. Middle class whites—many of whom were themselves "refugees" of a sort, having abandoned inner-city Miami for the suburbs—were often fearful. Their fear made them all but deaf to complaints, which arose from communities of color, about oppressive police tactics and even outright brutality. This was not an issue of racial hatred, but one of fear and panic contributing to an absence of understanding.[8]

But, make no mistake, not everything in south Florida was a fiction born of fear. Crime and violence really were features of daily life, especially in the poorer neighborhoods of Miami-Dade. While the residents of those challenged communities were overwhelmingly the victims of local crime and that violence, the mayhem did not always remain neatly and quietly confined within the borders of an Overtown or a Liberty City. As a result, all of Miami suffered economically as the city, long an international tourist destination catering to a wide variety of tastes, acquired a reputation as a very dangerous place, a place to be avoided. As late as 1993, after a German tourist who had inadvertently driven her rental car into an inner-city Miami neighborhood, was attacked, robbed, and killed, the German government issued a formal warning to its nationals planning a Florida vacation. The *Los Angeles Times* (April 7, 1993) quoted a German Foreign Ministry spokesman: "It's not as if we want to say that Florida is especially bad or more brutal than anywhere else. It's clearly no worse than New York." That was bad enough, but one major German newspaper, *Bild,* reported the story under this damning headline, "Miami: Death Trap Under the Palm Trees."[9]

Me? When I applied to Metro, I was less concerned about Miami being a world apart from Orlando than the fact that it was a three-and-a-half-hour drive via the Turnpike. I got off my shift at 11 p.m., came home, got a couple hours' sleep, and jumped in the car. My aim was to reach Miami when the doors of the personnel office opened at 8 a.m. I made good time from Orlando and drove up on the office in downtown Miami well before the doors opened. By the time they did, I was sleepy—sleepy, nervous, and hardly at my best. Maybe that's why I was the last applicant to complete the test. I just kept checking and rechecking my answers, worried that my drowsy self might have written down something monumentally stupid.

But I passed, and I reported for work at Metro Dade in April 1981. As a graduate of the police academy in Tallahassee, I was already state certified, but I did need some additional academy work for the new assignment. Because there was no class immediately available, I was relegated to the photo room for a month or so, filing and fetching mugshots and the like. It was not quite the thrill I had expected in policing a city with Miami's rep. But I put in my time there before I was assigned work only marginally more stimulating: background and investigations—a desk job vetting police department applicants, whose resumes were now pouring in. The requirement at the time was strictly quota and would not be acceptable under federal law today. Metro Dade wanted to recruit a third white officers, a third Latino, and a third black. I was really happy come August, when I was finally assigned to report to academy classes.

After two weeks, my coursework was complete and, like the other graduates, I was asked to indicate my preference of precinct assignments. I chose the Central Precinct. Universally regarded as the toughest in the Miami Metro area, it included Liberty City, which was predominantly black and overwhelmingly poor, except for an older section of middle class residents. As an African American officer, I would likely have been assigned to this precinct regardless of any expressed preference, but I wanted to make my feelings known. I was twenty-five, twenty-six years old. I had experienced the relatively calm universe of policing in relatively small towns. I was eager for the action of a more intense, more urban, more diverse setting.

There was another reason I wanted Central. On graduation day, a man by the name of Doug Hughes addressed our class. I was instantly impressed, and, after the brief ceremony, he and I made eye contact. He was a young man, charismatic. Reminded me of Robert F. Kennedy—lean build, with the unmistakable look of a forward thinker, progressive, idealistic, yet realistic at the same time. He was different, way different, from the typical police leader I had so often encountered. You could see that the minute you laid eyes on him, and the impression was rapidly reinforced by what he had to say. He was the major of the Central Precinct, assigned as its commander after the 1980 riots as part of a crash effort to address the crisis in Miami-Dade policing that had resulted in what everybody knew was the wrongful death of Arthur McDuffie, a tragedy that had triggered three days of fire, looting, and shooting. I wanted to be part of whatever solution Doug Hughes might begin to introduce. In Tallahassee, I had found a way to fit into—to coexist with—the kind of old school southern policing Sheriff Ken Katsaris was beginning to reform. Under his leadership, I found myself on the brink of the future. If old Sheriff Hamlin had opened the door for me, Ken Katsaris invited me in. I now believed that, working in the most challenged precinct in Miami, I had an opportunity to become part of the future.

I was not disappointed. Major Hughes marched into Central not as the commander of a new army of occupation, but as a builder of relationships with the neighborhood's key figures—clergy, community leaders, influencers—as well as anybody else who showed any willingness to be heard and also to listen. The Metro Dade police department had a reputation for brutality, and while that reputation was certainly not undeserved, it was unfair to what I know was the majority of good, decent officers. The main problem was that the department had few leaders like Doug Hughes, leaders who wanted to try new ways of policing, methods and policies that did not automatically pit officers against the very communities they were tasked to serve and protect.

I am not saying that the communities were innocently crying out to be served. Central Precinct could be a very dangerous place, both for the residents and the police. Practically every night I went out on patrol, I got into a fight. I often pulled my gun, though I never had to fire it. Our precinct was what patrol officers call "busy." Yes, very busy. It was all too easy to slip into the feeling that you were at war with the community. The trouble is that this perception makes for a self-fulfilling prophecy. Go into a neighborhood expecting a war, and that neighborhood will surely give you a war—because you will inevitably be acting like an invader.

Doug Hughes never minimized the real dangers. He did not ask us to deny that there were some bad people in the community. But he knew that indiscriminately treating everyone as an enemy was a sure way to make sure that *you* would be treated as an enemy in return. He certainly did not believe that building a few solid relationships in the community would magically convert adversaries into allies. But he was convinced that failing to build those relationships would ensure the permanent hardening of dysfunctional, dangerous, and destructive relations between police and community. Change was needed, and change had to start somewhere. Major Hughes wanted it to start with us.

There was no such thing as "community policing" when I joined Doug Hughes in Central. Many precincts had "programs" or "functions" they called "community relations" or "community services," and Doug Hughes himself used terms like "team policing" and "community-oriented policing." But the truth is that just about nobody wanted to be assigned to "community stuff," and few resources were dedicated to it. In the academy, absolutely no instructional time was devoted to community relations. Basically, it was all about runnin' and gunnin', kickin' ass and takin' names. At the time, community-oriented policing was about as far from a career path, let alone a career builder, as you could get—and yet Major Hughes was determined to make a start, to build relationships with people not just in the streets, but in places like Scott Projects, grim low-rise subsidized housing that had become shorthand for drugs, gangs, intimidation, and murder. Hughes had us treat Scott Projects like a community, and he led us into building relationships in a place where police had feared to tread.

Where Doug Hughes got his ideas from, I just don't know. I think a lot of it just came naturally to him. People were people, and he was masterful at working productively with people. The community loved him. There was still a fight every day and every night in that precinct. My shift might start off slow, but by the time it ended, I knew I had put in a full eight hours. It was hard on all of us. But the community-oriented approach gave us—and the people we served—direction as well as hope, hope that the "war," real though it was, would not be endless.

■ ■ ■

The move to the Central Precinct of Miami-Dade was exciting. It felt as if I had compressed years of policing into a matter of months. What is more, working under Doug Hughes and being part of a new way of policing was inspiring in the way that any important work with real meaning can be. I couldn't imagine leaving Central anytime soon—but then a position became available in a larger precinct, Northwest, which I just could not resist. It was an opportunity to go into investigations. Now, being a detective in most southern law enforcement organizations is not quite the promotion that it is up north, in New York City, say. In terms of pay, it's pretty much a lateral move. But I was sure it would present new challenges in my career, and my goal was always to keep moving forward. Even more, I not only liked working with people, I was deeply interested in what made them tick—what moved them, what prompted them to do good or to do bad. Investigations opened up the whole area of motivation and motive.

While I had no doubt that becoming a detective was a good career move, I seriously doubted I would be chosen for the spot. First, there were plenty of officers with more experience than I had. Second, Northwest was a very, very white precinct. Since the area itself was mostly white, department leaders saw little urgency in assigning minority officers to it.

As anyone in the profession will tell you, there is not a lot of money in law enforcement. Like many other officers, I held down an off-duty job. I provided security at Miami-Dade Community College. It was there that I first met Sergeant Fred Pelny. Rotund, white, and happy-go-lucky, he was very easy to like, and I liked him right away. I also knew that he worked in the Northwest Precinct. So, seeing him one day at the college, I asked him if he thought I should even bother to respond to the announcement of the detective slot in his precinct. Was it worth it? Did I even have a shot at it?

He broke into a wide grin. "Yeah! Sure. Put in for it!" he said.

My self-doubts may have been reinforced by my reluctance to leave a "busy" inner-city precinct and a commander I admired. Maybe that's why I almost didn't go up for the interview. My car was in the shop at the time, I could have used that as an excuse to take a pass, but my partner volunteered to drive me. I got in his car after my shift. It was a hot, muggy south Florida day, I had worn a heavy vest all through the shift, and I was just plain tired.

"You know what," I said to my partner, "just drive me home. I'm not going up there."

But he wouldn't hear of it. He saw an opportunity for me, and he just drove on up. Sometimes, we all need a little bit of understanding. Sometimes, what we need even more is a swift kick in the pants. I have always been grateful for that particular kick. Not everyone was so supportive, however. My lieutenant groused, "You ain't been here long enough to go into investigations!" Arguably, he had a point. But, that aside, I think he was just jealous.

Far more diverse economically, racially, and culturally than Central, the Northwest Precinct encompassed such areas as Carol City (today called Miami Gardens) and Miami Lakes—where football legend Don Shula lived. There were a few pockets of poverty, but the precinct was mostly solid middle class, a blend of Hispanic, black, and white residents. As I said, in terms of personnel, the precinct was very white. Florida's post-riot drive to create more diverse police forces by recruiting more Latinos and blacks was both laudable and necessary. If there was one flaw in that policy, however, it was the notion that "diversity" somehow meant putting minority officers in minority neighborhoods, so that the police on the streets looked more like the residents on those same streets. To me, however, this was hardly genuine diversity. Being a black officer in a black neighborhood was just fine, but it was not a demonstration of diversity. Being a good, respectful, empathetic white officer in a black neighborhood—or a white neighborhood, or a Hispanic community: *that* was diversity. I was born a black man. That is part of who I am. I was very glad that police departments were beginning to see that fact of my birth as an asset rather than as a liability or an obligation. But, for me, the ultimate expression of diversity was to be a good police officer in any and every community I served.

When the transfer to Northwest came through, I did regret leaving Major Hughes and the work we were just beginning to do together in community policing. As my commanding officer, he could have stopped my transfer, but he was the kind of leader who was all about developing more than his particular precinct. He wanted to build a great department, and that meant developing personnel, allowing and encouraging them to grow and to advance, to become the best officers they could be. He did not stand in my way, but endorsed the transfer and wished me luck.

My immediate superior in my new position as detective was none other than Fred Pelny, the very man who had encouraged me to apply for the transfer. In fact, although he never told me so, I suspect that he had put in a good word for me when I applied. He was a nice guy, a good guy, but very far from being another Doug Hughes. Let's just say that the polite word for him was "easy-going," but probably the more accurate, if less charitable, term was "lazy." But that was okay with me, because he pretty much just left me alone. Usually, I was the only detective on the 3 p.m. to 11 p.m. shift, which meant that I handled a lot of calls and handled them essentially unsupervised. Sure, Sergeant Pelny would tell me, "Cedric, if you need anything, call me on the radio. I'll be riding the north end." Now, even a newcomer like me quickly learned that the sergeant lived in Broward County, just to the north of Dade and our precinct. "Riding the north end" was nothing more or less than transparent code for "I'll be at home"! And that was perfectly fine with me. Sure, it wasn't proper, but I was confident that I could get him if I really did need him. Both he and I knew, however, that I would seldom need him. For a young detective like me trying to make a name for himself in law enforcement, Pelny was exactly the kind of supervisor I needed—or at least thought I needed. He left me alone, and I learned to live by my wits and do the job that was right there in front of me.

I handled every kind of investigation except for homicides, sexual assaults, and robberies, all of which were considered specialties and were handled by well-seasoned investigators dispatched from headquarters downtown, regardless of the precinct in question. Shootings that did not involve a fatality, as well as burglaries and non-sexual assaults—the most common offenses—all would come my way and were my responsibility.

I loved it. And it soon got even better. Within a few months of my transfer, Doug Hughes was transferred from Central to Northwest Precinct. It was a vote of confidence in him. He had done such a good job in the troubled Central Precinct, creating relationships with the community that began to turn that area around, that the leadership of the department sent him up to us. While Northwest was certainly less challenged than Central, it was maybe three or four times larger.

Not long after his arrival, Major Hughes called me into his office.

"Cedric, do you know what your closure rate is?" he asked.

I certainly knew what a "closure rate" was—it was a detective's personal scorecard, the percentage of cases he actually closed due to his investigative work—but, no, I really didn't know what *my* rate was. I hadn't given it much thought.

"It's 70 percent," the major told me. "National average is 30 percent."

Not bad for a novice detective! To me, every investigation was important. As different as I knew myself to be from a lawman like Raymond Hamlin, I have to admit that, from the day I met him—the first, last, and only day I talked with him, the day he signed the paper that opened the door for me—I carried something of his spirit with me. It was the spirit of law and order—of justice, even. When somebody commits a crime against somebody else, the whole community goes out of balance, even if just a little bit. If one person is wronged and does not find justice, no one in the community experiences justice. If the balance for one victim is not restored, everything is out of whack and no one is truly safe. It's just great when the police can deter, prevent, or successfully intervene in the commission of a crime. But, naturally, they cannot deter, prevent, or intervene every time. And so we investigate after the fact and try to make things right by asserting and affirming law and order, thereby restoring the balance of justice.

So, yes, every investigation was important to me. But some really stood out.

Sister Jeanne O'Laughlin was president of Barry University in the suburb of Miami Shores. She was a dynamic leader, who was bringing the small Catholic school into national prominence. Before her nearly two-decade presidency ended, her dynamism, both in the university and throughout the Miami community, would earn her the affectionate title of "the Power Nun."

One night, over in the Northeast Precinct, which included Miami Shores, Sister Jeanne was getting into her car when she was attacked by a strong-arm thief who smashed her in the face with his fist. Nearly crushed her face, and then robbed her. It was one of a rash of violent robberies that had been taking place in affluent areas like Miami Shores and Miami Beach, but because Sister Jeanne was a local celebrity, much admired, and much loved—and because she was a nun—it was big news throughout Dade County. When the days ticked by without Northeast Precinct detectives making any tangible progress in running down the perpetrator, Major Hughes called me into his office.

"Cedric, I need you to go to the Northeast Precinct and take a look at this case. See what you can find."

The detectives in our neighboring precinct were not exactly thrilled to see me. They answered my questions mostly in monosyllables. When I asked to see what they had, they sullenly dumped a bunch of banker's boxes on the desk.

"Here's *your* case," one of them said. His tone didn't invite thanks, but I thanked him anyway.

Okay, I thought. This is where I'm going to start from. Nowhere. Not a big deal.

I went back through everything, especially similar cases in Miami Shores—robberies with the same punch-in-the-face MO. A Miami Shores detective gave me a lead on a guy who was in jail for an assault virtually identical to the attack on Sister Jeanne. He was a short, stocky African American kid. Looked like a compact little running back. I put together a line-up. Now, the way this works is that you take your suspect and find five other guys who look more or less like him. You don't get this ensemble of characters by putting out a Hollywood casting call. You go to the local jail and ask for volunteers. I'd never done that before. In a jail, cigarettes are currency, and the jailer advised me to bring along some packs and offer smokes in exchange for participation in the line-up. Duly arming myself with cigarettes, I went into the blocks. When these guys see a new face attached to a suit, they make a lot of noise. How was I going to get their attention long enough to recruit my volunteers? I didn't ponder this quandary for more than a few seconds before one prisoner comes out and shouts down the cell block.

"Hey! Hey! Hey! Quiet down!" Then he turns to me. "What is it you need?"

"I need some guys for a line-up."

He nods once. "Some of you guys volunteer for a line-up!" he commands.

Before I knew it, I had my five guys. I distributed the cigarettes, we were joined by the subject in question, and we all filed down to the line-up room. The men were lined up on one side of a one-way mirror, and the assistant DA, me, the suspect's court-appointed attorney, and Sister Jeanne were on the other side. She was a very sweet, very patient lady. I've seen people injured, shot, beaten. I had stood guard over those two hospitalized survivors of Ted Bundy. That beating was as bad as it gets, at least on a person who's still breathing. But there was something about this nun—pale complexion outlining a livid black blotch covering most of her face, where the thief had struck her—that I'll never forget.

The line-up proceeds just like you've seen a million times on movies and TV shows. "Subject number one, step out" comes the command. He steps out. "Look left. Look right. Step back. Subject number two, step out …"

Then it was, "subject number three, step out."

Sister Jeanne very nearly slumped to the floor. It was my suspect, all right. No sooner did Sister Jeanne nearly pass out than the man's court-appointed attorney announces, "I invoke my client's rights against self-incrimination."

That's all I needed. I made an arrest for aggravated assault and aggravated battery.

■ ■ ■

Although the assault on Sister Jeanne O'Laughlin is an investigation that stands out vividly in my memory, I was actually no longer a detective when Major Hughes asked me to look into the case. Not very long after he was transferred to the Northwest Precinct, Major Hughes gave me an invitation—an invitation, I have to say, that few if any of my fellow officers would have coveted.

"Cedric," he said, "I would like you to join community services."

There was, at the time, still no such thing as "community policing," but that is what Doug Hughes was doing. Thirty-five years ago, *he* was what we see today. But even though his approaches had produced positive outcomes in Central, there was still widespread indifference and even outright resistance to them throughout much of the department. Certainly, unlike investigations, community-oriented policing was not a well-worn groove though which to advance a career. Pretty much nobody wanted to move from patrol to community services back in those days, and you probably needed to be frankly out of your mind to move into it from investigations. I was loving investigations. I loved being a detective. But I didn't hesitate a moment when the major asked.

"Yes," I answered, "I'll join."

I knew I was making a sharp left turn down a possibly lonely road. Looking back today, I don't know that a single one of my fellow officers would have taken that detour, which, I suppose, looked to any sensible officer like a dead end. What Hughes was doing didn't even have the status of a fad. It was at most a mixture of gut feeling and experimentation, this idea that police should make themselves known and familiar in the community, this idea that they should work in genuine partnership with clergy, community leaders, and neighborhood watch groups—either creating them from scratch or supporting and developing them where they already existed.

It was by no means a warm-and-fuzzy, touchy-feely approach to tough places. The idea was for the police to be bold, courageous, and firm—but fair, fair, respectful, and never, ever arbitrary or anonymous. Whatever we did in a community, we wanted to know the people we dealt with and we wanted them to know us. We wanted them to know what we were doing and why we were doing it. We talked, and we listened, and if we were really good at this community thing, we listened a whole lot more than we talked.

In the most troubled communities, the Liberty Cities and the Overtowns of Miami, for instance, police officers could expect to fight, draw their weapons, and sometimes even fire them. To some degree, community-oriented tactics had a reasonable hope of reducing violent acts and violent responses. But even in cases where the community-oriented approach failed to substantially reduce violent encounters, it could make those encounters mean something positive. Most of the most challenged communities are populated by good people who want to live in peace. Often, they are struggling just to put food on the table and keep a roof over their family's heads. They don't need the added looming burden of violent crime every time they set foot on the sidewalk. When they see police officers make an arrest—officers they recognize and maybe even have spoken with, either on the street or at a neighborhood meeting—they understand that these men and women are trying to protect them, defend the community, not simply throw their weight around and assert the authority of a badge over some neighborhood kid. Develop key relationships within a community, and the community comes to think of you as a guardian, not an invader.

■ ■ ■

I saw all this. With Major Hughes as a leader and a mentor, I really did see community policing not as *the* future, but as *a* future, a possible future, and a desirable future. Unfortunately—well, it seemed unfortunate at the time—Doug Hughes moved on from Northwest Precinct, and a new commander moved in to take his place. To the new man's credit, he did not trash everything that Major Hughes had built. He maintained a community services operation, and he did not actively discourage officers from getting to know the leaders in the community. But neither his heart nor his mind were into the broader community policing concept. Community policing was not a part of any academy course. It was not a tenet of department doctrine. It was certainly not standard operating procedure. Our new commander had neither the interest nor the vision to continue community work at the level to which Doug Hughes had brought it.

Maybe because I had drunk the Kool-Aid and was part of Hughes's investment in community policing, the new commander did not much like me or, at least, just couldn't figure out what to do with me. So he reassigned me—not to investigation, not back to patrol, and certainly not to community relations. Instead, he made me a school resource officer. Back then, if you wanted for some reason to hunt up a synonym for "school resource officer," you wouldn't have been far wrong to use the phrase "job nobody wanted." Me? I sure felt that way. I thought it was the worst possible thing that could happen to me and my law enforcement career.

Some people just don't like surprises. I have discovered, however, that surprises aren't all bad. Years earlier, I had walked into the office of Sheriff Raymond Hamlin expecting to be met with some combination of contempt, hate, rejection, insult, and ultimately indifference. I was surprised—stunned, really—to find that he was just a person, accessible, interesting, even wise, and certainly willing to do the right thing, to make the gesture that opened the door for me.

Being assigned as a school resource officer, with a big part of my beat being Carol City High School, resulted in the second big surprise of my law enforcement career. Far from being the worst thing that could have happened to me, it turned out to be the most rewarding. While Carol City was not nearly as challenged as Miami's inner city, the high school was troubled, burdened by a lot of drug use and a lot of violence. I approached the situation in the school as I had approached the situation on the street. I got to know the people I served. The difference was, they were all children. Whatever their problems, they were by definition the future. They were hope. They were potential. They all had stories, and I wanted to hear them. The more I got to know them, the more fun I had working with them. Of course, it was a joy always tempered by tragedy. Kids died on my watch. I don't mean that they were killed in school, but in the neighborhood. One day, a young man or young woman might pass me in the corridor and greet me by name—"Hey, Officer Alexander!"—and the next day, he or she would be gone. A person, a future would be shot, critically wounded perhaps, or even killed.

One day, I confided in Arthur Lindsey, the principal of Carol City High School. Tall, well-dressed, charismatic, open, and respectful, Mr. Lindsey was an educator to be admired. What particularly impressed me was the intelligence and care he always exhibited in building relationships with his students.

"I have to tell you," I said to him, "sometimes I'm stressed out, aggravated, and just plain worried over being around some of these kids who just don't seem to care. It's not that they don't care about school. It's that they don't even seem to care about their own lives."

"Cedric," Mr. Lindsey responded, "for some of these kids—not all, but a lot—school is the safest place in their lives. For many of our students, their lives outside of their six hours right here are played out in very dangerous places. For some, even their own home is no haven, no shelter. For some, in fact, home is the most dangerous place in a dangerous community."

We went on to discuss how kids, especially adolescents, struggle to find some kind of structure in their lives. If they don't find it in family or church or recreation center or something else positive in the neighborhood, they look for it in gangs or in dealing drugs. They need to belong. *We* want them to belong to something positive, safe, and constructive. *They* just want to belong, period. And they will affiliate themselves with whatever invites them first and strongest, good or bad. Because, even in the best of environments, trying to survive alone is next to impossible. And many of these kids were growing up in what was far from the best environment.

School, we agreed, offers structure, some basic medical attention, and a decent lunch—plus, of course, the chance to learn. Most of all, it offers an opportunity to be around people who care. We agreed: a lot of our students got more care and more positive attention at school than they ever received at home.

The conversation got me to thinking. One of the disciplinary tools the school had at its disposal, short of resorting to the juvenile justice system, was the ten-day outside suspension. Now, you would think that most kids who merited temporary exile from school would greet it more as a vacation than as a punishment. Actually, however, it was one of the worst things you could do to a kid. For ten days, instead of having safe, productive structure for six hours in their daily lives, they were on their own, rudderless, with nowhere to go. Most kids dreaded suspension, and this was evident because you would find them hanging out close to the school, shipwrecked sailors clinging to the wreckage.

In the most challenged neighborhoods especially, if you are young and unattached, you are in imminent peril. You feel that if you are not part of a gang or some other structured criminal enterprise, you are vulnerable, liable to be picked off any day or night. In the early 1990s, in Miami and many other American cities, street gangs were a major threat—a threat to the community, a threat to the kids in the community, and, most of all, a threat to the members of the gangs themselves. This is still the case today. But, today, thanks to technology, there is an added menace. What was once strictly a local problem has gone global. Today, marginalized, at-risk youth are not just vulnerable to affiliation with neighborhood gangs. With access to the Internet and social media, they are vulnerable to the lure of terrorist recruiters half-way around the world. Of these, as we now know, ISIS is the most adept at using social media to recruit youth from the West—especially from Europe and the United States. They offer the promise of belonging to some greater purpose. It is an offer too often irresistible to young people who feel no place in their own neighborhood, nation, or even their own family.

The groups trolling social media for recruits may be religious in nature, terrorist, physically based in the Middle East, or they may be home-grown hate groups, neo-Nazis, skinheads, whatever. They reach out to American kids of every social stratum, from desperately disadvantaged to highly privileged, from the likes of Compton and Camden to Beverly Hills and Greenwich. But it is the challenged communities that are most at risk because they seem to offer their young residents no tangible stake in belonging.

Belonging, structure, caring—these are things Principal Arthur Lindsey made me mindful of. Talking with him, working with him made me a better school resource officer as well as a better law enforcement officer. It made me a better—more informed, more aware—person. Both Sheriff Ken Katsaris and Major Hughes initiated me into the field of community policing. Principal Lindsey and my experience as a school resource officer got me thinking more deeply about what "community" really is—or should be—and how the police can work to make their communities stronger. A police officer by profession, I was unexpectedly back in school, and I was learning some very hard, very valuable lessons. It made me eager to do more, to learn more, to take yet another new road.

CHAPTER 3

Cop to Clinician

Community policing—or as Doug Hughes called it, team policing or community-oriented policing—took me out of the patrol car and to the people. It even took me and the rest of our team off the streets and into Liberty City's notorious Scott Projects. I was learning to do policing on a micro level, neighborhood by neighborhood, street by street, hallway by hallway, and, most important, person to person.

Person to person. When I traveled to Ferguson, Missouri, after the Michael Brown shooting in August 2014, I found missteps, mistakes, and dysfunctional policy in policing a challenged community. I did *not* find evil. I did *not* find premeditated injustice. It was clear to me that nobody planned—least of all Officer Darren Wilson—to shoot and kill a young black man that afternoon. When I met with Tom Jackson, chief of the Ferguson PD, I quickly felt that I was talking with a decent man and a conscientious administrator. At the time, some folks were comparing him to Theophilus Eugene Connor—better known as Bull Connor—Commissioner of Public Safety for Birmingham, Alabama, during the Civil Rights Movement in the early 1960s. Connor was a racist and segregationist, no two ways about it. In this, he was, partly at least, a man of his times. But those times, of course, needed changing. Television coverage of the Southern Christian Leadership Conference (SCLC) campaign in Birmingham in 1963, with its gritty black-and-white images of Connor's police using high-pressure fire hoses and fierce attack dogs against demonstrators, including the young children of those demonstrators, transformed Connor into a detestable national icon of what he indeed was.

But Tom Jackson was no Bull Connor. I know, because I talked to him—both in Ferguson and subsequently, many times—I talked to him person to person. That is how you get beneath and beyond assumptions, stereotypes, political icons, and cultural strawmen. You go person to person. And, as I reviewed hours of raw video footage from Ferguson, as I studied witness reports of the shooting—all three minutes of it—at least one major problem with policing in the community of Ferguson jumped out at me. None of the witnesses to the fatal interaction between Michael Brown, resident of Ferguson, and Darren Wilson, police officer patrolling Ferguson, was able to say the simple declarative sentence, "Darren Wilson shot Michael Brown." The reason? No one who came forth as a witness recognized Officer Darren Wilson. No one knew him, not by sight and certainly not by name. He was a cop. That's all. A uniform, a badge, and a gun.

And that was too bad for Darren Wilson. The fact that Wilson, for his part, did not know Michael Brown, by sight or by name—well, that was too bad for Michael Brown.

Ferguson is a small community—roughly 21,000 residents—and the Ferguson Police Department is a small department: 54 sworn officers, of whom perhaps half are regularly on the streets. People often lament the "good old days," when small towns were the backbone of America and everybody knew everyone else and the beat cop knew the neighborhood and the neighborhood knew him. Well, Ferguson is a small town, and the police force that patrols its streets consists of a mere handful of people, each with a face and a name. The two groups—the community's residents and the community's guardians—are small enough that individuals from both should be able to recognize each other, person to person. The encounter between Michael Brown and Darren Wilson proved that such mutual recognition was totally absent in the Ferguson community and in its police force. This absence is a symptom of a tragically dysfunctional relationship. There is, after all, no reason why the patrol personnel of a small police force in a small town must be anonymous, and there is no reason that the police who patrol the same neighborhoods day after day should, in turn, view residents as anonymous beings.

I'm not in the habit of deriving my life lessons from the likes of Soviet dictator Joseph Stalin, but there is a famous quotation attributed to him that applies here. "A single death," he said, "is a tragedy. A million deaths, a statistic." Get to know somebody—even slightly—and, chances are, you will feel some modicum of empathy and respect for him or her. I cannot tell you with certainty what would have happened and what would not have happened had Darren Wilson recognized Michael Brown as a person with a name or even as a familiar face and build—at six-four, 292 pounds, he should have made an impression on anyone in the community. I cannot assure you that Officer Wilson would not have backed up his patrol SUV alongside him and Dorian Johnson as they walked in the middle of the street, blocked them, and then brusquely ordered them onto the sidewalk instead of addressing them with at least rudimentary respect.

I *can* tell you that, had he recognized Brown, Wilson would have been far less likely to handle the situation the way he did. I *can* tell you that Officer Wilson would have been more likely to approach Brown person to person. And I *can* also tell you that, approached this way, person to person, Brown would have been less likely to have acted aggressively toward Wilson. Maybe Brown would have said, "Hello, Officer Wilson." Or it might have been, "Fuck you, Officer Wilson." Either way, the exchange would not have been anonymous. If Brown had actually recognized Wilson—as the cop who was on these streets day in day out, the cop who says hello to me, maybe even the cop who knows my name—I do not know for a certainty that Michael Brown would be alive today. But I do know it is far less likely that his life would have ended at 12:03 p.m. on August 9, 2014.

Getting to know people, actual people, in the Miami communities of Liberty City and Carol City made me a more effective police officer and a better guardian. I am also certain that knowing them and their knowing me also contributed to my own safety as I did my job in a tough, tough environment. I was wide open to the community policing concept because it made common sense and because I have always been interested in people both as members of communities and as individuals. When tight finances and family obligations prompted me to drop out of FAMU before finishing my undergraduate degree, I had been majoring in sociology. I could have received some scholarship money if I had majored in accounting, but I quickly realized that people, not numbers, were my thing. I mentioned earlier that getting an assignment as a school resource officer, working mostly out of Carol City High School, was for me an "unexpected" return to school. Actually, it was my *second* return. I started with the Miami-Dade Police Department in 1981, but leaving FAMU without my degree had always bugged me, and, two years after I started with Miami-Dade, I enrolled as a part-time student at what was then known as Biscayne College, a small Catholic institution now called St. Thomas University. In December 1983, I earned a Bachelor of Sociology degree.

Sociology had fascinated me back in the 1970s at FAMU, and, in 1983, it seemed like a great field of study for a police officer, especially one who didn't want simply to patrol communities, but also to understand their dynamics. As I became more deeply involved in community policing, I believe I became more deeply interested in understanding people as individuals, not just as members of a community. My colleagues on the Miami-Dade force often said that I was "good with people." Setting aside false modesty, I actually always knew that. In fact, *I* have the ability Raymond Hamlin told me *he* had: "I can talk to *anybody* about *anything.*" What is more, in doing this, I discovered that I could make people feel good about themselves. The more I talked with people and worked with people as a police officer in Miami, the more I came to believe that God had placed in my heart a desire to do something in the counseling field. So, in 1990, I enrolled at Biscayne College—now St. Thomas University— in a night school master's program in marriage and family therapy. My shift ended at three in the afternoon, and classes started at five or six in the evening. It was hard work, but it was gratifying work.

I had joined the Leon County Sheriff's Department in 1977. In June 1992, I received my Master of Marriage and Family Therapy degree. This meant that, after a fifteen-year career in law enforcement, I was in the process of taking a new turn. To anyone on the outside looking in, it must have seemed like a very sharp turn. To me, however, it was part of a single journey. To me, policing and counseling were different approaches to the same thing: helping people, person to person.

It was while I was working toward my Master's that I made up my mind to leave law enforcement. I also decided that the Master's would not be the end of the journey. As a police officer, I always tried to be the best officer I could be. When I joined the Miami-Dade force, I asked to be assigned to Central Precinct, policing the most challenged and challenging of Miami's communities. As I neared the end of the Master's program and realized that I had the chops to cut it academically, I began to apply all over the country to doctoral programs in clinical psychology. It soon became a discouraging experience. Going from marriage and family therapy to clinical psychology was a broad leap from a liberal arts-based concentration to a field rooted in more rigorous science. The university gatekeepers didn't make it easy. I applied to a host of schools, and I got rejected by a host of schools. After reaching my hand many a time into my mailbox, I caught on that a thin envelope bearing a university logo invariably contained a "letter of regret." It didn't take but a single sheet to say no. One after the other, all the big institutions sent me thin envelopes.

Among those was one from the University of Kentucky. I was prepared for that one, because a member of the department had called me to say that he'd been "pulling for me," but my GREs—Graduate Record Examination scores—"came up a little short." He advised me to take a test prep course, get my scores up, and apply again. I was encouraged by the call, but, in terms of enthusiasm, I was also running out of gas. Ultimately, I just could not bring myself to prepare for that test again.

Then I got a call from a member of the University of Iowa clinical psych department. He told me that the department wanted me to apply, but, he continued, "I've got a friend at Wright State University, and they're looking for good students, too, particularly minority students."

"Wright State," I asked, "where's that?"

It was in Dayton, Ohio. Well, I had heard about Dayton because I saw the name on a grocer's scale back in Pensacola when I was a kid. But "Wright State"? Total unknown. On the other hand, as far as Wright State was concerned, *I* was also a total unknown. So I applied—and I resigned myself to waiting for the arrival of another skinny envelope. And when I got fed up with waiting for it, I went ahead and enrolled at a very small, very local freestanding psych school in Miami. I even started classes there, but it was no use. As institutions of higher learning go, this one was strictly amateur hour and had little to offer me. After a couple of weeks, I just stopped going to class. A few days later, I pulled an envelope out of my mailbox. It was a big, fat packet marked Wright State University. I carried it upstairs, and I opened it.

"Congratulations," the cover letter began, "you have been accepted into the doctorate program ..."

"Whoa!" I said aloud.

I read the beginning of the letter at least three times, checking each time to make sure it was really addressed to me. After a steady diet of thin envelopes, this fat one was a little hard to digest.

Once I had convinced myself that I had actually been accepted, it occurred to me to find out just what Wright State University was. So I read the material in the packet and did some research at the library, too. To begin with, it wasn't in Dayton, but in a Dayton suburb called Fairborn. And it turned out to be a pretty impressive place: a public research university with major engineering and medical schools, and a Division One basketball team. What clinched it, though, was advice I had gotten from my father when I started applying to graduate schools.

"Where should I apply?" I asked him.

"You can never go wrong with a state school," he said. "As long as it's a state school, it doesn't matter."

Here I had been thinking Stanford, Harvard, but I sent applications to all the state schools I could find that had strong clinical psychology programs. Stanford? Harvard? Even University of Florida, in my own home state, rejected me. And then came the fat packet from Wright State. I could not have been more excited if I had just won the Nobel Prize. My feet, however, were very much on the ground. I had a high school-age daughter who lived with my ex-wife in Palm Beach County, and I wanted to be certain that I could continue to contribute to her support now that I was going to be a full-time student for the next four years. Like so many other students, I took out student loans—which, like so many other students, I am still paying for, nearly twenty-five years later. My training in marriage and family counseling also enabled me to secure a position as a drug addiction counselor at Dettmer Hospital, just outside of Dayton, in Troy, Ohio. In addition, my law enforcement experience earned me a post as adjunct instructor in criminal justice at the University of Dayton. Both of these jobs not only provided much-needed finance, but further broadened my experience in fields relevant both to my past and my future.

The Dayton winters were cold, and the absence of an ocean at my doorstep took some getting used to. Come October, I'm sitting in a classroom, and it's already snowing outside, gray, frigid, depressing. For someone accustomed to the balmy breezes and sunny skies of Miami, just looking out that window was enough to depress you. But, you know, it was all good. It was all conducive to the level of hard study a rigorous science-based clinical program required. Few distractions on a cold winter evening!

Just about anything worth doing requires sacrifice, and whenever I missed the sunshine and the excitement of urban Miami policing—and make no mistake, there was plenty there to keep the adrenaline pumping—I would remind myself of why I was making the sacrifice. I would focus on what I would gain and what I would be able to give back. Community-oriented policing, I believe, had shown me the true heart of police work, which required understanding and respecting people—*as people*—one person at a time. Policing is inherently dangerous. Ted Bundy was a real person. I know, because he sat chained up in my car more than once. Bad guys like Ted Bundy walk among us, and they need to be arrested, and, believe me, they don't usually go quietly. But beyond that and beneath that is another level of motivation. It is a desire to help people, to be a guardian of the communities we all share. It is also a desire to make individual lives safer, more secure, better. And this new path I was on, clinical psychology, was just another form of the guardian role. It had a connection to my undergraduate work in sociology, to be sure. But that study was *academic*, a way of understanding communities and other groups, whereas clinical psychology—like community policing—is *interventional*. Like policing at its best, it is about understanding human problems and then doing something about them, one person at a time.

So, yes, Ohio was not Miami—especially during fall and winter!—and the classroom was not the squad car. But the jobs, the roles, were surprisingly related. Fortunately, I understood that early on. In some ways, I was a stranger in a strange land. At thirty-seven when I got to Wright State, I was an old man to almost all of my classmates, who were in their early twenties and fresh out of undergrad school. I, in contrast, turned forty in graduate school! But, naturally, I got along with them all, one way or another. I could talk with *anybody* about *anything*. And I had a purpose.

As anyone who has pursued a doctorate in any field knows, the course work may be demanding, but the dissertation that is typically the culminating requirement for the degree is much more than an intellectual exercise. I would compare it to running a marathon, which is much more than an athletic endeavor. Whatever else they are, both a doctorate and a marathon are also stern tests of character and will. Spend any amount of time in and around a graduate school, and you are likely to meet more than a few ABDs—students designated "All But Dissertation"—folks who have completed all of their coursework and other requirements, but who were daunted and defeated by the prospect of writing a work of research. For me, the dissertation was a major challenge and just plain hard labor. While I embarked on the doctoral program with the intention of leaving the world of law enforcement, when the time came to find a dissertation subject, I just naturally fell back into my fifteen years of experience in that world. My dissertation was on police officer stress and burnout. Even in uniform, people are people. As police officers need to break through mutual anonymity to engage with the communities they serve, those communities must, in turn, see police officers as first and foremost people. Good community policing can make this two-way human relationship both possible and productive. Often, the greater difficulty is getting police personnel to see themselves and each other not just one dimensionally, as officers, but also as vulnerable human beings. An important step in this is to recognize and understand stress and burnout.

Few jobs are more inherently stressful than policing, and stress leads to fatigue and fatigue to burnout. That word, *burnout,* suggests a light bulb that works perfectly well one minute, only to go out the next. Well, that's misleading when it comes to people. If stress is not recognized and properly handled, officers become less efficient over time, which means that they, their fellow officers, and the public are put at risk for days, months, or even years. Fatigued officers are off the job more often, they make mistakes—in the field, with paperwork, and in the courtroom—they communicate less effectively, they get into accidents, they get hurt, and they may well hurt others. Citizen complaints of misconduct are often traceable to officer stress, fatigue, and some stage of burnout. And it is not just the job and the public who suffer. Stress is related to PTSD (post-traumatic stress disorder), to chronically impaired judgment, to unhealthy weight gain or weight loss, mood swings, problems with eye-hand coordination, depression, anxiety, substance abuse, chronic pain, and a general increase in health risks. Chronic stress has a direct bearing on problems such as diabetes and cardiovascular disease. Stress literally makes folks, police officers included, sick.

By no means did I find writing the dissertation a cakewalk, but the subject allowed me to approach both clinical psychology and the law enforcement profession in a whole new way, and it drove me to put in the work and pile up the pages. I defended my dissertation in 1996 and received my doctorate in clinical psychology in June 1997.

I could have hung out a shingle and started a practice or taken some other clinical job, but I was hooked on psychology and decided to look for post-doctoral programs. Back when I started at the Leon County Sheriff's Department, my *second* training officer rode with me for just two weeks before saying, "Cedric, you're ready!" Friends and colleagues were saying exactly the same thing after I got my degree from Wright State. "You're ready, Cedric!" And I *did* feel ready, ready to learn a lot more. When they told me, "You're ready. You don't need to go back to school!" I replied, "No, I'm going to get every bit of it I can get, and if there's something after post-doctorate, I'm going to go do that, too."

CHAPTER 4

Clinician to Chief

The University of Rochester, in Rochester, New York, had a great clinical psychology post-doctoral program. I was accepted into in in July 1997. Since it was a working program, I applied my specialty, marriage and family therapy, in a clinical context, counseling a lot of couples and families under the supervision of senior faculty members, who were practicing clinical psychologists and psychiatrists. My post-doc was supposed to last a year, but about halfway through, the head of the Department of Psychiatry, along with my director, offered me a job—or I suppose I should say "position": assistant professor, providing senior-level administrative and clinical leadership over a mental health services program that served police officers and firefighters, as well as their families, and members of the general population throughout western New York State. In addition to working directly with patients, I provided clinical supervision of post-doctoral fellows, medical residents, and medical students. I also provided clinical services and consultation to a number of school systems within the city of Rochester and Monroe County. The special focus on police and firefighters was pursuant to a contract between the University of Rochester Department of Psychiatry and the city of Rochester, under which the department provided counseling to personnel who had experienced any duty-related traumatic event. My background as a police officer and my dissertation on police stress and burnout made me a logical choice for the position, and what started off as a year-long post-doc became a five-year professional assignment. Usually, I worked directly with the officers and the firefighters. It was natural. Once a police officer always a police officer.

As other officers—and firefighters, too—see it, you and they are brothers. They opened up to me more readily because they trusted me. They knew that I understood the pressures of the job because I had experienced those pressures personally.

As familiar as I was with the unique demands of law enforcement, working clinically with first responders and their families was eye-opening. Not only was it fascinating and rewarding, it had the entirely unforeseen bonus of keeping me in the law enforcement arena. Because the Department of Psychiatry was contracted by the city, I got to know the mayor, William A. Johnson Jr., and we soon became friends, often eating lunch together. Bill Johnson knew my history, of course—that I was a former police officer—and one day, over lunch, he brought up some "issues" at the Rochester Police Department, including a recent string of three in-custody deaths. He knew and I knew that a series of such fatalities is not just an instance of tragic bad luck. It is, rather, a clear indication of something being done wrong. Rochester was an economically hard-hit rust belt town, whose biggest corporate employer, Eastman Kodak, had fallen on tough times in the late 1990s and continued to decline through the early 2000s. Poverty and crime were rising to critical levels.

That lunchtime conversation came in about 2001, and it proved to be the first of many about the community and its police. In April or May of 2002, Mayor Johnson and Robert J. Duffy, the city's police chief, asked me if I would consider coming onboard the department as deputy chief, specifically to focus on using the tactics of community policing to reduce the chronically high level of conflict between the community and the police.

Just how bad things were during this period can be gleaned from the headline of a *New York Times* article dated December 24, 2003: "Mean Streets of New York? Increasingly, They're Found in Rochester." John M. Klofas, a criminal justice professor from Rochester Institute of Technology who had made a fifteen-year study of the city's crime patterns, spoke of "an inability by the community to come together to address the problem"—especially the problem of homicide. The 2002 homicide rate was nearly 19 per 100,000 people, compared to New York City's rate of 7.3 per 100,000 and the national rate of 5.6 in that year. Interviewed by the *New York Times*, Professor Klofas cited the bad local economy, the flight of residents from the city, the number of abandoned homes that soon become centers of drug use and drug dealing, a local school system that was graduating no more than 25 percent of its high school freshmen, and a poverty rate among school-age children of 93 percent. Chief Duffy told the *Times* that poverty and drugs were fueling "an incredibly high number of homicides." He compared the situation to "a cancerous tumor, and it's growing." My friend Mayor Johnson cited the fact that, for young black Rochester residents, the risk of dying from homicide was 65 times greater than the national average.[10]

"These are horrible numbers," Bill Johnson said. "I've heard people talk about the city like it's a cesspool, a hellhole, a place to be avoided." He spoke of the need for the community to work together to "change the whole mind-set if we have any hopes of reducing" the number of murders and other crimes.[11]

In July 2002, I left the University of Rochester Medical Center and became deputy chief of the Rochester Police Department. When I had left Florida for Ohio and Wright State University to begin a doctoral program in psychology, I was as certain as certain can be that my days in law enforcement were at an end. I should have known better, I suppose, especially when I chose to write a dissertation focused on a police population. The fact is that I did not simply return to policing. I was coming into the job at Rochester from a new perspective, with a deep background in clinical psychology, and with a focused mission to understand and change a departmental orientation that was not working well in the community. If it was a return to law enforcement, it was a return with a difference. That said—and this may sound strange—I took the job with an uncanny sense of the spirit of Sheriff Raymond Hamlin hovering near me. Was I psychologist? Was I a police officer? Or was I police administrator? I realized that it was not the differences among these roles that mattered. It was how I could make them all come together, work together. "Cedric, I can talk to *anybody* about *anything*." That is what Sheriff Hamlin had said to me before he signed the papers that opened the door to a new career. Psychologist, police officer, police administrator—citizen, human being, member of the community. I could talk to *anybody* about *anything*.

Not that everybody in the Rochester PD greeted me with hugs and kisses. The police union—and it was a powerful one—protested loudly that I was disqualified as deputy chief precisely because I had worked with some of the officers as a therapist. "He knows about some of these offi-cers and their personal stuff," union spokespeople complained. As I saw it—as the mayor saw it, and as Chief Duffy saw it—this was *precisely* the reason for hiring me. But I did not simply dismiss the objection. It voiced a genuine concern.

So I explained that I had been a police officer for fifteen years, that I was a police officer before I became a psychologist, and that I understood what it meant to be a cop. I held the doctor-patient relationship as sacred, confidentiality as absolute, and trust as unbreakable. I assured all involved that any therapeutic relationship I may have had with any department personnel would not get in the way of my doing the job, and that I was prepared to recuse myself in any situation that might even remotely pres-ent a conflict or the appearance of one.

A therapeutic history with some of the officers was, as I say, a legiti-mate concern. But it also became clear to me that this was not the real heart of the union's objection to my coming on board. At that time, with a department locked in combat with a very troubled community, the last thing the union wanted was an "outsider" entering the force at a high level. The prospect of change is scary. The more change is needed, the scarier it is.

I don't know that my being black added to the apprehension. It is true that about a third of Rochester residents at the time were black and that the police department was predominantly white male. It is also true that diversity—racial, ethnic, gender, and general background—is highly beneficial to just about any organization, and especially to those that di-rectly serve communities. But it is a mistake to define diversity in policing as simply making the department "look like" the communities it serves. Back when I was starting out in law enforcement, in the 1970s, a lot of well-meaning city and department leaders wanted to recruit black officers to serve in black communities, Hispanic officers for Hispanic communities, and so on. This, of course, is the opposite of diversity. It is segregation. In a truly diverse department, officers of any race, ethnicity, gender, or back-ground should serve anywhere and everywhere in the city—any neighbor-hood. Black residents should be able to rely on and trust white officers because they are sworn and qualified and committed guardians, people helping people. The same applies to white residents and black officers or Asian officers or Latino officers. Back in Tallahassee, when I made that radio call about "three white males" in a pickup truck pointing a shotgun at me, it wasn't just black officers who responded. I had rushing to my aid a load of white deputies—as well as white civilian citizens in pickups adorned with Confederate battle flags! To them, I was not a black man. I was a deputy and a human being in need of help. And they all came, ready to save my life.

Do you want a good definition of diversity? It's a bunch of good ol' boys with rebel flags riding their pickups to save a black man's life.

No. I believe the union, simply afraid of change, wanted to protect its members from change—even though the status quo was failing miserably and tragically. The homicide numbers made that truth incontrovertible.

In any case, I did not see altering the racial makeup of the department as the immediate priority. There were two issues that cried out for rapid improvement, the first of which goes to the heart of the changing role of the police in our society.

If you grew up in America any time before the 1960s, you may remember that "state hospitals," "county hospitals," and other custodial facilities for the mentally ill were prominent features of just about every community. During the 1960s, however, the development of a growing array of psychoactive therapeutic drugs and antipsychotic medications led to the deinstitutionalization of a large segment of the population of facilities for the mentally ill and the consequent shuttering of many "state hospitals" and similar institutions. For many people, the new drugs were a godsend, restoring their freedom and allowing them to return to productive lives in our communities. Unfortunately, however, the drugs, while often beneficial, were not miracle cures. Many of our mentally ill fellow citizens need supportive counseling and treatment in addition to medication. Moreover, drugs, no matter how good, are effective only if they are actually taken as directed and their effects professionally monitored. For a variety of reasons, many persons with mental illness do not always take their medication as prescribed, regularly, or, sometimes, at all.

In many, perhaps most, of our communities, the rush to deinstitutionalize outpaced the creation and maintenance of facilities to provide ongoing support for those with mental illnesses. The result is that significant numbers of mentally ill persons have been cast adrift throughout America.

When they commit offenses or just behave in apparently bizarre ways or otherwise seem to pose a threat, it is usually the criminal justice system, not the medical community, that is called on to intervene.

According to a November 2014 report issued by the Treatment Advocacy Center, a national nonprofit dedicated to eliminating barriers to timely and effective treatment of severe mental illness, approximately 20 percent of inmates in jail and 15 percent in state prisons have serious mental illnesses.[12] While jails and prisons end up serving as de facto warehouses for mentally ill persons, it is police officers who encounter them first. It is bad enough that seriously disturbed people are incarcerated in facilities intended to house convicted criminals, but interaction between law enforcement personnel and the mentally ill on the streets can be even more dangerous, both to them and to officers. We can and must provide and fund facilities in our communities to support the mentally ill safely, adequately, and therapeutically. In the meantime, however, police departments need to face and to address the reality that officers are going to be called on—and called on often—to deal with disturbed persons. Rochester, New York, was no different from other urban areas in the United States. Police officers were often contending with disturbed persons, whether their condition was due to drug abuse, chronic mental illness, or a combination of the two. Officers who lacked the training necessary to deal with these people safely, effectively, and humanely were putting themselves and the mentally ill in danger. Too often, the result was an in-custody injury or even death.

The Rochester PD had about 700 officers when I came on board, of whom no more than fifty or possibly sixty had any training in how to work with persons who have mental health issues. My first move was to identify officers with the prescribed forty-eight hours of training and to put in place a mechanism that sent them to any call with a mental health component. I established this group as our "disturbed person emergency response team"—the go-to group for handling calls involving disturbed persons. It produced immediate and profound results. Citizen complaints, fights, and negative interactions resulting from calls to handle mentally ill persons went from a high rate to very close to zero. It wasn't that the fifty or so officers who were now designated for dispatch to these calls were any better than the other 650 men and women on the force. It was just that they were trained to deal more effectively with disturbed persons.

Based on the stats I now had demonstrating the positive results pro-duced by the disturbed person emergency response team, I argued that this specialized training would not only make citizens as well as officers safer, it would improve troubled relations with the community. We were able to show that the in-custody deaths in our department were all of mentally ill people. The officers involved were thus cleared of criminal wrongdoing. We persuaded the community that the deaths were not the result of any animosity, let alone policy. I am happy that we were able to clear those officers, but, of course, it would have been far, far better had the deaths not occurred. I argued that a robust training program in deal-ing, on an emergency basis, with disturbed persons was our best chance of preventing such deaths in the future.

In addition to the disturbed person response team, I brought Tasers into the department. This tactical alternative to deadly force had not been available to our officers, and I strongly believed it to be an essential and proven tool that, in confrontations, enhances the safety of officers as well as suspects and innocent bystanders. The emergency response team and the Tasers were not about making our department softer, kinder, or gen-tler. They were about dealing with reality, risk, and outright danger in ways that did not make a bad situation worse—worse by not only potentially causing unnecessary and unintended deaths, but by further alienating the community. Mayor Johnson was right when he told the *New York Times* that the *community* had to work together to "change the whole mind-set" and thereby reduce crime and murder in Rochester. The police are part of the community, they are stakeholders in the community, and they have to work with the community to make it possible for the community to work with them. Whatever other positive outcomes they might produce, the emergency teams and the Tasers were elements in building productive police-community relations.

I brought other initiatives and programs into the department, includ-ing scientific and analytical studies to determine the causes of new and emerging crime patterns so that we could better identify the patterns and assign appropriate personnel and resources productively and proactively. I also took the lead in working with other state law enforcement agencies to prepare and organize a team of more than a hundred officers operating collaboratively to locate and apprehend Rochester's one hundred worst criminal offenders. In addition, I worked to determine and implement sets of best practices to create definitive departmental policies governing police car pursuits and procedures following police-involved shootings.

The success of our emergency response teams led me to develop a department-wide mental health training program that took a best practices approach to instructing officers in safely engaging with mentally disturbed persons and offenders on the streets not only of Rochester, but in any and all of our cities.

It was an exciting time for me, and by 2005, I had built great relationships not only with the men and women of the department and with the Rochester community, but, yes, even with the union that had initially opposed my being hired. When Bill Johnson decided not to run for a fourth term as mayor, Chief Duffy decided to throw his hat into the ring, and Mayor Johnson appointed me as interim chief of police. I served in this capacity for some nine months, and when my former chief won his bid to become mayor, I decided it was time for me to move on as well. We had some essentially divergent views, and I did not want to work for him. I stepped down as chief of police at the end of the year, in December 2005, and was appointed by New York governor George Pataki deputy commissioner of the New York State Division of Criminal Justice Services.

I packed my bags and moved to Albany, where I now assumed responsibility for statewide public safety and homeland security training in direct support of all law enforcement agencies across New York State. To put it more bluntly, my job was to help a huge array of agencies reduce crime and violence in their jurisdictions. In carrying out this mandate, I oversaw the training of more than 6,600 law enforcement personnel annually. This included everything from U.S. Homeland Security training and training related to human trafficking to training in recognizing fraudulent documents. The position put me at the nexus of law enforcement and relevant state and federal officials. The training I oversaw ranged from officer training to executive development classes for police chiefs and sheriffs. In addition, I was responsible for delivering sensitive briefings on subjects of domestic and international terrorism. Whatever else I had to do on a given day, every day included working with a multitude of agencies to assess threats affecting the state based on the ever-changing national threat picture.

When Governor Pataki chose not to run again and Democrat Eliot Spitzer was elected governor, I expected to be shown the door, along with other Republican appointees. To my surprise, the new administration was very considerate and accommodating to me. Yet the philosophy of leadership and law enforcement that came with the new administration differed fundamentally from my own and was not a direction I wanted to take. So I applied for a position with the U.S. Department of Homeland Security. As I mentioned, my earliest ambition had been to get into law enforcement at the federal level. I was thinking FBI primarily, but Homeland Security seemed like the most viable target now. I was thrilled to be hired as the Transportation Security Administration (TSA) Federal Security Director for Dallas-Fort Worth International Airport (DFW), one of the largest airports in the world. I left the New York State Division of Criminal Justice Services in August 2007 and took up my new position in Dallas the very next month.

The move to Dallas and the TSA opened up to me the vista of Homeland Security. I was now obliged to look at law enforcement from a national and global perspective. Yet the job was also decidedly local. In many ways, an airport is a community, a neighborhood, even. I was in charge of more than 1,100 employees at DFW, a large organization. But, in the end, the security operation depended on each and every individual interaction between TSA officers and air travelers. That interaction, personal and even intimate, had potentially national and even global consequences. The very reason for a TSA was global. Airports are the places in which the world interacts with the local community. It is a situation that shaped my thinking about so-called local policing, policing on the level of a city or town, a precinct, a neighborhood, a block. No matter how closely you zero in on your particular corner of the world, it is still a corner of *the world.* These days, with just about everyone connected directly to the rest of the planet via the Internet, all policing has a global aspect. Organizations like al-Qaeda and ISIS realized this, I suppose, well before I did. They have both been precocious in reaching out to the marginalized and the impressionable through social media, and they reach out in this way all over the world. Yes, an airport like DFW is an interface between local community and the whole world, but, thanks to digital connectivity, most of us also have such an interface on our desks at work or at home, or on our laps, or in our hands.

At DFW, I did many things I had never thought of before, not as deputy, chief, or psychologist. I participated in long-term strategic planning for the TSA. I was part of a team that designed and developed the TSA Academy. Four times each year, I organized the Dallas/Fort Worth Criminal Justice Executive Luncheon—not to eat a good meal, but to promote productive information sharing across the entire law enforcement community. I did a stint as Acting Federal Security Director at the Baltimore-Washington International Airport even as I continued to run the TSA at DFW. I even served as TSA Federal Security Coordinator of Super Bowl XLV, which, in 2011, was played in Cowboys Stadium, located in the Dallas-Fort Worth metro area in Arlington, Texas.

All the new assignments and responsibilities I took on were related to law enforcement, of course, so they drew on my experience in the field. Yet they were also different in scope and detail from what I had done either in a patrol car or as a law enforcement executive. I enjoyed the new challenges, but I also felt that my role in meeting them was a quite familiar one. There was a common thread because every job I had held in law enforcement was ultimately about developing, projecting, and exercising leadership. I had been a good police officer, a good detective, a good community cop, and a good school resource officer. I began to understand, however, that my greatest strength was as a leader, a manager. I had never trained specifically for management. I briefly considered earning a degree in public administration, but, quite frankly, the subject held no interest for me—at least not academically. I simply took naturally to leading large organizations.

And I say "large organizations" deliberately, because the organizations I have led have all been large. They have not been mammoth, however. The direction in management I most naturally took was to lead organizations too large to micromanage. Like any competent leader, I work most directly with key subordinates, each of whom is directly responsible for some aspect of the organization's operations. Yet I have always tried to establish personal contact with most, if not all, of the people in the trenches and on the street. I want to meet each of my officers personally, and I want them, in turn to meet me. In an organization of 700 or 2,000 people, I can do that. I can lead a senior staff—chiefs, deputy chiefs, and the like—trusting them to lead smaller groups and individuals on a daily basis. But I can also make productive contact with the men and women on the ground. DFW just fit me. I was able to balance my skill in delegating responsibilities to key managers while maintaining a personal commitment to absolutely everyone in the organization. In mammoth organizations, the top executive cannot personally know everyone. But this does not relieve him or her of the responsibility of maintaining close contact with the ground level.

Micromanagement, wallowing in the weeds, is a leadership sin. But even worse is failure to maintain contact with ground level, to descend through the management hierarchy, to meet people on the front lines, shake their hands, look into their faces, talk to them, and, above all, listen to them. Any competent leader of a large organization manages through his or her top leadership. The really good leaders, however, combine this with a wariness about receiving a highly filtered view of what's really happening in the enterprise. It does not take any special genius to avoid the dangers of the filtered view. What it takes is getting up from behind your desk, going out your office door, and getting down into the front lines—physically, intellectually, and emotionally. *That* is the basis of good leadership, and there is no substitute for good leadership.

I spent five very happy and productive years in Dallas at DFW. The experience taught me to think of myself not as a psychologist or a police officer, but as a leader. But, of course, I used all of my experience in leading the TSA in Dallas. However, I wanted to be more than a generic leader. I soon realized that I wanted to "chief" again. As demanding and rewarding as being a Federal Security Director was, it did not have that fast-paced, 24-by-7 quality of non-stop engagement with situations that comes with leading an urban police force. I was attracted to that challenge, and I applied for the position of chief of police of the city of Atlanta. I made the shortlist as one of three finalists, but ultimately did not get the call. Three years later, in 2013, DeKalb County, Georgia, needed a chief. I applied, and I got the job. That was in April. Before the year ended, in December, I was named Public Safety Director, responsible not only for the police department, but for the fire department, the medical examiner's office, animal services, and 911 communications.

DeKalb is a metro Atlanta county, with about 10 percent of the city of Atlanta actually within the county. It is a vibrant community that is a study in ethnic and economic diversity, a home to people from all over the world. That at least begins to describe the *place*. The *time*? When I started the job, the county was reeling from revelations of widespread corruption, including bribery, abuses of taxpayer money, and theft. County leaders were eager to clean house, but morale throughout county departments, including the police, had taken a body blow. Such was the local snapshot. Nationally, we were at what has turned out to be an early point in a period of intense crisis in police-community relations across the country. For all the county's challenges in 2013, the DeKalb Police Department was not in critical condition, but it was demoralized, and I also knew we were by no means immune from the national crisis.

I had come a long way since Sheriff Raymond Hamlin opened the door for me, but, like him, I was (and still am) a law and order police official. The big difference between the two of us is this: I've learned to expect and demand much more from my officers and from my community in a nation that requires law and order to be 100% compatible with human and constitutional rights. However, my number one concern when I came on board in DeKalb was to address the issues of morale. A discouraged and depressed department can never be a great department, and I intended to lead nothing less than a *great* department.

When I took the oath of office on April 1, 2013, I made a speech[13] and pointed out that I had actually been on the job—without pay—for a couple weeks, getting to know the men and women of the department.

"We have a wonderful police department," I told everyone listening, "a wonderful, dedicated group of men and women." The average tenure of the command staff, I pointed out, was somewhere between twenty and twenty-five years. Some of these senior members asked me anxiously if I was going to bring in new senior command from the outside. "The answer to that question," I said moments after I had been sworn in, "was no then and it is no now, because the men and women whose blood is out there on the street, the men and women who have died being members of this department, are all friends of these folks who are going to help bring this police department back to where it was. Nobody can do that better than the men and women who are inside this police agency. So let's give them a round of applause," I said, turning to the audience. Nobody clapped louder than I.

I continued: "Coming in from the outside, I am just the coach of this team. … These guys are the players. We've had a few losing seasons here most recently, but this year and the years going forward, all of us are committed … we're going to win us some Super Bowl games. So I encourage all of us who are in this room, who are members of the community, to support the DeKalb County Police Department. They're wonderful people, who do an exceptional job every day."

I closed by saying I had noticed, in touring the county, many people "holding their heads down. That is not good. This is a great county with a great history. We have nothing to be ashamed of. … This is where you want to live …. My role as your chief and the men and women you see in uniform here … is to make sure that you have a safe community to work and play in. But we need your support, and we all need to hold our heads up … to stand rooted together as one community … one fight, one team, one community as we move forward."

Really, I would have said pretty much the same thing no matter what jurisdiction had hired me. A community, any community, has to find reason to feel pride in itself—or else it is not truly a community and never can be. If people are ashamed of where they live, or even if they are indifferent to it, they do not feel they have a stake in a genuine community. Those who live in a place but believe they have no stake in that place may be said to occupy that place, but they do not truly *live* in it. The place shows up on a map. It may be bounded by clearly visible rivers or mountains or highways or streets, but it is not a community. If it is hard work policing a community productively, fairly, and effectively, it is pretty much impossible to police a non-community, a mere place in which residents feel no interest.

On August 14, 2015, a Birmingham, Alabama, police detective pulled a motorist over for driving erratically. The motorist sucker-punched the detective, took his gun, and beat him unconscious with it. The incident did not happen on some lonely country road, but outside of a shopping mall in a bustling, predominantly African American urban neighborhood. Many bystanders watched the beating. Some took cell phone photos of the unconscious and bleeding detective, posting them on social media with such comments as "pistol pimped his face n um chillen now" and "Pistol whipped his ass to sleep #FckDaPolice …"[14] According to Heath Boackle, a Birmingham Police sergeant and president of the city's Fraternal Order of Police, "The officer was beaten and just left there. People were there long enough to take pictures of the officer full of blood and put it on social media.... No one stopped to help."[15]

Birmingham chief of police A. C. Roper told CNN that the reaction of bystanders "really speaks to the lack of their morality and humanity. People commented on the pictures in a celebratory fashion ... disregarding that this public servant has a family and is committed to serve in some of our most challenging communities." He continued, "The nobility and integrity of policing has been challenged. As a profession, we have allowed popular culture to draft a narrative which is contrary to the amazing work that so many officers are doing everyday across this nation."[16]

It is a terrible incident, a shocking incident. Both as a citizen and as a law enforcement officer and executive, I find it infuriating and disgusting. So I understand and appreciate Chief Roper's comments, but I believe that something Sergeant Boackle said reflects a more accurate understanding of the bystanders' response: "I feel that in today's society, both from law enforcement and the citizens, we have to trust in one another and do the best we can for this world as a whole."[17]

Yes, the callousness of the response—the failure to aid a seriously injured fellow human being—should cause us to ask questions about morality and humanity. And, yes, the "nobility and integrity of policing" *are* being challenged. But why? And just what is it that causes people who witness a beating to casually discard morality and humanity? The reason and the cause, I believe, is contained in Sergeant Boackle's comment. There is a breakdown in "trust," in trust between police and citizens, citizens and police, in trust that both police and citizens will "do the best we can" for the communities we share, for "this world as a whole."

The motorist who beat the detective fled, but was quickly apprehended. He had a record of multiple arrests and six convictions since 1996 (including convictions for robbery and assault). Clearly, his assault on the detective, especially when considered in the light of his criminal record, more than demonstrates that this individual is hardly motivated by a desire to do his best for the community or the world. On the contrary, his behavior reveals him as a threat to both, and the people of the community therefore have an urgent interest in seeing that he is taken off *their* streets. Yet, on that day, those bystanders did not *see* this. Certainly, they did not *believe* this. Those who failed to render aid and instead took and posted on social media photos celebrating the beating enthusiastically sided with the criminal rather than with the policeman. In effect, they expressed their feeling of having a greater stake in the beating of an officer than in the protection of the very place in which they live and work. Ultimately, they identified the officer, who happened to be white, as a greater threat than the criminal, who happened to be black.

Chief Roper is right. The integrity and nobility of policing are being challenged. But we in law enforcement must understand that integrity and nobility do not come with the uniform and the badge. They are assessments made by the communities we serve. We earn those assessments—we earn our very legitimacy—by the way we serve those communities. By the same token, those communities must do their part to enable us to do our work with integrity and nobility. The truth is that integrity and nobility cannot be the sole property of the police. They must be part of the fabric of the community. Police and civilians must both feel they have a stake in the communities they share. They both need to see themselves as proud guardians of those communities, with heads held high and with a willingness to serve together and protect together.

Our job as law enforcement professionals is complex, but our values have to be straightforward. They come down to respect: to showing it and to earning it. I expect my officers to maintain law and order, as we are all sworn to do, and, in so doing, to be courageous, bold, strong, caring, and totally professional—invariably and always. Biases and prejudices, we have them, all of us, police officers included. But our oath and our professionalism demand our being always aware of them and that we understand where they come from. We know we weren't born with them, but we got stuck with them nevertheless, maybe because of our own family of origin, maybe for other reasons. We know, however, that we were not born to be racist, sexist, or whatever. We were just born to be human beings.

Law and order is not just something we enforce upon the public. It is something we enforce upon ourselves. As professional guardians, we need to understand this and serve a vast and diverse public in a democracy, treating everyone with the same full measure of respect, regardless of who we are and where we're from.

The safety and prosperity of our neighborhoods, our nation, and "the world as a whole" cannot come from the police alone. When I was sworn in as chief of the DeKalb County Police Department, I told the citizens of the county that they have a responsibility just as we in the department do. But, as police officers, as *professional* guardians, we have a more acute responsibility. Without the good faith and hard work of the community, we alone cannot *sustain* trust. By definition, trust is a shared feeling, a mutual value and emotion. What we do have, as the professionals, is the potential and power to *initiate* the trust, the sense of common interest and common cause that is essential to building humane communities.

PART II
Officer-Involved

CHAPTER 5

Something's Happening Here

As any police officer well knows and will tell you, making a so-called routine traffic stop is about the most dangerous operation in law enforcement. We used to believe that the danger—the only real danger, aside from coping with the passing traffic—was the possibility that the driver was holding a weapon out of sight. As you walk toward the pulled-over vehicle, you really can see very little of its interior. Any good officer is keyed up at this stage in the stop. The emotion can't be helped. In fact, it's an asset. It's part of the survival instinct.

Several incidents over the last few years have made it necessary to add to the inventory of dangers inherent in the traffic stop. We think now not only of the very real possibility that an officer will get shot, but the equally real possibility that the officer will shoot an unarmed driver. It does not happen often. When it does, these days, the world may quickly come to know about it and, thanks to police dashcams, police bodycams, and bystander smartphone video, may also witness at least some part of it. The result of such exposure may be outrage—in a neighborhood, a community, or the nation. This is not necessarily bad. Outrage sometimes provides precisely the push that is necessary to overcome institutional and political inertia and thereby motivate positive change. Too often, however, emotions are not productively channeled and therefore do nothing more or less than widen the gap of trust between the public and the officers who serve them. This may further erode communities that, typically, already face daunting challenges.

From the immediate perspective of a police officer contemplating or making a traffic stop, the perception of danger is far more acute, of course. He or she might get shot—or might end up shooting an unarmed citizen. The consequences of getting shot are obvious. The consequences of shooting, quite possibly killing, someone who (it turns out) posed no lethal threat are also terrible and even more complex. There is the traumatic burden of guilt that comes with the knowledge of having ended a life, a life belonging to someone's child, brother, sister, wife, husband, father, or mother. Beyond this are legal consequences, up to and including the possibility of a murder or manslaughter conviction, and consequences for career and livelihood. It is also possible that such a shooting will ignite social unrest or outright rioting and all the loss of property and life that may entail.

Among the qualities I want in my officers—I expect in any law enforcement officer—boldness and courage rank very high. Today, more than ever before, we all know that officers are required to be bold and courageous not only in risking their own lives but in making decisions that may risk the lives of others and that, if they go wrong, may bring tragedy and catastrophe on both a personal level and to an entire community.

In the previous chapter, I focused briefly on a traffic stop that occurred in Birmingham, Alabama, on August 14, 2015. Spotting a vehicle driving erratically and believing the occupants might be connected to burglaries in the area, a city detective made a traffic stop in a busy strip mall called Roebuck Plaza. The detective radioed for backup, approached the vehicle, and instructed the driver, Janard Shamar Cunningham, and his passenger to remain in the vehicle. Given the possibility that the occupants were involved in a felony, he decided to wait for the arrival of a marked squad car. Cunningham got out of the vehicle, however, started questioning the detective about why he had been stopped, a physical struggle developed, Cunningham took the officer's service weapon, and he pistol whipped him into unconsciousness.

All of this was witnessed by bystanders in the Plaza. As Cunningham fled, none of them stopped to aid the injured officer, but several snapped photos with smartphones and even took the time to post them on social media, with Tweets and other messages of mocking approval: "Pistol whipped his ass to sleep" and the like.

As a law enforcement officer and as a citizen, I am sickened by this response. The taunting social media messages, the taking of pictures as he lay unconscious and bleeding—these are obscene. I can understand why no one attempted to intervene in a struggle over a gun. Nobody wants to run *toward* a loaded firearm. Police officers do this kind of thing every day, but when civilians do it, it's truly newsworthy, as when five unarmed passengers on a train from Amsterdam to Paris (August 22, 2015), including three young Americans, tackled a man armed with an AK-47 assault rifle, a handgun, and a box cutter.[18] But what excuse is there for failing to aid an injured fellow man—even as you take the time to photograph his suffering and broadcast it to the Internet? No wonder Birmingham police chief A. C. Roper said that it spoke of a "lack of morality and humanity."

I believe—I *know*—that most people who saw or read accounts of the Birmingham incident were revolted and enraged by its immorality and inhumanity. Yet we must get past our own feelings and our own natural impulse to condemn if we are to understand the sources of this cruel, heartless, and shocking response to a potentially deadly assault. If we chalk it up to a lack of morality and humanity and leave it at that, we cannot begin to understand it in a way that may help to prevent something like this from happening again—and probably again, and again.

Just as my gut feeling in response to the Birmingham incident is disgust and outrage at an act of callous inhumanity, so my natural reaction to the episode on the European train is admiration of straight-up old-fashioned heroism. And make no mistake, those people richly deserved the Legion of Honor decorations French president François Hollande pinned on them. I am not surprised, however, that all of the men so honored disclaimed any motive of heroism. For one thing—and let's face it—nobody gets up in public and declares, "Yup. I'm a hero! You got *that* right!" But I also believe that their disclaimers were more than just pro forma. When I take the time to reflect on the meaning of the events on that train, I can't help but believe that what united those passengers in an act of bravery was their perception that their welfare—their very lives—depended on what *they* could and would do. It was not an act of selfish self-preservation, but it was also more than absolute altruism. Tackling that heavily armed man was an act of collective self-preservation. In the blink of an eye, these passengers saw themselves as part of a community under attack. They responded not by hiding under a seat, or running into another railcar, or pausing to snap a smartphone image. They responded as the guardians of the community to which, at least for the duration of that train ride, they belonged.

Now flip the coin to its other side. Get off the train in northern France and take a trip to the Roebuck neighborhood in Birmingham. Did it just so happen by sheer dumb luck that five heroes were riding the same train from Amsterdam to Paris on August 22, 2015, whereas the officer pistol whipped and mocked in Alabama was surrounded by nothing but people who, as dumb luck would have it, just happened to be born deficient in morality and humanity?

Impossible.

Whereas the terrorist takedown on the European train was a triumph of community, the refusal to rush to the officer's aid, together with the social media celebration of his beating, was a failure of community.

The question is why did the community fail in that place, that time, and in response to that incident?

One obvious answer is that the failure is a symptom of profound distrust of the police, a distrust certainly amplified by the fact that the police officer was white and the driver he stopped was black and the neighborhood in which he stopped him was predominantly black. The absence of trust is manifest in the choice of the bystanders to side with a man capable of assaulting a police officer.

Now, the acid test of a police officer's professionalism is how he or she deals with disrespect and outright abuse. We in law enforcement often meet the public under the worst possible circumstances. Operating successfully in this intense environment requires a combination of empathy and a thick hide. After nearly forty years in law enforcement, I pride myself on my professionalism. But seeing those images from Birmingham and reading those Tweets, I find it nearly impossible to suppress my feelings. I would like to sit down with some of those bystanders and take them— figuratively, of course—to the woodshed. I would like to ask them, bluntly, if they truly believed that there was greater benefit to their community— more value, safety, and security—in embracing a criminal after he beat a policeman with a gun than in assisting and supporting that policeman, who has truly sworn to serve and protect the community.

I can imagine the kneejerk response to this imaginary question. It would be yes, *Yes, I trust the black man over the white cop.* So maybe I can also imagine what I would say next, to move beyond the kneejerk.

"Do you want that particular man, black or white—that man who just beat another man unconscious—as your neighbor?"

I can at least imagine that the answer to this would be no. Why? Because it is a question that forces an answer from the standpoint not of emotion and not of self, but of the community.

The fact is that I do not believe what happened in Birmingham can be explained away as some "inevitable" product of dysfunctional race relations and an institutional failure of social justice. We cannot simply dismiss these factors. They certainly play a part. But the even graver source of the shockingly callous response of those who celebrated the beating of a police officer is a lapse in the consciousness of living in a community. People who felt they had a stake in their community and who were continually mindful of that stake would have acted more like the men on that train. They would have acted to protect their community, not to celebrate a violent criminal for his act of violence.

The incident in Birmingham on August 14, 2015, was an inhumane and immoral act, no question. But it was not a symptom of anyone's inherent inhumanity or immorality. Take it instead as a warning of a toxic atmosphere that threatens to poison our communities.

I keep thinking about this incident, and I invite you to do so as well. The media has covered many, all too many, tragic encounters between police and citizens, encounters in which unarmed persons, most of them black, were killed by police officers, most of them white. These tragic encounters must be exposed, examined, discussed, and deliberated—in courtrooms, classrooms, legislative chambers, and by the public. Police misconduct and failures of procedural justice—the essential fairness of how police officers do their work in the community—cannot be excused or tolerated.

It is, of course, unfortunate and sometimes even tragic that the exposure of such misconduct and failures touches off civil disturbances that may erupt into vandalism and riot. The risk of such outcomes is one of the prices we pay for our free and open democracy. I must note, however, that the incident in Birmingham received much less attention from the media than incidents of officer-involved shootings and in-custody deaths. The Birmingham incident and other abuses against officers, up to and including their assassination, deserves—demands—much more attention, if we are effectively to address the problems we face in our American communities.

Back in the 1970s, before I dropped out of FAMU and became a sheriff's deputy, I was studying sociology. As friends and others have remarked to me from time to time, sociology is a good college major for somebody who goes into law enforcement. True enough. Sociology is the study of people in groups and communities. In law enforcement, we typically think of ourselves as working with various groups and serving the communities assigned to us. That is an accurate characterization, as far as it goes. But it does not go far enough. Once you are out on the streets as a police officer, you quickly realize that you are not actually working with "groups" or serving "the community." You are interacting with and building relationships with *individuals*. Policing is a person-to-person enterprise. Looking back, I'm sure that is one reason I left policing for a time, not to reenter the field of sociology—the study of groups and communities—but clinical psychology, which engages with individuals and often on the very deepest levels.

So let's set aside for a moment what that Birmingham encounter means for our communities and our society. Let's look instead at what it means for the individual, namely that officer who found himself on the receiving end of a beating—a beating with a weapon that could easily have been used to end his life. The detective later told CNN that he had deliberately hesitated to shoot his assailant. He might have claimed this as an altruistic, heroic action: he did not want to take the life of an unarmed man. But, instead, he was brutally honest with himself. "A lot of officers," he said, "are being too cautious because of what's going on in the media. I hesitated because I didn't want to be in the media ..."[19] Birmingham police sergeant and president of the city's Fraternal Order of Police Heath Boackle put it this way: "There is a saying that 'he who hesitates is lost' and that's why [the detective] lost, because he hesitated. If the officers on the streets were not in fear of losing their jobs, it wouldn't have gotten to the point it did yesterday. Officers are second-guessing every move because they're afraid they're going to be judged, by the media and by the public."[20]

Police officers make life-and-death decisions often. Such decisions are what we do. They are our stock in trade. Making them is the hardest, heaviest part of the job, and it is not going to go away. Officers—good officers (and I wouldn't want any other kind)—have always taken this central aspect of the job with utmost seriousness. They understand the potential consequences. Without denying the validity of what the Birmingham detective and the sergeant said, I would argue that police officers are far less concerned about losing their job than losing their life or causing someone else to needlessly lose his or hers. The decision to pull the trigger *should* be preceded by hesitation for evaluation of the situation. Correctly managing the duration of that hesitation becomes the difference between life and death for the officer, the suspect, and others. It is an incredibly difficult judgment to make. But no one said police work is easy. And, yes, every encounter that goes terribly wrong between police and public, between one officer and one civilian, makes it that much harder.

The more the media shines its harsh light, the harder some officers will find it to manage *necessary* hesitation. That the result may be fatal is a distinct possibility. What is an absolute certainty is that the morale of police officers is taking hits. As stories of fatal police shootings, which may be emotionally explicable but not legally justifiable, multiply and echo through the media, the community's support for its police erodes as trust decays.

In Birmingham, did an officer, fearful of getting into the media for the wrong reason, hesitate too long? He believes he did.

Did he get beaten? Yes.

Did members of the community make their judgment known, that he had it coming to him, got what he deserved? Yes, they did.

Will the next police officer who sees something or someone suspicious in that neighborhood close his eyes? Maybe, maybe he or she will blink.

Will that officer hesitate too long to use lethal force to save a life there? Possibly.

If so, will the community suffer a loss and be less secure? Definitely.

83

It is not just that "the police" or "law enforcement" cannot function without trust, it is that the individual officer cannot. The police are not going away. Without a relationship built on mutual trust, however, the police will function more as an armed patrol force occupying hostile territory than as a part of the community. Individual officers will not see themselves as respected guardians, but as grunts in an army of occupation. The relationship of enemy to enemy is neither desirable nor sustainable in an urban neighborhood. It certainly cannot be expected to produce positive results.

■ ■ ■

Back in 1980s, I was a detective in Miami—not for long, but long enough to discover that I was a very good investigator. Later, I became a practicing clinical psychologist. I believe I was good at that, too. In the spring of 2015, I traveled to Ferguson, Missouri, in what was then my capacity as president of the National Organization of Black Law Enforcement Executives (NOBLE). I talked to a lot of people, both in law enforcement and in the Ferguson community. I carefully reviewed what happened between Officer Darren Wilson and Michael Brown. I looked at the fatal encounter as both an investigator and a psychologist. As I mentioned earlier, what jumped out at me was the fact that no one who witnessed the shooting could identify Officer Wilson. He was just some cop.

If this incident had happened in nearby St. Louis or in some other sprawling urban area, the inability of witnesses to identify the officer would hardly have been remarkable. But Ferguson is small town of about 21,000 and the police force has no more than fifty-four sworn officers. Residents should have recognized Officer Wilson—by sight, if not by name—and Wilson should have recognized Michael Brown, six-four and nearly 300 pounds. That they did not, that the relationship between them was one of mutual and total anonymity, is significant in at least two ways. First, it is less likely that violence, lethal violence, would have erupted between an officer and a resident had there been at least some degree of mutual recognition. Second, the existence of anonymity in a small town policed by a small band of officers means that the residents do not consider the police to be members of the community, and that the police do not consider themselves members, either. The community sees the police as hostile alien invaders. The police see the community as a hostile alien land.

The prevailing anonymity is incompatible with trust. And if residents and police do not feel they have a mutual stake in the community whose very space they share, trust will never develop.

The shooting of Michael Brown and the unrest that followed, some peaceful, some amounting to riot, prompted the Civil Rights Division of the U.S. Department of Justice to investigate the Ferguson Police Department (FPD). On March 4, 2015, the division issued its report.[21] It was, in a word, scathing. In sum, the authors of the report found that:

- A "pattern or practice of unlawful conduct [exists] within the [FPD] that violates the First, Fourth, and Fourteenth Amendments ... and federal statutory law."
- "Ferguson's law enforcement practices are shaped by the City's focus on revenue rather than public safety needs."
- "City officials routinely urge [then-FPD] Chief [Thomas] Jackson to generate more revenue through enforcement." The report cited an example of a 2010 memorandum from the City Finance Director to Chief Jackson: "unless ticket writing ramps up significantly before the end of the year, it will be hard to significantly raise collections next year.... Given that we are looking at a substantial tax shortfall, it's not an insignificant issue."
- "The emphasis on revenue has compromised the institutional character of Ferguson's police department, contributing to a pattern of unconstitutional policing ..."
- The "emphasis on revenue generation has a profound effect on FPD's approach to law enforcement. Patrol assignments and schedules are geared toward aggressive enforcement of Ferguson's municipal code, with insufficient thought given to whether enforcement strategies promote public safety or unnecessarily undermine community trust and cooperation."
- The FPD culture is one in which officers "expect and demand compliance even when they lack legal authority. They are inclined to interpret the exercise of free-speech rights as unlawful

disobedience, innocent movements as physical threats, indications of mental or physical illness as belligerence."

- The city's municipal court "issues ... arrest warrants not on the basis of public safety needs, but rather as a routine response to missed court appearances and required fine payments." In 2013, for example, the court issued more than 9,000 warrants "on cases stemming ... from minor violations such as parking infractions, traffic tickets, or housing code violations."

- "Ferguson's approach to law enforcement both reflects and reinforces racial bias," with "harms ... borne disproportionately by African Americans ... due in part to intentional discrimination on the basis of race." During 2012-2014, "African Americans account for 85% of vehicle stops, 90% of citations, and 93% of arrests made by FPD officers, despite comprising only 67% of Ferguson's population."

The Justice Department report concluded that since the shooting of Michael Brown, "the lack of trust between the Ferguson Police Department and a significant portion of Ferguson's residents, especially African Americans, has become undeniable." The authors concluded that the distrust "is longstanding and largely attributable to Ferguson's approach to law enforcement," which includes "patterns of unnecessarily aggressive and at times unlawful policing; reinforces the harm of discriminatory stereotypes; discourages a culture of accountability; and neglects community engagement."

In recent years, [the report continues,] FPD has moved away from the modest community policing efforts it previously had implemented, reducing opportunities for positive police-community interactions, and losing the little familiarity it had with some African-American neighborhoods. The confluence of policing to raise revenue and racial bias thus has resulted in practices that not only violate the Constitution and cause direct harm to the individuals whose rights are violated, but also undermine community trust, especially among many African Americans. As a consequence of these practices, law enforcement is seen as illegitimate, and the partnerships necessary for public safety are, in some areas, entirely absent.

Restoring trust in law enforcement will require recognition of the harms caused by Ferguson's law enforcement practices, and diligent, committed collaboration with the entire Ferguson community.

Based on the Justice Department report, neither the government of the city of Ferguson nor the Ferguson Police Department gave the town's citizens—especially its black citizens—a reason for trust. Did the government and police therefore give them good cause to riot? The answer is no. What the failings, errors, betrayals, and constitutional violations did was to give that community reason to come together to create lawful change. Violent rebellion against the police, no matter how flawed they may be, will not create a better, more prosperous, safer community.

The abusive policies and practices of the Ferguson Police Department do not excuse the residents of Ferguson from their obligation to behave as the guardians of their community. This said, the Justice Department's findings make clear that any meaningful initiative to rebuild trust in Ferguson must originate with the police and the municipal government. This is true across the country. While both police and civilians need to accept the responsibilities that come with their mutual stake in the communities they share, the police, as trained professionals who have sworn to serve and protect, are in the position to take the lead. They have to demonstrate good faith. Although the law gives sworn officers authority, it is the people of the communities they serve who give them their legitimacy. Legal authority is conferred the moment the oath of office is taken and as long as the officer upholds it. Legitimacy, however, must be earned every day and by every interaction between the officer and the public. Earned legitimacy, not mere legal authority, is the foundation on which trust is built between the police and the community.

■ ■ ■

Policing is ultimately done person to person. Yet no matter how good—how trustworthy and trusting—a particular department's individual officers may be, we need, as a national community, to come together by changing the prevailing dialogue from one of division and opposition to one of unity within our diversity. Like the passengers on that train from Amsterdam to Paris, we are all in this together.

On August 28, 2015, Harris County (Texas) sheriff's deputy Darren Goforth was assassinated—I can think of no other word for it—while pumping gas into his patrol car at a suburban Houston Chevron station.

On August 30, during a Black Lives Matter march to the gates of the Minnesota State Fair, marchers chanted, "Pigs in a blanket, fry 'em like bacon."[22]

On August 31, GOP presidential candidate Ted Cruz issued a statement asserting that "vilification of law enforcement ... is coming from the top—all the way to the President of the United States and senior administration officials."[23]

A murder, a chant, a statement. Depending on their cultural background, politics, life experience, and—quite probably—race, different people naturally drew different connections among these three things. In the end, however, only one connection really mattered. None of the three—not the savage killing, the cruelly clueless chant, or the unsubstantiated political accusation—contributed to building and bettering our American community.

Make no mistake, the murder of Deputy Goforth was a direct attack on the community, *our* community, the community we all share and in which we all have a vital stake.

Police officers are sworn guardians of the community. That is their job, their profession, and their commitment. If and when individual officers fail to act as guardians, we may need to help them, we may need to discipline them, we may need to separate them from the profession, and in rare cases we may even need to refer them to the legal system. If and when an entire police department fails, we can organize peacefully, we can appeal to the state or federal government for assistance, and we can even secure a justice department investigation. To be sure, the community has a constitutional right to protest what it sees as police misconduct. Such protest can be positive, leading to productive and necessary change. Neither police agencies nor the communities they serve can tolerate misconduct. The "right of the people peaceably to assemble, and to petition the Government for a redress of grievances" is guaranteed not only in the First Amendment to the Constitution but existed in the Magna Carta, signed in 1215, 574 years before the Bill of Rights was written.

Yet even as we protest and seek redress, none of us can forget that the very existence of a police force—any police force—is a declaration of the values of the community. Among the very highest of those values is a commitment to law. When the community has a grievance concerning a single officer or an entire department, it must be dealt with in a lawful manner that reflects and upholds the values of the community. There is no legal or moral justification for a police officer to willfully abuse anyone. And there is no legal or moral justification for a deadly attack against a police officer.

In fact, more than the life of the officer is at stake. Even if you feel you have reason to resent the police—and as the example of Ferguson dramatically demonstrates, there are some people in some communities who have such reason—understand that an attack on an officer is an attack on you and your community. Believe it: the person who assaults a cop will not think twice before attacking anyone and everyone. Therefore, a community that tolerates, harbors, let alone praises those who assault the police invites its own destruction.

I am *not* suggesting that the police will stop protecting such a community. They will not stop. They will never stop trying. What I *am* saying is that when a community fails to support its guardians, it declares its support for the criminals who mean to destroy that community. No neutral position is possible.

We all need to do the simple but harsh math: Either a community supports law or accepts lawlessness. To support law is to proclaim the value of the community. To accept lawlessness is to surrender to the destruction of the community. Community and law enforcement must find ways to work together to improve law enforcement, communities, and the relationship between the two. Supporting the police does not mean ignoring, accepting, condoning, or defending bad police practices. On the contrary, supporting the police means working through government and the law to identify whatever is broken and to fix it.

The truth is that police and civilians are members of one community. Whatever their differences are as individuals, they share the community.

They have a common stake in it. Among other things, this means that those exercising their constitutional right of peaceful protest need to give serious thought to what they actually say in protest. If the unfairness, crudity, and cruelty of their words serves only to deepen and widen the gulf between community and police, they need to find other language, language that builds bridges rather than burns them.

As for public figures and politicians, whose moral responsibility is to shape laws and motivate actions that build a better and stronger American community, they need to ensure that their public speech educates and informs rather than merely inflames. As John Adams wrote to fellow Massachusetts Patriot James Warren in 1776, "It is much easier to pull down a government than to build [one] up ..."[24] In 2015, it was President Barack Obama who appointed me to the President's Task Force on 21st Century Policing. We issued our *Final Report* in May.[25] We pulled no punches in identifying issues in policing that cry out for reform, but our objective was to "build up," not just "pull down." Working closely with both communities and police agencies, we made extensive recommendations for improving community-police collaboration.

Our democratic society invites and thrives on argument. Coming together as guardians of our communities—police and civilians alike—does not require us to end all of our disagreements. We make progress through respectful debate. But we must come together completely in our mutual embrace of community. As we discuss, debate, and argue, as we defend and celebrate our diversity, we must be seamlessly united in our agreement that lawlessness is not an option, neither among the residents of our communities nor among the police who serve them.

CHAPTER 6

Raw Footage

I am a law enforcement executive in a community that is the headquarters of CNN, the network that invented cable news and created the 24-hour news cycle. That was an incredible innovation back in the day, but it is now a pervasive fact of daily life. As a long-time practitioner and advocate of community policing, I believe it is urgently important for members of the law enforcement community to reach out to the larger community to explain, discuss, and debate policing issues, values, aims, goals, problems, successes, and mistakes. As I see it, a big part of my job, whether in the media or in person, is to help the public "make sense of" what is unfolding between so many communities and their police. In the local as well as national community, the 24-hour cable news cycle can serve as a powerful amplifier for my voice as a public safety director.

So, in 2015, when CNN asked me to become one of their "Law Enforcement Analysts," I did not hesitate. In fact, since my arrival in DeKalb County, Georgia, I have appeared on all the national networks and have blogged regularly on the CNN website. As both a law enforcement executive and a CNN analyst, I have come to understand the social impact of the 24-hour news cycle, especially as it is fed by the potent technology of smartphone video combined with social media such as Facebook, Twitter, and YouTube. Together, these technologies have empowered ordinary citizens to witness and report on events that, in the pre-Internet era, often took place well out of the public eye.

Today, homicides and other crimes, as well as officer-involved shootings and even events leading to in-custody deaths, are broadcast to

American homes and to homes worldwide. On the plus side, this new-technology, new-media coverage raises public and national conscious-ness, stirring what I believe is in most of us an innate impulse to do the right thing, to act as the guardians of our communities. On the downside, the raw flow of images and sounds—broadcast on TV over and over again, available on the Internet potentially forever—creates the impression that police officers (mostly white) routinely take the lives of (mostly) young men of color.

It is an impression made all the more compelling by the common per-ception that raw, unscripted, unedited video footage necessarily presents objective reality. The truth is that both the coverage and the incidents covered involve complexly subjective issues of perspective, perception, motive, and judgment. These issues must be addressed both urgently and thoughtfully, which is far from an easy thing to do.

Well, nobody ever told me that law enforcement was an easy thing to do, and some forty years in the profession have proved this assessment true. If policing is hard, high-quality policing is harder. So, through my work on television and on social media, I try to give productive meaning to at least some of that raw footage. At times, what you see really is pretty much what you get. At times, the bystander smartphone video of an of-ficer shooting a suspect is, in fact, the straightforward record of an act of self-defense, or a tragic error in judgment, or an outright crime. At other times, however, there is much more to the story than what the raw foot-age conveys. I want to be there, present and accountable, whatever the "truth" of the footage may be. I want my community to see and hear a law enforcement official take responsibility when someone in his profession does the wrong thing. But I also want my community to understand that no act occurs in a vacuum. Every act has causes and effects—a context the raw footage alone rarely reveals.

"Liberation Technology"

Larry Diamond, a senior fellow at the Hoover Institution, a public policy think tank based at Stanford University, coined the term "liberation technology" as a label for what he calls "a striking ability of the Internet ... to empower individuals, facilitate independent communication and mobilization, and strengthen an emergent civil society." In a 2010 paper titled "Liberation Technology," Diamond explained: "Liberation technology enables citizens to report news, expose wrongdoing, express opinions, mobilize protest, monitor elections, scrutinize government, deepen participation, and expand the horizons of freedom."[26]

Diamond observed that liberation technology "is any form of information communication technology (ICT) that can expand political, social, and economic freedom." He described in his 2010 paper what he called a "watershed" instance of the Internet as "liberation technology."[27] I think this liberation concept is important to our understanding of the powerful potential of all modes of new technology and new media to create change in our communities.

In March 2003, Diamond relates,[28] police in Guangzhou (Canton), China, arrested Sun Zhigang, demanding to see his temporary living permit and identification card. Unable to produce these documents, he was packed off to a detention facility, where, three days later, he died in an infirmary. The cause of death in this twenty-seven-year old was officially stated as a heart attack. Sun's parents, however, ordered an autopsy, which revealed evidence of a severe beating. This sent the young man's father and mother to a local liberal newspaper, *Southern Metropolis Daily,* which launched an investigation that confirmed the beating. The local story was quickly picked up by newspapers and websites throughout China, and it became a national story as (according to *China Digital Times*) "chat rooms and bulletin boards exploded with outrage."[29]

In response to the public outcry amplified and spread by social media, the Chinese national government was spurred into conducting its own investigation. On June 27, 2003, the government's investigators determined that twelve officers were responsible for Sun's death. In a relatively closed society and government like those of the People's Republic of China, this was a remarkable result. As Diamond explains, however, it became even more remarkable as it created "a much wider and more lasting impact, provoking national debate about the 'Custody and Repatriation' (C&R) measures that allowed the police to detain rural immigrants (typically in appalling conditions) for lacking a residency or temporary-living permit." The Internet stories about Sun's death prompted "numerous Chinese citizens" to post Internet accounts of their own traumatic run-ins with C&R.

Universities began debating the constitutionality of C&R legislation, a petition to the Standing Committee of the National People's Congress was drawn up, and in June 2003 the government announced that it would close all—more than 800—C&R detention centers.

Tunisia

Social media amplified and ramified the Sun case until it produced a signficant legal and policy change. It was the kind of change that points the way toward a future in which adminstrative, legislative, and public policy will be routinely enabled and enhanced via the Internet and social media. Nevertheless, this instance of "liberation technology" fell well short of being revolutionary. The Chinese government of today is not essentially different from that of 2003. However, some of the events of the so-called Arab Spring (in the Middle East region itself, "Arab Awakening" is the preferred term) have been widely interpreted as the genuinely revolutionary application of liberation technology on a large scale. Beginning at the end of 2010 and lasting through late 2013, a revolutionary wave swept the Arab world, toppling autocratic regimes in Tunisia, Egypt, Libya, and Yemen, and igniting civil uprisings in many other countries. The results of this "Arab Spring" have ranged from positive and promising (in Tunisia, for instance) to nightmarish and cataclysmic (as in Syria).

With a wink and a nod to the 1970 Gil Scott-Heron song, "The Revolution Will Not Be Televised," former Peace Corps volunteer and independent scholar Mario Machado wrote a 2013 *Huffington Post* piece titled "The Revolution Will Be Tweeted": "The next revolution will certainly be televised," it began, "but, when it is, it will already be old news. Long before the cameras and the reporters arrive in the midst of the action, it will have been Facebook-ed and tweeted and Instagram-ed around the entire planet, probably even before any one has any idea what's really going on."[30] For those of us in government and in those agencies of government responsible for executing policy, enforcing laws, and serving and protecting people, this fact alone—the realtime aggregation of on-the-scene raw footage and its realtime dissemination, raw, across the global

Internet—should come as a wake-up call. We find ourselves in a perpetual race to draw abreast of events, let alone get ahead of them.

Before I return to the subject of America and its high-intensity Internet-and-24-hour-news-cycle stream of raw footage—ranging from smartphone video of a police officer shooting an unarmed man in the back and bodycam video of another officer shooting a motorist in the head, to a state trooper gunned down by a motorist he had stopped to assist—let me dive a little deeper into the evidence of what social media did in Tunisia, where the Arab Spring seems to have resulted in a mostly positive transformation of a society and its government.

In 2011, journalist Colin Delany reported on a discussion at National Public Radio's Washington, DC headquarters that was led by a young Tunisian protester named Rim Nour. The discussion, Delany wrote, "provided fantastic details on how Tunisians used technology to accelerate their revolution, and in the process gave us a preview of how other people around the world might do the same."[31]

A Tunisian with a background in technology and public policy, Nour argued that social media did not foment what Tunisians refer to as the "Jasmine Revolution," but certainly accelerated it. Perhaps even more importantly, digital tools helped Tunisians organize in ways that protected the political gains that had been made. Most of us in America probably know little enough about Tunisia, which, in 2010, was a country with a young, well-educated population struggling in an environment that offered few jobs of any kind and almost none for graduates with secondary and college degrees. Many Tunisians were enthusiastic users of Internet technology, with 85 percent of the population using cell phones—and 5 percent smartphones. About 2 million of the country's 10 million residents and 2 million expats were on Facebook at the start of the Jasmine Revolution. In America and other Western nations, journalists took to calling the Jasmine Revolution the "Twitter Revolution." Judged strictly by the numbers, this catchy nickname hardly seems justified. Twitter in 2010 had a vanishingly small Tunisian user base—just 500 accounts active within the country. But, at the NPR discussion, Nour pointed out that the raw number was misleading because most of the very few Tunisians who tweeted were seasoned political activists, who knew how to leverage Twitter to produce a social impact far beyond the platform's minimal presence within the country's borders. A more difficult impediment was the government's censorship of YouTube and other major Internet social media channels.

Nour laid out three main phases of Tunisia's "Jasmine Revolution." They reveal a lot about the potential roles of social media in social change. The first phase consisted of protests in the Tunisian interior, sparked by a man who set himself on fire in public. His name was Mohamed Bouazizi, a street merchant in the rural town of Sidi Bouzid. He eked out a living with his vegetable cart until December 17, 2010, when a policewoman seized the cart (for want of the required license), together with his merchandise. Bouazizi went to the local administrative authorities seeking the return of the cart and its contents, but the officials refused even to see him. Rebuffed in this manner, Bouazizi left the administrative building and returned a short time later. Dousing himself with an unidentified flammable liquid, he set himself ablaze outside of the building.

Before he died about two weeks later, he lingered in a hospital burn ward, gravely injured, unaware that he had become the inspiration for mass demonstrations throughout the country against the regime of President Zine el Abidine Ben Ali.

Although Bouazizi's self-immolation was not captured on cell phone video, the brutal police response provoked by the demonstrations was. Using Twitter and other means, activists saw to it that these images were broadcast online, both within Tunisia and, soon, throughout the region and the world. The dissemination of the response to Bouazizi-inspired protests and the government's attempts to suppress them initiated the second phase of the revolution. Tunisians all across the country—including its most affluent and well-educated areas—poured into the streets of Sfax and Tunis. These protestors coalesced into what Western commentators called a "smart mob," a political movement organized online by protesters who coordinated action via their cell phones and Facebook.

Thanks in part to social media, the uprising became sufficiently intense to prompt President Ben Ali to flee the country. At this point, Tunisia teetered on the verge of violent anarchy, but (Nour claimed) the people used social media to counter rumors and to further organize themselves to fight government security forces and diehard Ben Ali supporters as well as a fringe of violent protestors and looters within the movement itself.

To assess the extent of the motivating and organizing power of social media, it is important to note that the horrific self-immolation of Bouazizi provided the human, emotional spark of revolution. The demonstrations and the government crackdown on them were recorded on video, uploaded to the Web, and quickly went viral. Tunisia's tiny cadre of Twitter users accelerated this process with a #Bouazizi hashtag. The spread of the movement from the impoverished interior of the country to the more prosperous urban areas took no more than two weeks. At this point, Nour told the NPR conference attendees, Facebook became the center of action online. Whereas Twitter had but 500 users in Tunisia, Facebook had some two million, and they made extensive use of the videos that flowed in from the streets.

Facebook exposure also ensured that the Tunisian events would be seen across the world, not only among Westerners but also by a Tunisian expat community of at least two million. Operating far beyond the reach of any government censorship, these activists brought the Jasmine Revolution to the attention of the global mass media (especially Al Jazeera TV), news organizations, and governments. The global response, in turn, echoed strongly back in Tunisia, bolstering and building the movement there.

Belatedly, the Tunisian government began to play catch-up, embarking on a desperate media counteroffensive, not via the Internet but using the television and radio networks it controlled. By this time, however, the conventionally broadcast stories became easy targets for social media activists, who readily poked holes in their lies and propaganda. When government-controlled television broadcast images of a pro-Ben Ali demonstration, for instance, Jasmine revolutionaries were able to post on Facebook their own video footage, revealing just how few Ben Ali supporters actually demonstrated.

As Nour saw it, social media channels were vital in shaping revolutionary activity even in a highly fluid situation. When protestors were taken into custody, for example, social media coverage prompted other activists to argue promptly for their release. In addition, well-informed activists used social media to correct and counteract rumors, misinformation, and outright disinformation. They did an end run around the official government media channels. The same online digital technology that amplified

Bouazizi's desperate act of protest into a revolution kept the revolution alive, focused—and mostly non-violent.

Nour wanted to be clear. Social media did not *create* the Tunisian revolution. It *enabled* it. Interactive social media, with mobile technology, did not replace traditional broadcast mass media during the Arab Spring. In some cases, where the mass media was government controlled, social media provided a more trusted and trustworthy means of communications. Outside of Tunisia, in places where mass media was freer and more trusted, social media provided a source of information. Video from individual citizen cell phones was posted on websites and then picked up by major broadcasters worldwide, such as Al-Jazeera and CNN. Ultimately, social media and cable and broadcast mass media developed a synergistic relationship.

In Tunisia's Jasmine Revolution, the Internet facilitated the exchange of information among activists and made it possible to respond to real-world social and political developments in something very close to real time. In addition, mobile technology and the Internet—especially the interface between the Internet and conventional broadcast media—brought the whole world into events taking place in the Middle East. This, in turn, engaged expat communities worldwide and influenced public opinion as well as government policy in the West and elsewhere.

Ferguson
Officer Darren Wilson shot and killed Michael Brown just after noon on August 9, 2014. Some residents of the Ferguson, Missouri, community reacted almost immediately by creating a memorial with flowers and candles on the spot where Brown fell. Reportedly, a canine officer allowed his dog to urinate on the memorial, and police vehicles later crushed the display. Whether either of these occurrences was inadvertent or on purpose is not known, but the reported urination and the subsequent destruction of the memorial inflamed tensions. On the next day, neighborhood residents conducted a series of more formal observances, culminating that evening in a candlelight vigil. Police from St. Louis County came to Ferguson to reinforce the city's small department, and 150 officers stood ready in full riot gear. Soon, the observances turned

violent, as some people looted businesses and vandalized parked cars. The police dispersed the crowd on the street by 2 a.m. Unrest and outbreaks of violence nevertheless continued over the next several days, during which the police escalated their response by firing tear gas and bean bag rounds at protestors, including a Missouri state Senator, Maria Chappelle-Nadal.

Throughout the days of unrest, local, national, and international (most notably Al-Jazeera) television provided a steady stream of images. There is evidence that some police attempted to suppress the coverage, including video showing Ferguson officers firing tear gas into a residential neighborhood. But Ferguson is a city in the United States, not in Tunisia. The coverage by broadcast, cable, and Internet-based news organizations, as well as individuals with smartphones, continued. CNN recorded an unidentified officer shouting to protesters, "Bring it, you fucking animals, bring it." On August 12, a protestor—apparently peaceful—survived a gunshot wound to the head. The identity of the shooter remains unknown, but the victim criticized the police for delays in investigating the shooting.

On August 13, the unrest became more intense, and accusations of police attempts to suppress news coverage multiplied. On August 14, Ferguson police chief Tom Jackson denied the reports of attempted mass-media suppression, even as they continued to pour in. By this time, social media coverage—people recording events with smartphones and tweeting or otherwise posting what they saw—was showing up not only on the Internet but also on broadcast and cable news. One man documenting the protests for social media, St. Louis alderman Antonio French, was dragged out of his car by police and arrested for "unlawful assembly." On that same day, U.S. Senator Claire McCaskill (D-MO) blamed what she called the "militarization of the police" for escalating "the protesters' response."[32]

At this point, Missouri Governor Jay Nixon sent in the Missouri State Highway Patrol to take over the policing of Ferguson, with assistance of the Missouri National Guard. Highway Patrol captain Ron Johnson, an African-American who had grown up in the community, was assigned to lead state police operations there. He immediately engaged the protestors, walking with them and even leading a peaceful march.

The next day, August 15, six days after the shooting, Chief Jackson finally announced the name of the officer involved. His identity had gone undisclosed for six days, exacerbating unrest within the community. Even after the officer was identified, violence continued. On August 20, U.S. Attorney General Eric Holder traveled to Ferguson to meet with community residents and with Michael Brown's family. Apparently in response to Holder's visit, the unrest subsided significantly for some weeks, and Governor Nixon withdrew the National Guard from the city.

At about this time, a new presence developed on social media, an online crowdfunding campaign to raise money for Officer Darren Wilson. By August 25, some $400,000 had been collected—along with a number of racist comments directed against the black community. The owners of the website responded by shutting down the comments section. In the meantime, an online Michael Brown memorial fund had raised about $150,000.[33]

Broadcast and cable news video coverage as well as amateur witness or bystander video (much of it carried on cable and broadcast news programs) was prominent in the Ferguson story throughout August, September, and October. Images of crowd violence and police response—in riot gear and backed by military-style SWAT vehicles, firing tear gas—dominated, only briefly countered by the occasional positive image, as when Captain Ron Johnson walked and talked with peaceful protestors. It was not until November 24, when a grand jury was scheduled to announce its decision to indict or not to indict Officer Wilson, that social media fully emerged within the Ferguson community as a means of organizing a response to the decision.

In anticipation of renewed violence pending the grand jury announcement, Governor Nixon proactively declared a state of emergency. While awaiting word from the grand jury on November 24, protest organizers reached out to some 20,000 Twitter followers in an effort to shape and manage demonstrations. "We protest because we know that we will get killed if we are silent and the risks of speaking are worth it," one organizer tweeted. "We protest to live." In another tweet, he specified the locations where demonstrators were to gather. Another Twitter poster on #Ferguson provided a sign-up address where followers could receive free text alerts about the grand jury announcement. These were typical of social media actions within Ferguson. Throughout the rest of the country, the microblogging platform Tumblr was used to coordinate Ferguson-related protests in other cities and communities.[34]

When the grand jury announced that it was handing down no indictment, Ferguson was swept by a combination of peaceful protest and violent rioting. It is difficult to gauge the role social media played in these events—whether in organizing the peaceful protest or inciting violence. Researchers at New York University's Social Media and Political Participation Laboratory study the ways in which social media impacts an individual's decision to join a protest. Their work suggests that the biggest role social media plays "in facilitating protest [is] by making it easier for individuals to acquire information": location and timing of protests, safety/danger involved in participating, number of others who are currently participating in a particular protest or in related protests. Beyond this, the researchers say, social media triggers feelings of group identity, of injustice, and of anger and other emotions.[35]

The NYU researchers also point out that social media can actually make people *less* likely to participate in protests. They may decide that participation is too risky or too dangerous. Indeed, individuals and groups—potentially including police and other government agencies—can use social media to discourage particular protests, either by presenting factual information or fabricating disinformation.

Events in Ferguson raised another issue of interest to the NYU researchers: Does social media have a *unique* impact on the decision to participate in protest? Or do other sources—such as broadcast and cable news—deliver the same or similar impact? The evidence from Ferguson and elsewhere suggests that "the use of social media has effects that are different from simply receiving information via more traditional forms of media."

- Social media delivers information more or less in real time, which usually is not possible in the case of mass media.
- Unlike mass media, social media is interactive, allowing potential protesters to participate in planning events.
- Social media allows people to search for information specifically relevant to themselves.

- In most cases, social media provides information relevant to the user's network. This information has a word-of-mouth quality that gives it increased credibility.
- Social media gives protesters the ability to share information, including information about protests, demonstrations, and actions traditional mass media either misses or chooses not to cover.

In Chapter 10, I will have much more to say about how law enforcement can use social media and other aspects of the Internet to work more effectively with communities. For now, it is important to observe that, just as social media facilitated and accelerated the organization of truly revolutionary protest in Tunisia and other Arab nations during 2010-2013, it has the potential for facilitating social change in the United States. Events such as those in Ferguson only begin to suggest that potential, both for civil violence and for positive civil reform. In Ferguson, the effect of social media as well as broadcast and cable media has been mixed, but four things are certain:

First, in a free society like ours, efforts by governing and police authorities to suppress the flow of information are not just unlawful, they are doomed to fail.

Second, the only productive way for authorities to manage the flow of images, words, ideas, tweets, 24-hour news cycle reports, and the like is to respond to them as quickly and as transparently as possible—even if the only prudent and responsible available response is to admit that "we are aware of the reports and are investigating them, and we promise to deliver further information as soon as we have it."

Third, authorities—especially first responders—need to monitor social media, to make use of it as a valuable source of on-the-ground intelligence.

Fourth, traditional methods of communication—press conferences, official bulletins, news interviews, and the like—cannot keep pace with social media, which is interactively geared to real time.

Governing and police authorities need to create a strong online presence, not just for the sake of PR, but to improve ongoing operations.

Tool or Weapon?

Writing in 2011, Internet socio-economist Clay Shirky observed that the more developed Internet-enabled networks become, the more information they open to "the networked population," providing "more opportunities to engage in public speech ... and ... undertake collective action." This gives "loosely coordinated publics [the power to] demand change."[36]

It is an accurate observation—if you happen to be an "Internet socio-economist." By the same token, if you are a carpenter who sees a hammer, you identify it as a tool for building things. If, however, you are a homicidal criminal (or a homicide detective!), you are more likely to see that hammer as a weapon. The point is that the Internet and all the technology that connects to it, such as smartphones with photo and video capability, are, like a hammer, components of a neutral, agnostic technology. They are neither inherently good nor evil. Like hammers, they can be used as constructive tools or as a lethal weapons.

Some videos depicting officer-involved shootings and violent encounters with suspects may reveal mistakes, misjudgments, and even outright crimes. Others, however, show nothing more definite than the tragic outcome of events that transpired either before the recording was started or outside of the range or frame of the camera. Because such videos are generally produced by bystanders, not paid professionals, we assume we are standing in the shoes of a disinterested eyewitness. We assume we are seeing a dispassionate transcript of reality precisely as it unfolds. The fact is, however, that bystander videos are never wholly objective. Somebody decided when to start recording and when to stop. Somebody decided who to include in the video and who to exclude—or perhaps the physical position of the bystander determined this. As much as a bystander video may include, a great deal is left out. We never see most of the *context*—the before and the after. Often, we don't hear the dialogue between or among the subjects in the video. Most of all, we cannot feel what any of the participants felt. We may imagine their feelings, but we cannot know them. What made the officer shoot? What made the suspect run—or refuse to obey the police officer's commands? ("Stay in the vehicle!" "Get on your knees!") What exactly did the officer hear or see that prompted him to pull the trigger?

Perhaps the best-known example of bystander video, its power, its limitations, its potential, and its dangers comes from the days before the ascendency of the Internet and social media. George Holliday lived in a first-floor apartment overlooking the corner of Foothill Boulevard and Osborne Street in Los Angeles. He also happened to be the proud owner of a brand-new VHS camcorder, and when, on the night of March 3, 1991, he saw flashing lights and heard the sound of sirens followed by discordant voices, he went to his balcony. What he saw prompted him to break out his camcorder. Looking at the video Holliday made, the case appeared in 1991 and appears now to be an open and shut instance of police brutality. Four white officers whale on a black man—his name was Rodney King—with their flailing batons. Visually, the tape presents a level of violence that was and remains shocking.[37]

Naturally, the video does not—cannot—show what led up to the beating, which included (according to trial testimony) a speeding car, a high-speed pursuit on the freeway, the motorist refusing to pull over, and continued pursuit at high speed (55-80 miles per hour) through residential neighborhoods. Rodney King later admitted that he had been drinking and that a DUI would have violated his parole on a prior robbery conviction. When the chase finally ended, King at first refused to exit his car when told to, and when he finally emerged, he giggled, patted the ground, and waved to a police helicopter hovering overhead. King then grabbed his buttocks, which made at least one officer think that he was reaching for a gun.[38]

At this point, there was a real danger that King—who proved to be unarmed—would be shot. Instead, the ranking officer on the scene, LAPD Sergeant Stacey Koon, ordered everyone to holster their weapons and directed four of the officers to "swarm" King—that is, to grab him with their empty hands, subdue him, and handcuff him. King resisted. Officers later claimed they believed King was under the influence of the powerful street drug PCP—he was not—and Sergeant Koon used his Taser on him. It was only at this point that Holliday began videotaping.

Fully two days after the incident, Mr. Holliday contacted the LAPD to inform them of the existence of the videotape. Incredibly, he was ignored. So he took the tape to the KTLA television station, which chose to edit the first ten seconds of the video, presumably because it was extremely out of focus. What the blurry image revealed, however, was King charging at the officers.

Did Rodney King need to be struck repeatedly? Based solely on the videotape as broadcast, the answer is a resounding no. But when more of the story is told, the context developed more fully, and the first ten seconds of video restored, the answer becomes more difficult. A California state jury found sufficient reasonable doubt to acquit three of the four officers who had been charged with assault with a deadly weapon and use of excessive force. The jury acquitted the fourth on assault with a deadly weapon but deadlocked on use of excessive force. Subsequently, all four were additionally tried in federal court on charges of having violated King's civil rights, a federal crime. Two were found guilty, and two acquitted. In the meantime, the state acquittal triggered the so-called Rodney King riots (April 29-May 4, 1992) in Los Angeles, in which 53 people were killed and more than 2,000 injured.

The Social Media Opportunity

Bystander video can trigger needed reform, or it can spark a riot that still stands as the worst American urban violence, in terms of death toll, since the infamous Civil War "Draft Riots" of 1863 in New York City.

Police officials and local governments must become more sophisticated in responding to on-the-scene video, especially today, when it can be instantly disseminated through social media—something not possible in 1991. They must act quickly and persuasively to assure the public that the matters in question are being investigated vigorously and fairly. They must explain, in a transparent and frank manner, the need to understand the context of each video. They cannot do what the LAPD did back in 1991, which was to ignore recorded evidence any eyewitness offers.

The police should use the availability of bystander video as an opportunity to reach out to the public. Bystander video should be regarded as evidence, and people should be asked and encouraged to come forward with video. The police need to be clear that they are grateful for the cooperation of the community in whatever form it takes.

Beyond this, government and police agencies need to counter the inherent subjectivity and selectivity of bystander video by collecting evidence from other video sources. In addition to fixed surveillance video cameras mounted on buildings, streetlight posts, and the like, all police vehicles should be equipped with dashcams and the officers themselves with bodycams. Both devices should be activated during any interaction with the public. The more perspectives that can be recorded, the greater the objectivity of the video record.

But let's not approach "citizen journalism," bystander video, and traditional broadcast and cable news video defensively. While it is true that news organizations in particular tend to report on bad things more often than on good things—"If it bleeds, it leads" has long been a journalistic rule of thumb—leaders in our communities and the agencies that serve them should do all they can to highlight and celebrate "raw footage" that documents the good.

During the manhunt (June 6-June 28, 2015) for the two convicted murderers who escaped from Clinton Correctional Facility in Dannemora,[39] not far from the Canadian border in upstate New York, I was impressed by the televised coverage of the massive and protracted police search. I realized at the time that we Americans were watching the unfolding story of a productive and positive collaboration of a community and law enforcement in a search and patrol endeavor that involved 1,300 officers fanning out over a wide and rugged area during twenty-two tense and grueling days. The community enthusiastically supported and cooperated with police who, after all, were significantly disrupting their daily lives. Vigilant citizens supplied investigators with thousands of tips—many submitted via social media or on websites set up for the purpose. For their part, police officers from many jurisdictions and backgrounds, under tremendous pressure, treated residents with respect and empathy. If attitudes had been different on either side, the entire scenario might truly have resembled that of an enemy army occupying conquered territory. But such was not the case, as both police and the community embraced the role of guardians and acted with true heroism.

I studied and worked for years in western New York. I knew the police in those communities to be dedicated, courageous professionals. The wider public, however, rarely sees the best of law enforcement. I was heartened by the coverage of the Dannemora manhunt, but I also fear that government and law enforcement are mostly losing the battle to create a constructive image of their role, their presence, and their mission.

The Social Media World War

That battle—the struggle to win the hearts and minds of our communities, especially those that are most challenged, those whose residents feel marginalized and, in fact, *are* marginalized—that battle is one we cannot afford to lose.

In Ferguson—and in other communities—law enforcement and other public agencies have been slow to understand and use contemporary media technologies. As a result, police departments that are often already perceived as detached from the community if not in outright opposition to it, are growing increasingly out of touch with public they serve. According to the NYU researchers, among the sentiments that social media "triggers," feelings of group identity, of injustice, and of anger are the most powerful. If our law enforcement agencies have been slow to recognize and act on this fact, they can look to social media as it was used during the Arab Spring for both inspiration and a wake-up call.

Or they can look to something far more extreme.

Months "after the [U.S.] State Department signaled that it was planning to energize its social media campaign against" ISIS/ISIL, *The New York Times* reported on June 12, 2015, the State Department's own internal assessment concluded "that the Islamic State's violent narrative — promulgated through thousands of [social media] messages each day — has effectively 'trumped' the efforts of some of the world's richest and most technologically advanced nations."[40]

Earlier, a June 8, 2015 report in *The Daily Signal* detailed how ISIS/ISIL uses social media platforms to recruit followers (a/k/a, terrorists) far beyond the Middle East. ISIS/ISIL posts on YouTube high-quality videos with Hollywood-level production values, shares videos of its gruesome operations on Twitter, and even publishes an online magazine.[41] (Called *Dabiq*, after the town in northern Syria where, according to one Muslim tradition, Christian and Muslim are destined to face each other in final battle, the magazine is published in English and other languages.)

The generation rising all over the world has come of age with digital media, whether in the portions of the Middle East now controlled by ISIS/ISIL or in Paris, France, or in Ferguson, Missouri. For these young people, connections made through the Internet are often more compelling and more influential than those made in their own geographical neighborhood. If their proximate community offers them little or nothing, no relevant values, no stake in itself, and if the most visible representatives of society's values and laws—the police—are perceived as enemies, these young people will find other communities to join. They may turn to criminal gangs. These, after all, have served as alternative "communities" for many years. Today, however, disaffected youth may also turn to the online "gang" that is the likes of ISIS/ISIL. Its remote location halfway around the world, bound up in a culture with beliefs and traditions to which most American youngsters have never been exposed, does not diminish the effectiveness of the organization's social media outreach. A connection with faraway terrorists can be as close as a laptop, tablet, or smartphone screen.

Values, technology, and perception put us all in a continual contest for hearts, minds, and lives. The stakes in this struggle are incredibly high. When the police fail to earn trust and legitimacy, they are seen not as guardians with a common stake in the communities they serve, but as armies of invasion and occupation. If they fail to act as representatives and servants of the community, if they are perceived as the enemy of minority youth who already feel themselves marginalized economically and culturally, the likely result will be the all-too-familiar *domestic* tragedy of crime that reinforces a cycle of poverty and alienation, which, in turn, reinforces the criminal choices too many young people make.

Those are terrible consequences. Today, these *American* consequences also have a *global* dimension. As I discuss in the next chapter, the cycle of alienation today presents local threats with global connections and potentially grave national consequences.

CHAPTER 7

American Consequences

I came of age during t 1960-1970, a decade during which violent crime in the United States increased by 126 percent. People were scared. I remember. I remember that talk about "gang violence," "murders," "muggings," and the like was routine yet urgent. Besides, between the soaring crime rate, the protest movements growing out of the struggle for civil rights and the backlash against the Vietnam War, a seemingly endless series of political assassinations (JFK, Malcolm X, MLK, RFK), and the general sense that "young people" had no respect for the values of their elders, there was a nearly universal sense that America was coming apart at the seams. When I joined the Leon County Sheriff's Department in 1977, the rate of increase in violent crime was slowing down, but it was still rising—and a lot: 64 percent between 1970 and 1980. People were still scared—and, based on the numbers, they had right to be.[42]

In 2013, the violent crime rate fell to its lowest point since 1970, and according to the Department of Justice's National Crime Victimization Survey, published in September 2014, violent crime in the United States declined from 79.8 to 23.2 victimizations per 1,000 people.[43] Yet people are still scared. In fact, I'd say they're generally even *more* scared than they were back in the 1960s, 1970s, and 1980s, the years in which I was either growing up or patrolling the streets. Even with the recent upticks in violent crime in some cities, the numbers do not justify the fear.

This does not, however, give us license to ignore the fear. We need to understand it.

But, first, what caused the crime decline? The 2015 report published by the Brennan Center for Justice at New York University School of Law (my source for most of the statistics I just cited) uses that very title, *What Caused the Crime Decline?* The *greatest* contributing factors, the report's authors found, were an aging population, changes in income, and decreased consumption of alcohol. But increased numbers of police officers and the widespread use of CompStat, a policing approach that helps law enforcement officers gather data used to identify crime patterns and thereby more effectively target resources, also played significant roles in the decline. At the same time, what many people (erroneously) regard as the end product of good policing—"adding individuals to the prison population"—contributed "essentially zero" to the decline in American crime.[44]

The bottom line is that crime is lower these days than it has been in a long time, and police have played a measurable, if not leading, role in that decline. Yet people are, if anything, more frightened about crime than ever. What accounts for the disconnect between the empirical data—the objective numbers—and the subjective emotion?

In a *Huffington Post* blog, two of the Brennan Center study's authors, Lauren-Brooke Eisen and Oliver Roeder, blame the media for adhering to the traditional "if it bleeds, it leads" approach to reporting the news. Anecdotal evidence is always more emotionally compelling than statistical trends, and by highlighting this or that particularly violent crime, the media creates the perception of crisis.[45]

Doubtless, Eisen and Roeder have a point. But, as a long-time street cop and law enforcement executive, just as I want to make sure that the police get their fair share of credit for bringing down crime, I can't help thinking that we should also share at least some of the blame for the lingering—and disproportionate—public concerns about crime. I am not alone in my willingness to shoulder a slice of the blame. Judging by the numbers, today's police departments succeed more than they fail, yet, as reported in *Legitimacy and Procedural Justice: A New Element of Police Leadership* (published by the U.S. Department of Justice, Bureau of Justice Assistance in March 2014), many police chiefs these days feel compelled to take "on a new challenge: applying the concepts of 'legiti-macy' and 'procedural justice' ... to policing." Performance numbers are not enough. Legitimacy and procedural justice are different "measure-ments of the extent to which members of the public trust and have con-fidence in the police, believe that the police are honest and competent, think that the police treat people fairly and with respect, and are willing to defer to the law and to police authority."[46]

These two concepts, legitimacy and procedural justice, are not just desirable adjuncts to the profession of law enforcement. It feels good to be respected and trusted, and who doesn't like to feel good about the job they do? Who doesn't want to be appreciated? But, as observed in *Legitimacy and Procedural Justice*, "Because the effectiveness of police operations often depends at least in part on the public's willingness to provide information to and otherwise help the police, police leaders in-creasingly are seeing legitimacy and procedural justice as necessary con-ditions of success ..." Or, as we members of the President's Task Force on 21st Century Policing put it, "People are more likely to obey the law when they believe that those who are enforcing it have the legitimate authority to tell them what to do. ... The public confers legitimacy only on those they believe are acting in procedurally just ways."[47]

Policing is never a solo act. The community must play its part, must be engaged, must cooperate, collaborate, and, in a word, care. My col-leagues and I on the Task Force recommended that law enforcement cul-ture "embrace a guardian mindset to build public trust and legitimacy."[48]

And departments are listening. Radley Balko, author of *Warrior Cops*, one of the best books on the militarization of the police,[49] pro-filed Lieutenant Chad Goeden, commander of the Alaska Department of Public Safety Training Academy, in *The Washington Post* on July 28, 2015. Goeden hung a sign over his office door with a quotation from Sir Robert Peel—the British home secretary who established London's Metropolitan Police, the first modern urban police force, in 1829. (*Robert* Peel is the reason British cops are nicknamed "Bobbies"!) "The ability of the police to perform their duties is dependent upon public approval of police ac-tions," the sign says. Goeden told Balko that he chose that quotation because he "thought it was important to remind myself, my staff and the recruits why it is we do what we do, who we serve, and who it is we are beholden to." This means rejecting the notion of officers as warriors. "If we're warriors," he asks, "who are we at war with?" He tells his staff not to use the term *warrior* and instead speak of *guardian*. When Balko asked if this was "just semantics," Goeden replied, "Words matter." To each of his academy classes, he explains, "We are Guardians—of our communities, our way of life, our democracy, the Constitution."[50]

Los Angeles Police Department Deputy Chief Bill Scott recently told an assembly of his officers, "We were warriors," evoking the notorious LAPD of the 1970s and 1980s, which reporter Kate Mather described as "a hard-charging, occupying force that raided poor neighborhoods and rounded up anyone in sight." Those officers were *trained* to think of themselves as "soldiers in a never-ending war on crime." Today, Scott tells his officers to think of themselves as "guardians watching over communities—not cracking down on them." He adds, if being a guardian means "we've got to take somebody to jail, we'll take them to jail. ... But when we need to be empathetic and we need to be human, we've got to do that too."[51]

As a thirty-year trend, the declining crime rate in the United States is real, but so is the recent uptick in murders in some American cities. "Murder Rates Rising Sharply in Many U.S. Cities," a *New York Times* headline warned on August 31, 2015.[52] Yet, as *Washington Post* reporter Max Ehrenfreund correctly observed a few days after the appearance of the *Times* article, "Overall, most cities are still far safer than they were two decades ago, and virtually all of that improvement has remained." He quotes University of California, Berkeley, criminologist Franklin Zimring: "Crime and violence in most big cities in the United States are pretty much as they've been lately." Zimring added, "Boy, is that good news."[53]

Ehrenfreund wants us to know that the country is not going to hell in a handcart, but he also points out that at least three cities do show "deeply worrisome" statistics: "If current trends continue, Baltimore, Milwaukee and St. Louis this year [2015] stand to lose more than 20 years of progress in preventing homicide." Ehrenfreund observes that all three of these cities "have been the site of protests over the deaths of black residents at the hands of police, which has led some law enforcement officers and commentators to suggest that police are now too cautious to do their jobs properly." He quotes Carnegie Mellon University criminologist Alfred

Blumenstein, who calls public pressure for police accountability a "good thing," but "What we've seen is, because police are being held accountable, a tendency or possibility that the police are backing off."[54]

Just as we cannot attribute the long decline in violent crime exclusively—perhaps not even primarily—to improved policing, so we cannot exclusively (or even primarily) attribute the recent homicide uptick in some cities to overcautious police work. Neither reporter Ehrenfreund nor any other criminologist I've read has pointed to sufficient data to definitely nail the causes of the uptick. I do, however, have an opinion about it. It is an opinion based less on any hard data than on my instinct and feel for what's going on "out there." The overall crime decline is real, and the uptick in homicides documented in certain cities is likewise real. I believe the uptick is strongly associated with another *real* decline—the declining perception of police legitimacy and procedural justice in some of our most challenged communities.

LAPD Deputy Chief Scott's exhortation to his officers to be guardians, not warriors, is part of a new program of training in that department, which, in turn, is part of a national movement that has been significantly inspired, I'm proud to say, by the President's Task Force on 21st Century Policing. It is all about productively and positively reforming law enforcement. As the *Los Angeles Times* reported on August 21, 2015, "Departments across the country are taking steps to replace the warrior mentality with a different approach, one that emphasizes protection over suppression, patience instead of zero tolerance. It's a fundamental shift, one that could affect issues such as how often officers fire their guns and the way they walk down the street."[55]

The LAPD training, in particular, comes "as several police shootings have strained [police-community] relationships." Some of these incidents have drawn national and even international attention, including the officer-involved shootings of a homeless man, Charly Keunang, in LA's skid row (March 1, 2015); Brendon Glenn (May 7, 2015); and Ezell Ford (July 19, 2015)—all unarmed, all African American, all widely covered on broadcast and social media, and all prompting community protests. The *Los Angeles Times* reported that Mac Shorty, chairman of the Watts Neighborhood Council, "said the department should have invited residents and local community leaders who have concerns about LAPD officers to the [new]

training. Doing so, he said, would have added legitimacy to the training."
Note that word: *legitimacy.* Mac Shorty "said many in his neighborhood
have lost trust in the LAPD after the recent shootings, adding that he
thinks twice before calling 911."[56]

Mr. Shorty observed, "Right now, the LAPD could never be the guardian of the community because there's too much distrust. Every time we
get to the point we can trust them, there's another shooting."[57]

■ ■ ■

Even as the overall rate of violent crime has declined, the spike in homicides in mostly poor neighborhoods of color continues to reflect the feelings of desperation and marginalization among many, the harsh realities
of financial hardship, and the strong presence of gang culture. We will
talk about these in a few moments. But I believe that activists like Mac
Shorty should be listened to. A big urban police force wants to reform
itself. It wants to shift from a dysfunctional "warrior" model of policing to
the forward-looking, 21st century "guardian" model. This is great news!
Yet: "Right now, the LAPD could never be the guardian of the community
because there's too much distrust."

In many communities across America—mostly those that are not ben-
efitting from the general decline in violent crime, but are enduring spikes
in violent death—the police are suffering a crisis of legitimacy.

Let's define our terms carefully. *Legitimacy* reflects the community's
belief that it is proper, acceptable, and desirable for the police to exercise
authority in the community. This belief flows from three judgments ordinary people must make.

1. The people must judge the police to be deserving of their trust.
    Trust, in turn, requires public confidence in the honesty of the po-
    lice officers, their sincere effort to perform their duties well, and
    their commitment to protect the residents of the community.
2. For a community to invest the police with legitimacy, residents
    must be willing to defer both to the law and to the authority of the
    police to enforce it.

3. The community must believe that the actions of the police are moral, ethical, and appropriate to the circumstances in which they take place.

In recent years, many criminologists have suggested that the public perception of legitimacy also depends largely on the procedural justice police exhibit in their interactions with a community. There are at least four essential components to procedural justice:

1. In any interaction with the police, people want to be able to tell their side of the story. They want to explain the situation. They want to present their point of view, their arguments, *before* the police decide what action to take. The community and its residents want a voice—both with regard to any given interaction and in the development of police policy generally.
2. People want the police to act impartially, without personal bias, and on the basis of the law—the application of legal principles to the facts of a particular situation or incident. This requires the police to be clear, open, and transparent about what they are doing and why they are doing it. People may or may not like or agree with an officer's decision, but, at minimum, they need to know the reason—in law—for it. People need to believe that police decisions are made on the basis of neutral, unbiased judgment informed by law.
3. Everyone wants to be treated with respect, with dignity, and with common courtesy. Treated in this manner, they are more likely to believe that their rights are being respected and safeguarded.
4. People respond favorably to authority figures who exhibit a trustworthy, caring, and benevolent character. These traits are demonstrated through action, speech, and demeanor. Showing empathy does not mean "going soft" on anybody or failing to enforce the law, let alone violating the law. It does mean communicating in ways that demonstrate a concern for the other person's feelings and humanity. People want to believe that whatever decisions police officers make or actions they take are made or taken from

motives of benevolence—not punishment, not vengeance, not the mere exercise of power and authority.

To the degree that an individual or an entire community is convinced of the procedural justice of police actions, behavior, demeanor, and speech, that individual or community will tend to accept the legitimacy not only of particular law enforcement decisions and actions, but of the police themselves. To the degree that individuals grant law enforcement legitimacy, they will not only comply with police instructions, they will more generally cooperate with and support the police in their community. Their default response will be to *defer* to the police, not resist them.

Procedural justice is not rocket science. In almost every situation, it comes down to acting on the basis of commonsense fairness by implementing fair procedures. Individual officers and entire departments that *consistently* implement fair procedures tend to create a climate in which community members voluntarily defer to the police and accept both the law and their application of it. This, in turn, tends to enhance the community's confidence in and respect for the justice system as a whole. It gives communities a stake in the system, which, in turn, promotes greater lawfulness as people become more willing to take responsibility for abiding by the law. This benefits both the community and the police. The community is safer, police officers are safer, and both the community and the police are spared the necessity for frequent interventions by law enforcement.

Neither the United States Constitution nor the statute books of individual states and jurisdictions make any mention of the concepts of legitimacy and procedural justice. These documents are concerned only with legality. It is necessary for the police to follow the law. From this, their legal authority is directly derived. Yet, while *necessary*, legality is not in itself *sufficient* to the effective exercise of police authority. Legality is defined by statute. Legitimacy is defined by the myriad judgments ordinary people make every day concerning the police and what they say and do. The law is objective. Legitimacy is subjective, which can make it something of a moving target.

Understandably, some police officers do not like the idea of being judged according to subjective standards—just as the people they serve do not like feeling that the police treat them according to some arbitrary feeling, impression, bias, or whim. But the fact is that the police have a legal responsibility to apply the law as objectively as possible, without bias, whereas the public has no such sworn obligation. How could they? Most people know relatively little about the law, especially as it applies to police practices. The only means they have for judging the procedural justice and legitimacy of what officers say or do to them are subjective. How did the officer's behavior, action, and words make them feel? Did these things seem fair? Were they reasonable? Did they make sense? Was the interaction respectful? Did the officer or officers listen? Did they explain themselves? Were they transparent? None of these questions are matters of law. All of them concern legitimacy. Yet if an officer fails to earn legitimacy as the result of a given interaction, the ordinary person who evaluates the interaction subjectively will judge it not merely as illegitimate but also as illegal. This judgment may bring a formal complaint, or it may simply erode police-community relations one more notch. In either case, the perception of illegality—valid or not—will make individuals and, ultimately, entire communities that much less willing to defer to police actions, even when they are both legal and necessary. The police officer will be perceived not as a guardian, but as a warrior—or, more accurately and even worse, as a soldier in an enemy army sent to invade and occupy the neighborhood.

For communities, the feeling that they are being oppressed by an invading army tends to exacerbate crime, which, in turn, reinforces a vicious cycle of poverty and alienation. Not every poor neighborhood is a crime-plagued neighborhood, but most high-crime neighborhoods are poor. To the degree that police in these neighborhoods fail to earn legitimacy, residents feel no incentive to cooperate with law enforcement to build and safeguard their community. Yet lawlessness is not a viable option. It leads rapidly to the disintegration of the community as violent crime increases. The perception that social values bring benefits to the community breaks down, and with the breakdown of this perception, social values themselves erode within a community in which any substantial number of residents feel they have no stake in adhering to them, much less defending them.

I have a degree in sociology, but it was hardly necessary for me to study the subject to understand that human beings are naturally social beings. It's obvious. We see it every day. If one social structure breaks down, if the neighborhood, the community, and the nation are seen as valueless, offering no tangible stake, people will search for alternative social structures. Sometimes, the strongest-seeming structure available is the criminal gang. In the absence of a personal connection with the broader community, membership in a gang offers identity and fellowship. In a violent environment, it also offers protection from attack by rival gangs. Not that gangs are benevolent. Recruits may also be forced into joining by threat, assault, and other coercive means.

Gang violence transforms many neighborhoods into hell on earth. Gangs often finance themselves through organized extortion of residents, especially local merchants. When doing business in a neighborhood becomes too dangerous or too expensive, providers of goods and services pack up and go elsewhere. The neighborhood loses places to shop as well as sources of local employment. In cities, high-crime Zip codes often become "food deserts," communities underserved or even wholly unserved by supermarkets and markets. Residents may resort to "convenience stores," if these are available, and pay top dollar for a meager, often unhealthful, selection of goods.

In addition to extortion, gangs typically deal in drugs, firearms, and other forms of so-called organized crime. But it is the *disorganized* crime—anarchic drive-by shootings and violence that erupts when members of rival gangs rub up against one another—that bring the greatest terror, random, swift, and devastating as the involved and the innocent alike are caught in the crossfire. On October 1, 2015, a six-month-old girl was shot on Cleveland's East Side. She was being driven by her grandmother, strapped safely in an infant car seat. She was the youngest of three children shot and killed in that neighborhood within a month's time, collateral damage in a perpetual gang war.[58] *This* is domestic terrorism.

■ ■ ■

Every life in every neighborhood matters, white, black, brown, old, young, or in between. In our most at-risk neighborhoods, all of these lives are in danger—in terms of quality, in terms of survival itself. At greatest risk, however, are the lives of young black males, who are both the victims and perpetrators of violent crime at rates wildly disproportionate to other groups. They are—and feel themselves to be—marginalized in their communities and therefore see themselves as having little or no stake in the community. This is neither an exclusively African American problem nor exclusively an American problem. "Youth marginalization" is a *worldwide* phenomenon, and in March 2014 it was even the focus of a Columbia Global Policy Initiative jointly sponsored by New York's Columbia University and the Office of the United Nations Secretary General's Envoy on Youth. Throughout the world, youth are excluded from many rights, from political participation, and from participation in community affairs. Their employment options are limited, and their educational opportunities often inadequate.

Indeed, marginalization, especially of youth, is likewise a global phenomenon. While many of the poorer neighborhoods in America's cities seem remote, obscure, and out-of-the-way, they are part of a global community. The immediate reach of a street gang may be locally defined, but the cycle of alienation in challenged communities presents both a threat, on the neighborhood level, and also a more general threat to homeland security. Youth who feel no value connection with their immediate community are unlikely to develop such a connection with the broader, national community. Citizens—guardians—are forged within neighborhoods, and those neighborhoods constitute the fabric of the nation. A fabric is only as strong as its most distressed, worn, and abraded sections.

As local alienation and marginalization eventually aggregates to have a national—and global—effect, so international terrorist gangs reach out to youths worldwide, wherever they happen to live. We see this, for example, in Paris—renowned as among the world's wealthiest, most glamorous, sophisticated, "civilized," and cosmopolitan cities, yet ringed by *banlieues*, suburbs or urban districts that are often poverty traps, home to foreign immigrants as well as French citizens of foreign descent. Geographically on the margins of the city, they are places of the marginalized.

With marginalization comes a devaluing by those on the inside as well as those on the outside. The ultimate expression of this devaluation is a lack of social identity bordering on anonymity. The very phrase *"les banlieues"* is commonly used by the European French not to describe particular suburbs or outlying neighborhoods, but the blocks of low-income housing within them. The two young self-proclaimed jihadists who killed twelve and injured eleven at the Paris-based offices of the satirical magazine *Charlie Hebdo* on January 7, 2015, were Paris-born French citizens, the children of Algerian immigrant parents. They lived in one of the outer—marginalized—*arrondissements* (administrative districts) of Paris. They felt no positive connection with the city or nation of their birth, but they did make a very passionate connection with the "community" of radical Islamism and jihad (holy war) associated with al-Qaeda.[59]

Two years earlier, in the great American city of Boston, at 2:49 p.m. on April 15, 2013, brothers Dzhokhar and Tamerlan Tsarnaev—Dzhokhar, the younger, a US citizen, Tamerlan, a Russian and Kyrgyz citizen with permanent US residence status and a US citizenship application in progress—detonated two powerful homemade pressure cooker bombs near the finish line of the crowded Boston Marathon. Three spectators were killed in the blasts and an estimated 264 people were wounded, some sustaining permanent disabilities, mostly amputations.

The boys' parents were grateful to the United States, which had granted them refugee status after they emigrated in 2002 from war-torn Kyrgyzstan. They settled in Cambridge, Massachusetts. Tamerlan Tsarnaev attended Bunker Hill Community College before dropping out to become a boxer. He had dreams of competing on the US Olympic boxing team, he married a US citizen, Katherine Russell, who was pregnant with his daughter, and yet he said he "didn't understand Americans" and claimed to have no American friends.[60] After the bombing, authorities came to believe that April 15, 2013, might not have been the first time Tamerlan had killed. He may have been involved in an unsolved 2011 triple homicide in Waltham, Massachusetts. One of the victims was Tamerlan's sparring partner. Tamerlan's connection, if any, to the other two is unknown; both of those men were Jewish.[61] In 2009, he had been arrested for assaulting his girlfriend.

While Dzhokar seemed far better adjusted than his older brother to life in general and American life in particular—he attended the University of Massachusetts Dartmouth as a marine biology major and was regarded as a friendly, quiet young man—he greatly admired Tamerlan, emulated him, and wanted always to please him. By 2009, Tamerlan became deeply involved in the ultra-conservative, jihadist Salafist movement within Sunni

Islam. He subscribed to a YouTube channel devoted to it, and he seems to have influenced Dzhokar in this direction.[62]

The Tsarnaevs slipped through law enforcement's antiterrorism network. They had kept a low profile. They had made no overt threats. While it is easy to second-guess authorities and criticize them for having failed to prevent an act of domestic terrorism, I find it far more remarkable that law enforcement foils so many apparent plots-in-the-making. The public usually does not learn about these, partly because the law enforcement operations are secret, but also because a foiled plot is far less likely to make the 24-hour news cycle than a violent plot that reaches fruition or comes very close to it.

One such story that did, however, make it into the news was headlined by *The New York Times*, "Young Mississippi Couple Linked to ISIS, Perplexing All."[63] Nineteen-year-old Jaelyn Young and her fiancé, Muhammad Dakhlalla, twenty-two, were arrested on charges of trying to travel from Mississippi to Syria to join ISIL. "Perplexing All" speaks volumes about this case. "Friends and strangers alike said it was difficult to imagine two less likely candidates for the growing roster of young, aspiring American jihadists."

Jaelyn was a high school cheerleader and honor student in Starkville, Mississippi, home of Mississippi State University, a tranquil college town noted for a level of tolerance and affluence the rest of the country does not typically associate with Mississippi. The daughter of a Starkville police officer, she was a member of her high school's homecoming court, and she aspired to a career as a physician.

Known to his friends as Mo, Muhammad Dakhlalla, was a psych student at MSU, who planned to go on to graduate school at the university. His father, Oda, a kind of "patriarch" of Starkville's small Muslim community, was well known for his "personable air and habit of sharing food with friends and strangers," which "made him seem like a walking advertisement for Islam as a religion of tolerance and peace." Oda Dakhlalla, had come to Mississippi as a young man to study civil engineering at the University of Mississippi. His wife, a New Jersey native, was a Muslim convert. The couple raised three sons in Starkville, all natural born American citizens. Mr. and Mrs. Dakhlalla ran a successful Middle Eastern restaurant in the college town, and Oda also served the community as a math tutor.

According to Starkville's mayor, the family was a veritable fixture in the town. Oda even made it a habit to come to City Hall with free lunches for workers there. Active in the local mosque, he sometimes delivered sermons, to which he invited his non-Muslim friends and neighbors.

Both Mo and Jaelyn had been born in America. Mo had never expressed "radical" Islamist opinions, and Jaelyn Young had been raised "in a Christian household." She nevertheless found herself "drawn to the Quran's teachings" because, unlike the often-translated Bible, she believed the Quran "had been unchanged since it was first written." She and Mo met each other about a year before they were arrested, and she converted to Islam in April 2015. By May, according to an FBI affidavit, she was "identified … 'through social media platforms' as a supporter of ISIL.'" A pair of what the agency affidavit identified as FBI employees, posing as ISIL (ISIS) members, engaged online with both Jaelyn and Mo, who "repeatedly stated their desire to join the militants," Jaelyn with an offer of "medical aid" to the organization and Mo as a fighter.

"On June 6, the couple performed an Islamic marriage ceremony," but the marriage was not valid under Islamic law, because Jaelyn's police officer father, who had served in the US military in Afghanistan, "refused to sign a marriage contract." On July 17, 2015, one day after a young Muslim man in Chattanooga shot and killed five members of the US military, Jaelyn "rejoiced" about the shootings in a message to an FBI employee posing as an ISIL (ISIS) supporter.

On July 30, the couple received US passports and, a few days later, Turkish visas. "Alhamdulillah [praise God], soon we will taste the freedom of Khalifah [the Islamic State]," Jaelyn posted online. On August 8, 2015, Mo Dakhlalla and Jaelyn Young were arrested at Golden Triangle Regional Airport in Columbus, Mississippi. Both admitted to attempting to travel to Turkey with the intention of joining ISIL.[64]

If convicted of attempting to join a terrorist group, the pair face the potential of twenty-year prison terms. This would be a tragedy for them—although it could have been worse, for both of these two young Americans living deep in the heart of America, and also (as the people of Boston discovered) for the nation. Clearly, America is catching up to Europe in terms of the terrorist affiliation of alienated young people for whom the promises of ISIS, operating remotely via websites and social media, hold a stronger appeal than a connection with their own neighborhood, community, and country.

In the twenty-first century, the police and community alike have an urgent role in creating national solidarity and mutual security. The police must act in ways that demonstrate procedural justice and thereby foster the community's perception of their legitimacy. This will help to create the level of trust that will both strengthen and protect the community.

Yet, of course, the police cannot do it all. Creating a strong and secure community also requires the community to find value in itself, to respect and value its own residents, and to set high expectations for them. Such a community must whole-heartedly accept that there is no viable, sustainable, or desirable alternative to working productively and in concert with a police department that has earned its legitimacy and the community's trust. While the police must reach out to the community, so the community must also reach out to the police.

Communities cannot do this alone, police agencies cannot do this alone, and, even working together, they cannot achieve the level of solidarity, security, and value that will trump the hollow, lethal, and fraudulent value proposition of the local street gang or the global terrorist organization. Police and communities alike need national political leaders committed to addressing issues of social injustice and marginalization in our society. The only way to find such leaders is to demand them, and the only way to do that is to elect them. Democratic governments are, after all, built by the people, the electorate. The glory and the curse of a democracy is that its people pretty much get the government they ask for, whether through their votes or by grim defaults, through a misguided willingness to settle for whatever happens to present itself. To administer and enforce a just society, we need first to create that society.

For it will not be given to us. If we want an "American Spring," we need to build it, together, as guardians of ourselves, our families, our neighborhoods, our towns and cities, and our nation. If we all set out to be guardians of the community, we will find the common ground on which to build the society we want and the government we deserve.

When Sheriff Raymond Hamlin opened the door that admitted me into the *sworn* role of community guardian—a deputy sheriff of Leon County, Florida—he set me on a journey that led, among many other places, to a place on the President's Task Force on 21ˢᵗ Century Policing. Back in 1977-1980, the Florida Panhandle community I served in the capacity of guardian was essentially bounded by what I could see through the windshield and windows of my patrol car. Today, the opportunity to serve on the President's Task Force has given me a much broader field of vision. But my basic role—as guardian—is still the same. The concluding chapters of this book draw on my work with the Task Force to outline the responsibility of 21ˢᵗ-century policing to reform and improve itself while helping our communities to build the best, most secure, and most promising America that can be.

PART III
Officers, Involved

CHAPTER 8

Connect Policies to Values

Think of *Hamlet,* and you think "To be or not to be." Think of "The Declaration of Independence," and most of us get only as far as "We hold these truths to be self-evident, that all men are created equal," or maybe a little further, to the "unalienable Rights ... Life, Liberty and the pursuit of Happiness." Of course, there's a lot more to the document's preamble, which concludes with author Thomas Jefferson submitting "Facts ... to a candid world" to prove that the "history of the present King of Great Britain is a history of repeated injuries and usurpations." In fact, most of "The Declaration of Independence"—the part to which few of us give much thought—is a long rap sheet on King George III. I count twenty-eight items in Jefferson's presentation of the king's criminal record. Four concern keeping "among us, in times of peace, Standing Armies without the Consent of our legislatures," rendering those armies "independent of and superior to the Civil Power," and "Quartering large bodies of armed troops among us" while also "protecting them ... from punishment for any Murders which they should commit on the Inhabitants of these States."

Since even before there was a United States, Americans have deeply distrusted and resented the presence of uniformed armies among them. One of the first urban riots on record in America, the Boston Massacre of March 5, 1770, was provoked by this very thing. It began when some Bostonians taunted a Redcoat sentry, and he shouted for help. A Redcoat squad responded, and the Boston mob grew. They pelted the soldiers with snowballs and ice balls and anything else they could get their hands on. In response, the soldiers fired their muskets into the crowd, and, in an instant, five Boston residents lay mortally wounded or dead (including Crispus Attucks, a runaway black slave) and six more were injured.

Even after the Revolution was fought and won and the United States had rid itself of Redcoats forever, a lot of people—politicians and citizens alike—wanted no part of any permanent army, even a *United States* Army. A citizen militia was all the nation needed, they believed. Although those favoring the creation of a standing army ultimately got their way, for nearly a hundred years, that army was kept very, very small. When the Civil War broke out in 1861 and when two world wars were fought in the twentieth century, the U.S. Army was quickly built up using a combination of recruitment and conscription. But during the intervals of peace, the military was always very quickly demobilized, drastically reduced in number.

Since the end of World War II, the onset of the Cold War, and then the growing violence emanating from the Middle East, it has been necessary to maintain a very substantial "peacetime" military. We Americans tolerate this. We sometimes even express gratitude for the 1 percent of us who choose to serve in what is now an All-Volunteer Force. Yet, unless we happen to live in a Navy, Army, Air Force, or Marine town—a town that hosts a large military base—we see remarkably few uniformed service members walking among us. Most of the time, they are out of sight and pretty much out of mind, much the way Thomas Jefferson and the signers of "The Declaration of Independence" wanted it.

In fact, the only uniformed armed personnel most Americans see on a daily basis are police officers. Traditionally, the uniforms they wear are deliberately designed to distinguish them from soldiers or sailors or airmen or marines. This follows a tradition that began with the world's first "modern" urban police force, which was established in London in 1829 by British Home Secretary Sir Robert Peel. Street crime was rampant in London back then, and Peel believed the capital desperately needed a disciplined force to counter it. He also understood that, like the American colonists in 1770, English men and women in 1829 hated the idea of a large, possibly armed, military-style force "quartered" among them. They feared the very thing the colonists, some six decades earlier, had endured:

the presence of a force capable of suppressing political protest and propping up unpopular rule. So Peel—or, more precisely, the two commissioners he appointed, Charles Rowan and Richard Mayne—drew up nine principles that London's Metropolitan Police were to follow.[65] They are very much worth reading, studying, and, yes, even applying today. (In fact, New York City Police Commissioner claims to "carry" a somewhat paraphrased version of them "with me everywhere. My bible."[66])

The Nine Principles of Policing, 1829

1. To prevent crime and disorder, as an alternative to their repression by military force and severity of legal punishment.

   > Far from "quartering" an army among the people, Peel wanted the police to serve as an alternative to "military force." Moreover, he saw timely intervention by the police as an alternative to the "severity of legal punishment." Today, state-of-the-art policing prioritizes "de-escalation" tactics, which aim first and foremost at reducing or avoiding violence, thereby reducing the severity of both the human and legal consequences of crime and of police intervention in crime. Also, Peel and his commissioners were careful to specify distinctive uniforms for the police that were quite different from nineteenth-century military garb. The unique "high helmet" uniformed British "police constables" still wear on dress occasions looks nothing like any headgear worn by members of any military force in the world. It instantly marks the wearer as a "bobby," the affectionate nickname for a British police officer that pays tribute to Robert "Bobby" Peel.

2. To recognise always that the power of the police to fulfil their functions and duties is dependent on public approval of their existence, actions and behaviour and on their ability to secure and maintain public respect.

Peel declared, "The police are the public and the public are the police." For him, it was all about shared values between the community and those appointed to enforce the community's laws. Authority is conferred on the police by law, but the ability of the police to exercise that authority is derived from the public, who approve "of their existence, actions and behavior," thereby conferring legitimacy on them.

3. To recognise always that to secure and maintain the respect and approval of the public means also the securing of the willing co-operation of the public in the task of securing observance of laws.

   Successful policing is not something that is done to a community. It is done with "the willing co-operation" of the community." The people have to do their part.

4. To recognise always that the extent to which the co-operation of the public can be secured diminishes proportionately the necessity of the use of physical force and compulsion for achieving police objectives.

   Where the police and the community can work as partners, "the use of physical force and compulsion" diminishes—a lot.

5. To seek and preserve public favour, not by pandering to public opinion; but by constantly demonstrating absolutely impartial service to law, in complete independence of policy, and without regard to the justice or injustice of the substance of individual laws, by ready offering of individual service and friendship to all members of the public without regard to their wealth or social standing, by ready exercise of courtesy and friendly good humour; and by ready offering of individual sacrifice in protecting and preserving life.

   This principle is all about procedural justice—not just fairness and fair treatment as defined by law, but fairness and fair treatment that everybody can see, understand, and appreciate.

6. To use physical force only when the exercise of persuasion, advice and warning is found to be insufficient to obtain public cooperation to an extent necessary to secure observance of law or to restore order, and to use only the minimum degree of physical force which is necessary on any particular occasion for achieving a police objective.

On September 9, 2015, retired tennis star James Blake, an African American, was quietly texting on his phone as he awaited a limo beside the doorway of a Manhattan hotel. Without warning, he was rushed and tackled to the ground by a white plainclothes NYPD officer, James Frascatore. The officer misidentified Blake as a suspect in a credit card fraud (identify theft) case. Frascatore exhibited no badge and did not announce himself as a police officer. He handcuffed Blake and was soon joined by four other plainclothes officers, all white. After about fifteen minutes, Blake was released when a retired officer happened to walk by and recognized Blake as "the tennis player."

Blake, who suffered a cut to his left elbow and bruises to his left leg, received no apology from Frascatore or any of the other officers. Far more serious was the injury done to procedural justice and the perception of the legitimacy of the NYPD, since a surveillance camera captured the entire incident, and—as is almost always the case these days—the video found its way both to the Internet and broadcast TV. The only good thing about this incident—which was otherwise a textbook lesson in excessive force (the crime in question was non-violent, and Blake did not threaten or resist)—is that it could easily have ended up a lot worse. Because the officer had failed to identify himself, Blake would have been justified in defending himself with whatever force he thought necessary. The officer, Blake, or both could have been injured or killed. And for what?[67]

7. To maintain at all times a relationship with the public that gives reality to the historic tradition that the police are the public and that the public are the police, the police being only members of the public

who are paid to give full-time attention to duties which are incumbent on every citizen in the interests of community welfare and existence.

> *The police are members of the community—"the public"—who are paid to do "duties ... incumbent on every citizen in the interests of community welfare and existence." Police officers and "the public" must recognize that they share the same values, the same goals, the same duties. Policing cannot succeed as a solo performance.*

8. To recognise always the need for strict adherence to police-executive functions, and to refrain from even seeming to usurp the powers of the judiciary of avenging individuals or the State, and of authoritatively judging guilt and punishing the guilty.

> *The police protect and serve the public, and they enforce the laws that apply in their jurisdiction. They do not determine guilt, and they do not punish anyone.*

9. To recognise always that the test of police efficiency is the absence of crime and disorder, and not the visible evidence of police action in dealing with them.

> *One standard on which police performance may be evaluated is the safety of the community—the "absence of crime"—and not any "quota" of arrests, stop-and-frisks, or traffic tickets.*

Ever since the Declaration of Independence, we Americans have claimed the right to be free from domestic military occupation, and since at least 1829, the standard model of a police force has been specifically designed to avoid any appearance or implication of hostile, militaristic occupation. For more than a hundred years, American police forces invariably adhered to this British model. They wore uniforms that made them look like police officers, not shock troops. They walked beats or cruised in squad cars that were clearly civilian police vehicles, not Humvees, not armored personnel carriers, not tanks. To be sure, through that hundred-plus-year-period, some police officers did offensive things, bad things, criminal things, stupid things, and brutal things. But, most of the time, these were recognized as aberrations, denounced, and treated accordingly—if necessary, through the justice system. Recently, however, an impression has emerged that misbehavior, brutality, racial profiling, and the like have become more the rule than the exception. There is a widespread sense in the nation that many police officers and police departments think of themselves as being at war with the communities they supposedly serve. In turn, many communities—our most challenged communities, typically poor communities of color—see the police as an implacable enemy, a hostile military force. It is not unlike the way Bostonians, circa 1770, thought of the Redcoats quartered among them.

Both perceptions—that police abuse of the public has become standard operating procedure and that the police and the community are locked in chronic mortal combat—are grounded not in reality, but in *certain* realities. Both perceptions, I believe, originate in an actual historical movement toward the militarization of police departments.

■ ■ ■

The Third Amendment to the Constitution forbids the quartering of soldiers in private homes without the owner's permission. In modern times, the amendment has come to seem a quaint relic of the past, so absurd is the notion that the U.S. Army would someday decide to forcibly quarter troops in the family bungalow. But recently, the Third Amendment made a rare appearance in court and in the news. In July 2011, Henderson, Nevada, police arrested a family for refusing to allow officers to use their homes as lookouts during a domestic violence investigation. The family members brought suit against the police for violating their Third Amendment rights by attempting to forcibly "quarter" the equivalent of "soldiers" in their homes. A federal court rejected the suit in 2013 on the simple grounds that "a municipal police officer is not a soldier for the purposes of the Third Amendment."[68]

That made for an interesting news item. The *real* news, however, came from reporters and commentators who pointed out that, while a federal court explicitly ruled that municipal police officers were not soldiers, more and more of those officers were nevertheless equipping themselves in a manner almost identical to soldiers—wearing BDUs (battle dress uniforms), carrying tactical gear, wielding assault weapons, driving up in APCs (armored personnel carriers)—and also behaving more like troops than cops.

By 2013, the nation was increasingly taking notice of the "militarization" of American police forces, and it sometimes became a topic of heated conversation. Stories like the one relating the death of Sal Culosi stirred amazement and outrage. He was killed in a SWAT raid "because he bet on a football game":

> Several months earlier at a local bar, Fairfax County, Virginia, detective David Baucum overheard the thirty-eight-year-old optometrist and some friends wagering on a college football game.... After overhearing the men wagering, Baucum befriended Culosi as a cover to begin investigating him. During the next several months, he talked Culosi into raising the stakes of what Culosi thought were just more fun wagers between friends to make watching sports more interesting. Eventually Culosi and Baucum bet more than $2,000 in a single day. Under Virginia law, that was enough for police to charge Culosi with running a gambling operation. And that's when they brought in the SWAT team.
>
> On the night of January 24, 2006, Baucum called Culosi and arranged a time to drop by to collect his winnings. When Culosi, barefoot and clad in a T-shirt and jeans, stepped out of his house to meet the man he thought was a friend, the SWAT team began to move in. Seconds later, Det. Deval Bullock, who had been on duty since 4:00 AM and hadn't slept in seventeen hours, fired a bullet that pierced Culosi's heart.[69]

This is only one of many, many similar accounts of tragically inappropriate applications of SWAT or other military-style force to non-violent or low-violence situations found in Radley Balko's 2013 book, *Rise of the Warrior Cop: The Militarization of America's Police Forces.* The sheer volume of such accounts Balko presents gives the impression that American police forces are now thoroughly convinced that they are soldiers engaged in a war with the communities they are supposed to serve. It is as if the "Declaration of Independence," Third Amendment, and Peel's principles never existed. Fortunately, the impression is ultimately misleading. Although voluminous, the incidents Balko relates remain the exception in American policing, not the rule. Nevertheless, the book makes for valuable reading. First and foremost, it shows what can happen when force is misapplied; second, it relates the history of the *partial*—and I stress that adjective, because Balko fails to—militarization of America's police forces; third, it draws the critically important connection between militarization and the alienation of police from community and community from police. If a police department thinks of itself at war with the community, it is going to go to war with the community, and many community members will respond to the police as they would to any hostile occupier. The wrongful shooting of anyone is tragic, horrific, and completely unacceptable. The even greater harm is to allow anything resembling a permanent state of war to exist between the police and the community.

When police act like the Redcoats at the Boston Massacre, citizens have both the right and the responsibility to hold them accountable to the same laws to which they themselves are held accountable. They are justifiably enraged even by the appearance that brutal officers are being unfairly shielded or when attempts are made to justify a militaristic response by claiming that "it's a war out there." Make no mistake, the level of violence in some of our most troubled communities does at times approach a level resembling warfare. It is also true that, post-9/11, police departments do have to be prepared to handle potential terrorist situations, battles in a "war on terror" that can break out on any street corner, any building, any neighborhood any time. But it is a catastrophic error to confuse either of these warlike scenarios with an actual state of war in our communities. To do so, transforms the *metaphor* of war into something very like the *reality* of war. Treating a community as enemy territory creates a community of enemies.

We need to put the phenomenon of police militarization in perspective, but that does not mean minimizing or denying it. A permanently militarized police force is alien to American government and society, and, so far, no American police agency has been thoroughly or permanently recast in the military mode. Nevertheless, as authors like Balko document, military equipment and tactics are applied more often than they should be in situations that do not warrant their application and in which a military approach creates unnecessary and immediate danger to police and citizens as well as enduring damage to the trust that should exist between police and community.

"9/11," our political leaders tell us over and over again, "changed everything." I've never agreed with that simple sentence. 9/11 did *not* change everything. We, in our response to 9/11, changed—well, not everything, but a lot of things. Among these was the hitherto inviolable separation between the military and the police. Suddenly, police felt themselves on the frontlines of a global war on terror—and if you were a cop in New York City or the Washington area on September 11, 2001, it was impossible to feel any other way. In the wake of 9/11, the U.S. Department of Defense actively encouraged law enforcement agencies nationwide to request military-grade weapons, vehicles, and other equipment from surplus and other stocks of DoD hardware. This materiel was not suddenly made available after 9/11/2001. The so-called 1033 Program had been created four years earlier by the National Defense Authorization Act of Fiscal Year 1997. Its sole purpose was to transfer "excess military equipment to civilian law enforcement agencies." By 2014, the program had transferred some $5.1 billion in military hardware. Between 1997 and 9/11/2001, the most-requested commodity was ammunition (which still remains the number one request) followed by non-weapon-related materiel, such as cold weather clothing, medical supplies, sand bags, and so on. After 9/11, military weapons and vehicles—everything from grenade launchers to armored tactical vehicles to helicopters—were called for.

Over the years, the 1033 Program has had its detractors. The DoD's own Inspector General criticized the program in 2003 for waste and fraud, and the ACLU and other rights organizations protested police use of weapons and vehicles designed for the battlefield against domestic demonstrations and protests in urban America. Broadcast and cellphone video from the streets of Ferguson, Missouri, in 2014, after the killing of Michael Brown and after the grand jury's decision not to indict Officer Darren Wilson, the man who shot Brown, showed SWAT teams and an array of armored vehicles that, at the very least, gave the appearance of military-style force being used to suppress the exercise of First Amendment rights to free speech and protest. On January 16, 2015, President Barack Obama issued Executive Order 13688, which led to the recall of some surplus military equipment (vehicles, specialized firearms and ammunition, riot equipment, and so on) granted to police departments under the 1033 Program.[70]

Both the 1033 Program and 9/11 accelerated the militarization of many American police forces, but neither caused that militarization. It had been, in fact, a long time coming. It dates back to the middle and late 1960s, when many felt that the civil unrest associated with the Civil Rights movement and protest against the Vietnam War demanded a greater show of force than most police departments could muster. During August 11-17, 1965, the predominantly African American neighborhood of Watts in Los Angeles erupted into violent riots—34 killed, 1,032 injured—after the arrest of a black motorist for DUI. Among the LAPD officers who responded during the riots was a detective named Daryl Gates. He was appalled by what he saw as the department's tactical inadequacy to cope with the situation. "We did not know how to handle guerrilla warfare," he wrote in his autobiography. "Rather than a single mob, we had people attacking from all directions."[71]

Convinced that the police were engaged in "guerrilla warfare," Gates sought advice from another organization fighting guerillas at the time— the U.S. Army, which was locked in combat against insurgents in Vietnam. Gates's dialogue with the military resulted in his formulation of the Special Weapons and Tactics concept: SWAT. What was "special" about the weapons and tactics was that they were military—submachine guns, assault rifles, sniper rifles, armored vehicles, and so on. Gates did not invent the SWAT concept. Rather, he used what he learned from the military to build upon the example set by a unit already in operation in Philadelphia, created in 1964 to counter a rash of violent bank robberies. The Philadelphia team's mission was not to chase the bad guys after the robberies, but to intervene *during* them—and that mission required special weapons and tactics. Gates created the first LAPD SWAT team in 1967. He said that "SWAT" originally stood for "Special Weapons Attack Team," but bowed to his boss, LAPD Chief Edward M. Davis, who wanted him to soften the acronym by substituting "and" for "Attack."

As the 1960s and 1970s saw rising rates of violent crime and drug use, more and more Americans felt that police needed to "crack down" on a restive and rebellious population. The SWAT concept became popular, and police agencies across the nation adopted it. One of the problems with the 1033 Program is that acquisition of "excess" military hardware is often unaccompanied by the necessary training and formulation of policy to ensure that the equipment is used appropriately—to deescalate or end dangerous situations rather than exacerbate them. From the beginning, SWAT was about equipment *and* tactics, which meant that training was at the heart of it. There is no doubt that, in some very dangerous situations, SWAT has been a lifesaver. But such situations were and are few and far between. This means that departments heavily invested in full-time SWAT teams have tended to deploy them in situations that could and should be more appropriately handled by "ordinary" officers who are dressed and equipped like police officers, not soldiers. Nevertheless, the public became increasingly accustomed to seeing military-style police officers on their streets, and, in 1971, when President Richard M. Nixon began using the phrase "War on Drugs" to describe an initiative to combat what he called "public enemy number one," most of the public believed that SWAT was just the "army" to fight this war. To give President Nixon due credit, he also asked Congress to fund programs for the prevention and treatment of drug addiction. These initiatives, however, did not capture the popular imagination as powerfully as the idea of war, which was so compelling that a majority of Americans freely accepted the acquisition of military-grade materiel, weapons, and vehicles to win victory in this war. Radley Balko points out that, since the 1970s, most militarized police operations have targeted suspected drug dealers—most of whom were not heavily armed.

Introduced in the campaign against drugs, the war metaphor soon bled over into all aspects of policing, especially in poorer communities of color, which were also often the areas in which drug dealers were concentrated. Moreover, not only did the federal government provide low-cost and even no-cost military hardware to fight the War on Drugs—equipment that hard-up, cash-constrained police departments could never have afforded to pay for on their own—the federal government encouraged aggressive prosecution of the drug war by authorizing local police to keep much of the property seized as "asset forfeitures" in drug raids. Thus the War on Drugs became a cash cow in many jurisdictions. As we saw in chapter 5, the scathing March 4, 2015 report by the Civil Rights Division of the U.S. Department of Justice on the Ferguson Police Department criticized the city's disproportionate reliance on judicial fines, mostly for traffic violations and other infractions and misdemeanors, as a source of revenue. The truth is that the War on Drugs has long been an even greater source of revenue in many jurisdictions and has fostered the militarization of some police departments.

Balko's book is perhaps most valuable not so much for criticizing the militarization of the police, but for exposing and exploring the *inappropriate* militarization and the *inappropriate* use of military-grade tactics, weapons, and force. Even today, the public thinks of SWAT as an elite force reserved for only the most dangerous missions against heavily armed adversaries. In fact, SWAT teams are sometimes used in operations against informal (but illegal) gambling activities and other non-violent criminal enterprises—even civil matters, such as bars operating with expired liquor licenses. Such inappropriate uses of SWAT not only push the bounds of constitutionality, they are dangerous far beyond the level of conventional police operations. Even worse, in the long term, they reinforce the most negative images of the police and their role in American society. A militarized police force looks like a police force at war with the people it is supposed to serve. Add to this the fact that military equipment is applied most frequently in poor neighborhoods of color. Now it begins to appear that the police are disproportionately waging war against African American and other minority communities.

As I do not want to lay down a blanket condemnation of SWAT and other military-style tactics—they do have value, often life-saving value—neither do I want to condemn the military. One of the lessons of Vietnam and, even more, of counterinsurgency in such places as Iraq and Afghanistan is that the indiscriminate use of military violence tends to exacerbate rather than suppress insurgencies. Today's American military puts the emphasis on restraint rather than on relentless attack, and on constructive "civic action"—building trust in war zones by (for example) ensuring a remote village adequate access to water and food. We police officers and police executives have much to learn from the American military about power and the powerful effect of restraint, as well as about the exercise of leadership to encourage good judgment, courage, and a service orientation.

•••

Those of us in law enforcement need to find ways to connect our policies with the values of American democratic society. In principle this is simpler than it may at first seem. As a member of the President's Task Force on 21st Century Policing, I was privileged to work with other law enforcement executives and with community organizers, legal scholars, educators, criminal justice experts, civil rights attorneys, leaders of police officer organizations, and others to outline future directions for policing in America. This has been challenging. But here's the simple part. We can begin to shape the future by going back to the future, back to 1829 and those remarkable principles of policing drawn up under Sir Robert Peel. All of them are about connecting policy to values—the values of the "ordinary" citizen, from whose ranks the police, after all, are recruited.

In the United States, we hope that these values—the values of the citizen, the values of the community—coincide with the values of American democracy, and then it becomes our task in law enforcement to ensure that *our* values and *our* policies harmonize with and support those of the nation and the neighborhood. But here's the hard part. Our communities are diverse and some are deeply troubled. There is no guarantee that the values prevailing in any given neighborhood reflect those of our democracy. In what we call our "most challenged" communities, many residents are alienated from national values because they feel themselves cut off from the promise of those values. They feel cheated by the American mainstream, including the American government. In some of these communities, hope has given way to despair, a feeling that America's political and economic leaders have forgotten or even betrayed them. The representatives of mainstream government authority with whom members of these communities most often come into contact are the police. Plagued by poverty and crime, it is the roughest neighborhoods that have the greatest need for the police. Yet, because they have been alienated from much of the American promise, many residents of these communities, particularly young residents, see the police as uncaring at best and enemies at worst.

By applying the objectives and tactics of community policing, law enforcement agencies can do a lot to build trust. But they cannot do everything. They cannot build a better, kinder economy. They cannot improve the schools. They cannot ensure that the nation has wise leaders rigorously dedicated to governing in good faith and with good sense. In 2015, the Chicago Police Department came under heavy national criticism for a series of officer-involved shooting incidents that, on their face, suggested a highly dysfunctional relationship between the police and the predominantly black communities of the city's south and west sides. There were the 2014 shooting of Laquan McDonald, shot by a police officer sixteen times in the back—all but one of the rounds delivered *after* McDonald (who was armed only with a small knife) was face down in the street; the shooting on December 26, 2015, of Quintonio LeGrier, an unarmed nineteen-year-old and, in the same incident, the "accidental" shooting of Bettie Jones, a 55-year-old grandmother, also unarmed. These shootings were fatal. Although the killing of Laquan McDonald occurred in 2014, release of a dashcam video of the incident was successfully suppressed by the police and the Cook County district attorney for thirteen months. When it was released late in November 2015, it resulted in the firing of Chicago police superintendent Garry McCarthy and widespread calls for the resignation of Mayor Rahm Emanuel because the video contradicted virtually every detail of the official 2014 account of the incident. The police shootings of the nineteen-year-old young man and the 55-year-old grandmother on the day after Christmas 2015 came hard on the heels of the release of the McDonald video. Twelve hours after those shootings, 26-year-old Mikel Lumpkin was critically wounded when he was shot five times—reportedly *after* he had complied with police commands to drop the gun he was, in fact, carrying. Whatever these tragic incidents may reveal about Chicago police practices and about relations between Chicago officers and the communities they serve, what may be even more significant is what they imply about the civilian administration of the city of Chicago. There is a reason for the calls for the resignation of Mayor Emanuel. Many Chicagoans have come to feel alienated not only from the police, but from their own city government. The city and county fought in the courts to prevent the release of dashcam video in the McDonald case—a video that is incompatible with the official version of the 2014 incident. The mayor and other civilian officials were slow to respond in the shootings of LeGrier and Jones and Mikel Lumpkin. At first, it did not seem that Rahm Emanuel was going to cut short his family's vacation in Cuba—but, after a day's delay and despite inclement weather that disrupted air travel, he did return to Chicago.

A constructive police-community partnership cannot be built if the city's civilian leadership fails to behave like part of the community and, what is more, fails to create the perception that it *is* part of the community. The police can enhance the sense of community. They cannot singlehandedly create a healthy, functioning community. The police cannot simply decree and proclaim social justice. In a democracy, it is the community itself, in partnership with local government, that must provide the will and the impetus to do these things.

Even under the best of conditions, this takes time. And, in places like Chicago, conditions are far from "the best." So, more urgently, the community has to find the hope, the will, and the courage to improve whatever can be improved right now. Like the police, the community has to make that journey back to the future that was 1829 and accept the "duties which are incumbent on every citizen in the interests of community welfare and existence."

The work of harmonizing the values of police and community begins when both community and police recognize that they actually share the same job—doing what is "in the interests of community welfare and existence." This commonality of purpose is the only relationship between community and police that can be productive in a democracy like ours. It is desirable. It is normal. A relationship of hostility and outright war may at this moment in time represent the status quo in many communities. It is, however, unacceptable, abnormal, and intolerable. Before we can move forward together, we all have to accept the desirability and normality of the common cause that exists between police and community. Having accepted this, those of us in law enforcement can then create a sound strategic basis for demilitarizing policing—without reducing the effectiveness of the police in emergencies and without unduly endangering the lives of officers and citizens. This, in turn, will build greater and greater trust between police and community, community and police. Without such trust, procedural justice becomes difficult to establish and legitimacy almost impossible to earn.

This journey toward trust won't be easy for anyone, I promise you.

On October 23, 2015, the *New York Times* reported on an address FBI Director James B. Comey delivered at the University of Chicago Law School, in which he observed that the additional scrutiny and criticism of police officers that followed a series of highly publicized episodes of apparent police brutality during 2014-2015 may have contributed to a spike in violent crime in some American cities. Comey acknowledged that he had no specific data to back up this assertion, but he said that he nevertheless possessed "a strong sense that some part of the explanation [for the spike in crime] is a chill wind that has blown through American law enforcement over the last year."[72] Some in the media refer to this "chill wind" as the "Ferguson effect."

The Obama administration expressed disagreement with Director Comey's assessment, as did a number of top police officials throughout the country. My assessment is based on my own observation of the men and women of the DeKalb County Police Department. Like other officers across our nation, they are aware of public scrutiny. They also understand that they will be second-guessed by the media, politicians, and members of the public. They accept that their careers and maybe even their larger future can quite possibly hang on a dashcam, bodycam, or smartphone video—a document that reveals a slice of time from a narrow perspective but that is widely regarded as a purely objective transcript of truth. They are aware of all these things—and yet they go out, day after day, determined to do their job to the best of their ability. I never heard from my officers what Director Comey said he heard—that officers who used to stop to question suspicious people are now deciding to remain in their patrol cars, fearful that their encounters will end up as global video scandals.

"Lives are saved when … potential killers are confronted by a police officer, a strong police presence and actual, honest-to-goodness, upclose 'What are you guys doing on this corner at 1 o'clock in the morning' policing," Director Comey told his University of Chicago audience. "We need to be careful it doesn't drift away from us in the age of viral videos, or there will be profound consequences."[73]

No, I have not heard my officers express this kind of hesitation, but I do appreciate that police officers these days have reason for doubt and reason to second guess their own judgment. I've already pointed out the dangers of war metaphors applied to policing, but I cannot help commenting that today's officers work in conditions that remind me of the combat environment the great German military theoretician Carl von Clausewitz described in the early 1800s. He wrote of the "fog of war." In times and places of intense, potentially deadly conflict, there is always a fog of doubt. For police officers, technologically enabled scrutiny in the era of the viral video only serves to make that fog thicker, that doubt more urgent and more complex.

It won't be cleared up anytime soon. Yet "lying down"—stepping back from taking appropriate action—is unacceptable in police work. The police, like the public they serve, have to *try* to do the right thing despite their doubts. The "fog of war" is real. Soldiers and their commanders learn to operate within it. The police have to do the same, and the public is best served by trusting them. The fog of war, this atmosphere of physical danger and moral complexity, close scrutiny, and second guessing, engulfs the police and the community alike. Both need to function within it and despite it. Neither can take time out in the hope that the situation will somehow resolve itself. What will make the uncertainty easier to navigate is transparency and communication on an immediate and ongoing basis. The police need to persuade the public that they are working together toward the same goals—to achieve safety, security, respect, and justice. If our communities then work with the police to implement, honor, and defend those shared values, I know that officers nationwide will perform the way my department's officers do: boldly, honorably, and decisively, creating relationships, building trust, and saving lives—through the fog and despite the doubts.

■ ■ ■

In our work on the President's Task Force, we emphasized the urgent necessity for police policies that reflect community values, and we formulated a series of practical recommendations to assist law enforcement agencies to achieve this. Among these, I believe the following are key to aligning community and police:[74]

- There must be active collaboration between law enforcement agencies and community members in developing policies, strategies, and programs to better serve neighborhoods disproportionately impacted by crime. Both the police and the community need to take ownership of important policy initiatives.

- Police agencies need to formulate and transparently articulate policies on the use of force. The policies need to be comprehensive, addressing everything from officer training to performance in the field. The rationale behind force policies should be fully explained. It is critically important that these policies be open to public inspection, most conveniently on a departmental website. People understand and accept that the police sometimes need to use force and that force is a tool used to protect the community. What they will *not* accept, however, is force applied inappropriately or for no clear reason. In such cases, people are quick to attribute the use of force to the uncontrolled emotions of the officer or to racial or other bias.

- We learn from our mistakes. Police agencies should implement non-punitive peer reviews of officer-involved incidents that negatively impact community relations, even if these incidents do not involve violations of policy. "Following policy" should never be used as an excuse to ignore incidents that threaten to damage police-community relations. In fact, such incidents likely indicate a need to modify policy.

- We must frankly address issues of bias involving race, religion, culture, ethnicity, gender, and sexual orientation proactively through data-based procedures that have been scientifically validated. For instance, adopting identification procedures scientifically designed to minimize bias will do a great deal toward preempting, within the community, suspicion of racial and other profiling. Likewise, police departments should collect, report, and make readily available data on the demographic composition and diversity of the department. They should collect and make available similar demographic data relating to all detentions (stops, frisks, searches, summons, and arrests). Data is powerful because the truth is powerful. Candor and transparency are critical to creating

DR. CEDRIC L. ALEXANDER

trust. Of course, police agencies should adopt and strictly enforce policies defining and prohibiting all forms of profiling based on race, ethnicity, gender (including gender identity and expression), sexual orientation, immigration status, disability, housing status, occupation, or language fluency.

- Tactical equipment, including protective gear, special weapons, and armored vehicles, have their place in law enforcement. Ours can be a very dangerous world. Nevertheless, in policing mass demonstrations and other public assemblies, law enforcement agencies should take steps to avoid presenting the appearance of a military operation. The "optics" of tactical, military-style equipment are inherently provocative and inherently negative. We Americans have a constitutional right to peaceful protest, and the police must not only honor and protect this right, they should demonstrate through their actions, appearance, and equipment that they share the democratic values this right embodies.

- As community outrage in Ferguson, Missouri, and other places has amply demonstrated, municipal and law enforcement agency practices that rely on citations and summonses to generate revenue must be discontinued and avoided. Recall Sir Robert Peel's ninth principle of policing: "the test of police efficiency is the absence of crime and disorder, and not the visible evidence of police action in dealing with them." Officers should never be required to issue a predetermined number of citations or make a predetermined number of stops, frisks, and other investigative contacts not immediately related to issues of public safety.

- We are all familiar with the concept of Karma—the cosmic version of what goes around comes around. Officers who treat the people with whom they come into contact with respect—suspects included—stand a good chance of getting respect (and, with it, compliance) in return. Departmental policy should require officers to seek consent before a search and to clearly explain to the subject that he/she has the constitutional right to refuse consent (in the absence of a warrant or probable cause). Officers should be capable of articulating their probable cause for a search, and they should be willing to explain clearly and respectfully their reasons to the person who is being searched. This is essential to creating the true impression of procedural justice and legitimacy. Officers should always identify themselves by rank, name, and command. Announcing oneself as a police officer is not only respectful, it is necessary to the safety of both the subject and the officer. It is a good idea for all officers to carry official business cards and to distribute them to everyone involved in any encounter. This enhances transparency and respect, and it facilitates all follow-up investigation.

People enter law enforcement for many reasons, but, in my experience, most officers consider themselves members of a "helping profession." Consider that word, *helping*. It expresses a vital endeavor and a worthy goal, but it is not the equivalent of "fixing" or "curing." And it should not be. The police cannot do everything. They can help, but they cannot promise to fix, to cure, or to work any other miracle. Nevertheless, a dedicated officer can do a lot, and I am convinced that following the principles and policies discussed in this chapter—those from 1829 as well as those formulated specifically for the twenty-first century—will go a long way toward forging a stronger and more productive relationship between law enforcement and communities, resolving some of today's doubt and uncertainty by introducing clarity, transparency, and trust.

CHAPTER 9

Do Community Policing

James Q. Wilson and George L. Kelling were both social scientists in the early 1980s—Wilson, the Shattuck Professor of Government at Harvard, and Kelling, a criminologist and fellow at Harvard's Kennedy School of Government. Although Kelling had been a probation officer early in his career, neither man was a police officer, but both knew that "social psychologists and police officers tend[ed] to agree" on a certain homely theory. It was this: "if a window in a building is broken *and is left unrepaired,* all the rest of the windows will soon be broken."[75]

You can be forgiven if this "theory" leaves you underwhelmed. Admittedly, it's not Darwin on evolution, Einstein on relativity, or Freud on the unconscious. But break it down. The existence of a broken window is not a crime. To leave a broken window unrepaired is not a crime. It is, at most, a sign of disorder. A window left broken is a signal that no one cares, which, in turn, is a sign of local disorder. Yet this symbol, this sign, *is* capable of generating a crime. It will almost assuredly spawn more broken windows, and the act of willfully breaking a window that is not yours is vandalism, a criminal act.

What is particularly interesting about this "broken windows theory" is that it is as true, Wilson and Kelling observed, "in nice neighborhoods as in run-down ones." This is not a judgment based on anecdotal evidence or mere opinion. In 1969, Philip Zimbardo, a Stanford University psychology professor, conducted some experiments testing the broken window theory. He parked an automobile, without license plates and with its hood up, on a street in a tough neighborhood of the Bronx. He did the same in Palo Alto, California, home of Stanford—a neighborhood that was not only a continent away, but, in terms of prevailing socioeconomic conditions, even more distant. Within ten minutes of the automobile's abandonment in the Bronx, the car was attacked. "The first to arrive were a family— father, mother, and young son—who removed the radiator and battery. Within twenty-four hours, virtually everything of value had been removed. Then random destruction began—windows were smashed, parts torn off, upholstery ripped. Children began to use the car as a playground. Most of the adult 'vandals' were well dressed, apparently clean-cut whites."[76]

Pan cross-country to Palo Alto. After a full week sitting on this sunny street in an upscale neighborhood, the abandoned car remained unmolested. Then Zimbardo intervened, smashing part of it with a sledgehammer (one tool I never thought of using in my own career as a psychologist!). Suddenly, passersby began joining in.

> Within a few hours, the car had been turned upside down and utterly destroyed. Again, the "vandals" appeared to be primarily respectable whites.
>
> Untended property becomes fair game for people out for fun or plunder, and even for people who ordinarily would not dream of doing such things and who probably consider themselves law-abiding. Because of the nature of community life in the Bronx—its anonymity, the frequency with which cars are abandoned and things are stolen or broken, the past experience of "no one caring"—vandalism begins much more quickly than it does in staid Palo Alto, where people have come to believe that private possessions are cared for, and that mischievous behavior is costly. But vandalism can occur anywhere once communal barriers—the sense of mutual regard and the obligations of civility—are lowered by actions that seem to signal that "no one cares."[77]

Wilson and Kelling argued that "no one cares" signals contribute to what they called "untended behavior," which, in turn, leads to the actual "breakdown of community controls":

A stable neighborhood of families who care for their homes, mind each other's children, and confidently frown on unwanted intruders can change, in a few years or even a few months, to an inhospitable and frightening jungle. A piece of property is abandoned, weeds grow up, a window is smashed. Adults stop scolding rowdy children; the children, emboldened, become more rowdy. Families move out, unattached adults move in. Teenagers gather in front of the corner store. The merchant asks them to move; they refuse. Fights occur. Litter accumulates. People start drinking in front of the grocery; in time, an inebriate slumps to the sidewalk and is allowed to sleep it off. Pedestrians are approached by panhandlers.[78]

Wilson and Kelling observed that, at this point, "it is not inevitable that serious crime will flourish or violent attacks on strangers will occur. But many residents will think that crime, especially violent crime, is on the rise, and they will modify their behavior accordingly."

They will use the streets less often, and when on the streets will stay apart from their fellows, moving with averted eyes, silent lips, and hurried steps. "Don't get involved." For some residents, this growing atomization will matter little, because the neighborhood is not their "home" but "the place where they live." Their interests are elsewhere; they are cosmopolitans. But it will matter greatly to other people, whose lives derive meaning and satisfaction from local attachments rather than worldly involvement; for them, the neighborhood will cease to exist except for a few reliable friends whom they arrange to meet.

As a single broken window, left unrepaired, tends to spawn crimes of vandalism—additional windows broken deliberately—so the appearance of disorder, the signals that "no one cares," begin to produce behavior that, quite literally, destroys the neighborhood as a community. Seeing the signs that "no one cares," people actually stop caring—about everything except their fear of crime. In their fear, they give up on their community.

> Such an area is vulnerable to criminal invasion. Though it is not inevitable, it is more likely that here, rather than in places where people are confident they can regulate public behavior by informal controls, drugs will change hands, prostitutes will solicit, and cars will be stripped. That the drunks will be robbed by boys who do it as a lark and the prostitutes' customers will be robbed by men who do it purposefully and perhaps violently. That muggings will occur.[79]

In the mid-1970s, George Kelling was part of an experiment in policing conducted in the gritty city of Newark and twenty-seven other New Jersey communities. It was called the "Safe and Clean Neighborhoods Program," and it was a simple, ultra-low-tech program based on the humble broken windows theory. The state gave funds to cities to enable them take officers out of their patrol cars and put them on foot patrol.

Foot patrol! The cops mostly hated the very thought of it. In fact, in many departments, foot patrol was a form of disciplinary punishment. Even most academic criminologists doubted it would have any significant impact on crime—except perhaps to increase it because police, deprived of their vehicles, would be hindered in responding to calls for service. But the state was funding the program, and local jurisdictions willing to forgo free money are few and far between. So the experiment was on.

And it went on for five years before the Washington, D.C.-based Police Foundation published an evaluation, focusing most intensively on Newark. The crime rate was unaffected by foot patrol. There must have been a lot of *I told you so's* in response to that result. But the numbers didn't tell the whole story. The fact was that "residents of the foot-patrolled neighborhoods seemed to feel more secure than persons in other areas, tended to believe that crime had been reduced, and seemed to take fewer steps to protect themselves from crime (staying at home with the doors locked, for example). Moreover, citizens in the foot patrol areas had a more favorable opinion of the police than did those living elsewhere." Even more surprising, "officers walking beats had higher morale, greater job satisfaction, and a more favorable attitude toward citizens in their neighborhoods than did officers assigned to patrol cars."[80]

How could this be? How could people *feel* safer when the crime rate had not declined? Even the remarkably progressive Sir Robert Peel, back in 1829, had said that the effectiveness of the police was measured strictly by the reduction in crime their presence produced. What the Newark foot patrol experiment demonstrated is that crime, especially the prospect of violent crime, is one source of fear within a community. Another source, however, is "the fear of being bothered by disorderly people." These are not necessarily "violent people, nor, necessarily, criminals, but disreputable or obstreperous or unpredictable people: panhandlers, drunks, addicts, rowdy teenagers, prostitutes, loiterers, the mentally disturbed." The foot patrol officers managed "to elevate … the level of public order in these neighborhoods." Moreover, although "the neighborhoods were predominantly black and the foot patrolmen were mostly white, this 'order-maintenance' function … was performed to the general satisfaction of both parties."[81]

It was not a matter, strictly speaking, of enforcing the law. Kelling followed the Newark officers, who quickly acquired a feel for the neighborhood. They became attuned to the values of the community, its needs, its fears, and its desire for order—the sense that *someone* really did care.

> The people [on the officer's beat] were made up of "regulars" and "strangers." Regulars included both "decent folk" and some drunks and derelicts who were always there but who "knew their place." Strangers were, well, strangers, and viewed suspiciously, sometimes apprehensively. The officer—call him Kelly—knew who the regulars were, and they knew him. As he saw his job, he was to keep an eye on strangers, and make certain that the disreputable regulars observed some informal but widely understood rules.

For example, "Drunks and addicts could sit on the stoops, but could not lie down. People could drink on side streets, but not at the main intersection. Bottles had to be in paper bags. Talking to, bothering, or begging from people waiting at the bus stop was strictly forbidden." The "rules" sometimes pushed the envelope of what was strictly legal: "If a dispute erupted between a businessman and a customer, the businessman was assumed to be right, especially if the customer was a stranger. If a stranger loitered, Kelly would ask him if he had any means of support and what his business was; if he gave unsatisfactory answers, he was sent on his way. Persons who broke the informal rules, especially those who bothered people waiting at bus stops, were arrested for vagrancy. Noisy teenagers were told to keep quiet."[82]

The "rules" were a form of collaboration with the neighborhood "regulars." The rules were not imposed by the patrol officer, nor were they demanded by the community. Instead, they were something the two, in collaboration, informally agreed upon. Over the course of five years of familiarity, these rules became the integument of procedural justice. By enforcing them, the patrol officer earned legitimacy. To be sure, some of this enforcement was *law* enforcement, but much of it was extralegal—not illegal—but outside of the law nevertheless. The officer took "steps to help protect what the neighborhood had decided was the appropriate level of public order."[83] Thanks to him, the neighborhood made sense, and because it made sense, it seemed safer and more secure. People felt cared about, not marginalized. Feeling cared about, they were empowered to care about each other, their community, and the officers who served it.

The broken windows theory has drawn and still draws significant and important criticism. Many critics rate physical disorder low on the scale of crime rate influencers. Others see "fixing windows"—addressing issues of physical disorder—as a superficial and short-term response to crime and the social conditions that contribute to crime. Some critics argue that the broken windows approach is inherently biased against African Americans and disadvantaged minority groups and that low-level interventions are used as cover for racist policing behavior. There is also a danger, critics say, of criminalizing the poor and homeless. Moreover, it is all too easy for the broken windows approach to become an excuse for harassing behavior by law enforcement, behavior that is anything but respectful and therefore violates community values.

Whatever the doubts and drawbacks, however, the broken windows concept was a major impetus to community policing, the approach to which I was introduced in Miami-Dade during the 1980s and early 1990s.

To me, it seemed a viable solution to the conundrum at the heart of modern policing: the most urgently troubled communities present the most urgent demands for public safety yet tend also most strongly to resent and resist the methods police employ to provide for public safety. In too many instances, the result is precisely the opposite of what was achieved in the Newark foot patrol experiment during the 1970s. Instead of the values of the officers and community residents meshing, so that the two parties are—and perceive themselves to be—on the same side, there is often an adversarial relationship between police and the community. The two come to see one another as enemies, and that perception is often magnified by policing policies based on military models. In the worst cases, opponents become belligerents in an outright and never-ending war.

■ ■ ■

The basics of community policing are what they were when I learned and practiced them in the 1980s under Major Doug Hughes in Florida—a time before the phrase "community policing" was even in general use. Those of us who served on the President's Task Force on 21st Century Policing were unanimous in identifying community policing as essential to building the positive relationships between police and members of the community that are essential to crime reduction.

On the big-picture level, community policing is a law-enforcement philosophy that advocates organization strategies to support police-community partnerships and pragmatic problem-solving techniques to proactively address immediate conditions that give rise to such public safety challenges as crime as well as those "broken windows" issues of social disorder and fear of crime.

Although you could never tell it from reading the newspaper or watching TV news, violent crime rates have indeed dropped dramatically over a period of decades. "High-crime neighborhoods" certainly exist, and many of them are poor neighborhoods of color. Statistically, however, these areas are on the margins in that they are the exceptions to the general decline in crime. On the statistical margins, these neighborhoods are almost always on the socioeconomic margins as well. As they have not benefitted from the national decrease in crime, so they have not benefitted from most of the social and economic opportunities many Americans enjoy. In these neighborhoods, the threats to safety are real, and they are tragic. By the numbers, they are unquestionably crime hotspots. Accordingly, law enforcement must—and does—concentrate efforts in these places. That concentration, however, often arouses resentment, and police are put in a painful and dangerous situation. They are scorned by the very people they are trying to protect. Many in the community refuse to cooperate with police efforts to reduce the rate of violent crime afflicting residents.

During 2014, living—or trying to live—in some Chicago neighborhoods was more dangerous than living in Honduras, the nation with the dubious honor of being the world's leader in homicide. Chicago's West Garfield Park neighborhood, with 18,000 residents, had 21 murders in 2014. That's a rate of 116 per 100,000. Honduras, during the same period, had 90 homicides per 100,000. Another tough Chicago neighborhood, West Englewood, compiled a 2014 murder rate of 73.3 per 100,000, beating the 53.7 rate in Venezuela, which is second only to Honduras in homicides. At 58, Chicago's Chatham neighborhood beat the 44.7 of Belize. Englewood, with 52.6 homicides per 100,000, outdid El Salvador—41.2—in 2014. To put this grotesque competition in context, the United States, on average, has "only" 4.5 murders per 100,000.[84]

On November 2, 2015, at 4:15 in the afternoon, Tyshawn Lee added one more digit to the grim statistics. The nine-year-old boy was lured into an alley in the 8000 block of South Damen Avenue on Chicago's South Side, where he was executed by gunfire because of his "family relationship with a member of a gang," according to then-Chicago Police Superintendent Garry McCarthy. Asked by the press to identify the family member, Superintendent McCarthy explained, "Tyshawn's father has ties to a certain gang that is in conflict with another gang."[85]

Superintendent McCarthy characterized the boy's murder as "probably the most abhorrent, cowardly, unfathomable crime I've witnessed in 35 years of policing." The boy's father, Pierre Stokes, would undoubtedly agree. He also told the *Chicago Tribune* that he was sure his son had been targeted—otherwise "he wouldn't have got hit so many times in the back and face. I think he was targeted."[86] On November 5, Superintendent McCarthy told reporters that "Stokes might know who killed his son but he has refused to cooperate with police."[87]

Stokes told reporters that he had nothing to say to police. "The only thing I can do to help is to help my son. Lay him down peacefully."[88]

Asked by TV reporters what Stokes said to police investigators who had approached him, the Chicago police superintendent responded that he had used "words that 'you can't say ... on TV.'" McCarthy explained that, because he did not believe Stokes was a witness, he did not know if Stokes could supply information that would help the police, "but I could tell you this, I'm a father, many of us here are fathers. My reaction would be a little bit different."[89]

I don't know Pierre Stokes. I am not going to either condemn or defend his response to the police. Like the Chicago superintendent, I, too, am a father, and I, too, would react differently. My human tendency is to assume that just about *any* parent would move heaven and earth to help law enforcement find their child's killer or killers. Precisely because I feel this way, I can begin to appreciate the level of fear and distrust of the police that must prevail in Mr. Stokes's world. This is the challenge 21st century policing must meet and overcome.

It is a daunting challenge—and yet, as Camden County, New Jersey, Police Chief J. Scott Thomson told the members of the President's Task Force, "community policing starts on the street corner, with respectful interaction between a police officer and a local resident."[90] Moreover, Chief Thomson noted, the discussion need not be related to a criminal matter. Indeed, it is important that interactions between officers and citizens *not* be *exclusively* based on emergency calls or crime investigations. The foundation of community policing is not some expensive, complex program. This isn't NASA, and this isn't a trip to Mars. Community policing is not rocket science. It begins by doing what every one of us is qualified to do: act like a civilized human being, demonstrate interest in others and empathy with them, have a friendly, caring conversation.

Community policing develops partnerships with the community. Partnerships include developing working relationships with community leaders (faith-based leaders such as local clergy, businesspeople who live and work in the community, and community organizers) and also with agencies outside of law enforcement. For example, Philadelphia's Police Diversion Program, a partnership between the police department and the Philadelphia Department of Human Services, the school district, the

Office of the District Attorney, Family Court, and others, is a collaborative initiative that has reduced the number of arrests of minority youth for minor offenses. But, most of all, community policing develops relationships between officers and neighborhood residents—and by "relationships," I mean something positive and friendly that "starts on the street corner."

At one extreme in our nation are police forces that consider themselves at war with the community. They are occupying forces struggling to "keep a lid" on what they consider a powder keg. It is naïve to deny that some communities more closely resemble war-torn towns in a Middle Eastern desert than they do communities in Middle America. The objective of the police in these communities is, first and foremost, to protect the public. But this cannot be the exclusive objective. Law enforcement has to find ways of partnering with the community to bring the war to an end. It is not a sustainable model for policing. Worse, it is not a sustainable model for an American community. Yet even in departments and communities that do not feel themselves to be engaged in war, police recruits are often trained with the sole objective of "fighting" crime.

Well, what could possibly be wrong with that? Again, Sir Robert Peel in 1829 said that the absence of crime is the only meaningful measure of the effectiveness of a police force. This is not sufficient for policing in the 21st century, however. Today's police force must not only protect public safety, it must also respect the constitutional rights and the dignity of everyone. The public is not going to study crime statistics to judge the police in its community. They are going to reflect on how they *feel*. Do they *feel* safer? Do they *feel* that the police among them have their well-being uppermost in heart and mind? Do they *feel* that the officer walking a beat, riding a bike, or cruising in a patrol car is an ally, not an enemy?

The 1970s Newark policing experiment encouraged police officers to look for opportunities to interact with individuals in the community that were not directly related to crime, intervention in crime, or investigation of crime. Officers were encouraged to greet people, to ask about their health and welfare, to engage in brief conversations. On a more elaborately organized level, police agencies often sponsor community organizations, such as the Police Athletic League (PAL), which provides a safe environment within the community for young people to play sports and engage in other activities, or Law Enforcement Exploring (also called

Police Exploring), a program affiliated with the Boy Scouts of America that gives young adults an opportunity to explore law enforcement as a career.

The fact is that most contact between the police and the public takes place under stress or even duress. Often, the officer is helping someone, obtaining information from a witness or victim, or, quite possibly, intervening in a crime or other situation—writing a summons, making an arrest. The President's Task Force on 21st Century Policing recommended that police agencies and police officers seek ways to "prevent and reduce crime through informal social control," and that police "agencies should consider adopting preferences for seeking 'least harm' resolutions" in appropriate situations.[91] Diversion programs can be used to avoid incarcerating certain offenders or otherwise putting them into the criminal justice system and to avoid criminal charges and the criminal record that goes with them. For minor infractions, a warning may be adequate or a written citation without arrest. The objective of such measures is to recognize the infraction, so that the offender understands he or she has violated the law, but not to make the consequences of the infraction worse than the infraction itself.

Today's world is permeated by media—smartphone video, social media, and broadcast/cable media. In consequence, a national—doubtless, an international—audience has borne witness to numerous instances of the tragic consequences of a few officers' failure to act professionally and with the intention of doing the least harm. On April 4, 2015, a bystander used a smartphone video camera to record a white North Charleston, South Carolina, police officer shoot an unarmed African American, Walter L. Scott, in the back—eight times. The officer had pulled Scott over because his taillight was burned out. Scott, probably fearing that he would be arrested for unpaid childcare payments, bolted from his car. That is when Officer Michael Slager shot him. Now an unarmed man is dead, and a police officer is (as of this writing) awaiting trial for murder, having been released on a $500,000 bond.[92]

In another incident, on July 10, 2015, a white Texas State Trooper, Brian Encinia, pulled over an automobile driven by Sandra Bland, an African American woman, because she had failed to signal a lane change. The trooper wrote a citation. His dashcam and audio recording portray what begins as an uneventful, reasonably polite interaction that rapidly develops into a heated exchange. Either Trooper Encinia or Ms. Bland could have descalated the encounter, but, for whatever reasons, neither did. The result was an arrest, during which Ms. Bland ended up on the ground claiming that she could not hear and that Encinia had slammed her head against the ground. Allegedly, the arrest came when Ms. Bland kicked Officer Encinia, and what had begun as a traffic stop for an infraction ended with an allegation of assaulting a public servant. Ms. Bland was taken to the Walker County Jail, where she was held on $5,000 bond. Three days later, she was found dead, having apparently hanged herself in her cell.

After her arrest, Sandra Bland made a phone call and left a voice message: "How did switching lanes with no signal turn into all this?"[93] The only reasonable answer is that it never should have. Was it worth stopping Sandra Bland for failing to signal? The officer made his judgment. The exchange between Ms. Bland and Trooper Encinia began to heat up when he asked her to put out her cigarette and she responded defiantly, demanding to know why she should be required to put out *her* cigarette in *her* car. Should she have simply complied? Compliance is certainly the most effective way to prevent a simple traffic stop from escalating into something far worse. But, as the dashcam video reveals,[94] something pushed Encinia's buttons, and the encounter soon spiraled out of control. The woman's suicide was an unforeseeable and certainly unintended consequence of the encounter, but it is difficult to avoid coming to the conclusion that this final tragedy was not only avoidable but unnecessary. Yes, Ms. Bland could have prevented it. But it is the job of the police officer, the professional, to take the initiative by deescalating potentially violent situations rather than fan the flames.[95]

There have been more incidents of routine, even innocuous interactions resulting in tragedy. On July 19, 2015, Ray Tensing, a white University of Cincinnati police officer stopped Samuel DuBose, an African American man, because he failed to display a front license plate. As Tensing's bodycam video shows[96], the officer repeatedly asked DuBose for his driver's license. DuBose repeatedly failed to produce it. Finally, when the officer pulled open the car door, DuBose pulled it shut, started the engine, and put the car in drive. On the bodycam video, we hear Tensing yell "Stop! Stop!" He drew his pistol, and he shot DuBose at pointblank range.

Tensing claimed that he was being dragged. In charging him with voluntary manslaughter, however, prosecutors alleged that the bodycam video disproved this. (At this writing, a trial has yet to begin.)[97]

Traffic stops, as every law enforcement officer well knows, always have the potential for danger. Usually, of course, it is the officer who is at risk, but, as these recent incidents show, there is danger to the subject of the stop as well. There were 32,719 motor vehicle deaths in the United States in 2013.[98] Clearly, traffic regulations and laws need to be enforced, and police officers are the people society assigns to do it. But they must do it with the awareness that the danger in stopping a driver for a non-functioning taillight or failing to signal a lane change or failing to display a front license plate is potentially as great as stopping a speeder or a reckless driver, individuals who pose an imminent threat to their own safety and the safety of others. In the course of the stop, the officer needs to understand that his or her interaction with the driver has the potential for creating an outcome far graver than the outcome of driving with a bad taillight. It is a question of proportionality.

Even interactions that do not result in arrest, injury, harsh words, or death can have a negative impact that is way out of proportion to the reason for the interaction. In Ferguson, Missouri, for example, black motorists were ticketed disproportionately for traffic infractions. This was routine. Ferguson depended on revenue from citations to meet its operating expenses, and officers were therefore encouraged to write summonses. The result was a revenue stream for the town. Was the money worth the dysfunction that was created in the relationship between the police and the community?

The police cannot guarantee the safety of communities. They can and must, however, work to build the capacity of a community to reduce and even prevent crime through fostering informal social control. While formal, judicially imposed punishment for wrongdoing certainly has a deterrent value, that value should not be squandered by a quota-driven focus on issuing citations for petty infractions. Moreover, many years of law enforcement experience, bolstered by research, demonstrates that informal social control, inculcated within the community, is often more effective than formal punishment, at the hands of the justice system, at reducing crime in a neighborhood. A community's behavior is shaped by its values.

Those values can—and should—be modeled by the police in that community, but the police cannot *impose* values on a community. Values need to arise from the members of the community itself. The police can and should reinforce them, both formally, through law enforcement, and, just as importantly, by informal means, through more casual interactions.

While it is possible to gauge the effectiveness of the community-based, informal approach by analyzing crime statistics, the numbers do not tell the whole story. We can only guess at how many opportunities for criminal acts are passed up on a given day because of the influence of the community's values. When the broken windows are repaired—when members of the community show that they do care about their community—the sense that it is okay or acceptable to commit crimes tends to dissipate.

■ ■ ■

Individual officers can do a great deal to create positive relationships with the community, but, ultimately, community policing has to be a mode of policing for the entire force in a community, not just the product of a particular officer's goodwill and affable personality and not even the work of specialized unit within the force. Community policing depends heavily on the relationships individual officers build with individual members of the community; however, community policing is also about the relationship between police agency leaders and the leaders and influencers within the community, especially the leaders of churches, businesses, and schools.

In addition to partnering with community leaders, police leaders need to reach out into the professional community as well. As first responders, the police are often called on to address problems that cannot be resolved by the police alone. For example, many calls for service involve dealing with mentally disturbed persons. Police officers can be trained to do this. I instituted such training when I was deputy chief and then chief of the Rochester, New York, Police Department. But it is impractical to train every officer as a professional psychologist. While officers can be trained in ways that help them prevent a disturbed person from harming themselves and others, they cannot be expected to resolve mental health issues. A team approach is called for, in which law enforcement, social services providers, and community support networks work together to provide the appropriate resources and expertise for a given situation. The police must most immediately protect the subject and the community. For this intervention to have a *sustainable* positive effect, however, the police must be able to direct the subject or the victim—perhaps a disturbed person, or a parent distraught because they lack the means to care for their child, or a child in an abusive environment—to the helping professionals who are in the best position to help. Police departments don't just need to keep the phone numbers of hospitals, social services, and community centers handy on a computer or a Rolodex, they need to develop close, ongoing working relationships with these institutions and the mental health professionals, the social workers, substance abuse specialists, and crisis counselors who work within them.

Positive relationships are both top-down and top-up, they are institutional and individual. This means that police departments must embrace community policing wholeheartedly and in good faith. The principles, attitudes, and tactics of community policing have to permeate the entire force. Those of us on the President's Task Force heard Camden, New Jersey, police chief Thomson testify that community policing, to be successful, cannot be relegated to a single program or unit. It cannot be a single strategy or mere tactic in a manual. It must be one of the department's core principles. It has to form part of the foundation of the department's very culture.

Working on the President's Task Force, we began speaking of police agencies and the neighborhoods they serve as "co-producing public safety." This is a useful way of defining a successful police-community relationship. It is one that produces—that *co-produces*—a precious product called public safety.

Police agencies need to listen to their officers as well as community members to identify problems and to collaborate on formulating and implementing solutions to them. As professional guardians, the police need to be willing to take the initiative in this effort, but, having taken the initiative, they also need to invite, encourage, and embrace the community's participation, collaboration, and feedback.

Community policing is proactive rather than reactive policing. Years ago, in Miami-Dade, this is the quality that drew me to what was then called community-oriented policing. It was proactive, aimed at least as much at prevention as it was at response. In Miami-Dade, we were able to put ourselves in a position to work proactively by listening to the members of the community and treating them with respect. We reached out. Our goal was to transform adversaries into partners mutually dedicated to curing the community conditions that promote crime, fear of crime, and general social disorder. Now, at that time, in the 1980s, SWAT-style and military-style policing also laid claim to taking a proactive approach to public safety. Do not get me wrong, SWAT has its place, especially in an era in which terrorism poses potential danger to every community. But it is a mistake to apply the military model to everyday policing. It confuses force and intimidation with proactivity, and it thus inevitably creates collateral damage in the form of amped-up alienation, anger, hostility, and violence. Community policing, in contrast, works collaboratively to solve community problems before they result in criminal acts. When violence erupts, the community-oriented approach aims to deescalate rather than aggravate.

A proactive approach to any situation depends on timing. The proactive approach to safety on the road requires preventive maintenance—brakes, steering, lights that work perfectly, tires with proper inflation and plenty of tread. The proactive approach to a leaky roof is performing repairs at the first sign of a drip rather than waiting for a torrent of water that ruins your sofa or shorts out your big-screen TV. The proactive approach to health combines healthy habits—healthy eating, healthy exercise—with regular visits to the doctor to prevent sickness before it strikes.

In "co-producing public safety," the *most* proactive approach is to create "policies and programs that address the needs of children and youth most at risk for crime or violence and reduce aggressive law enforcement tactics that stigmatize youth and marginalize their participation in schools and communities."[99] Much of who we are as adults is formed, maybe even determined, in childhood and youth.

Youth, that period between childhood and adulthood, is both wonderful and dangerous. It is a time in which a young person has many of the responsibilities of an adult and is, in many respects, expected or even required to act like an adult, yet enjoys few of the privileges of an adult. We have seen in the Middle East, in Africa, in Europe, and in the United States the horrific consequences of marginalizing youth. If they feel wronged, abused, or simply powerless within their own geographical community—their neighborhood or their nation—youth will find another community that will accept, welcome, and (seemingly, at least) empower. This alternative "community" may be a criminal gang or an international terrorist organization, an ISIS or an al-Qaeda.

Communities need to give their youth a voice in community decision making, and this is something in which the police can help with collaborative programs as well as frank dialogue with young people. Such listening and empowerment strategies are doomed to fail, however, in law enforcement, judicial, educational, and community environments that emphasize zero-tolerance policies. Policies that encourage open communication yet link it to the inevitability, let alone likelihood, of punishment cannot succeed. Prosecuting children as adults does not reduce crime, it only turns up the spigot on the school-to-prison pipeline. It is absolutely necessary to respond to and to correct childhood behaviors and actions that are antisocial, offensive, or dangerous. And while it is true that such acts committed by an adult might well warrant judicial punishment including incarceration, similar acts committed by children usually do not. Neither our neighborhoods nor our nation can afford to criminalize the behavior of children. Recall another shocking smartphone video recorded by a student at Spring Valley (South Carolina) High School in 2015, showing a school resource officer arresting a student for having failed to relinquish her cell phone when a teacher asked her to. It is bad enough that the *child's* show of misbehavior and disrespect was escalated by an *adult* teacher into a police intervention ending in arrest, but the manner of the arrest—in which a large, burly, muscular officer used what he described as a "muscling technique" to effect a remarkably violent takedown of a slightly built girl—was stunning to watch and wholly unacceptable.[100] As the *Final Report of the President's Task Force on 21ˢᵗ Century Policing* observes, "Noncriminal offenses can escalate to criminal charges when officers are not trained in child and adolescent development and are unable to recognize and manage a child's emotional, intellectual, and physical development issues." Moreover, "School district policies and practices that push students out of schools and into the juvenile justice system cause great harm and do no good."[101]

My last assignment as a deputy sheriff in Miami-Dade was as a school resource officer in a tough school district. It was an extraordinarily rewarding experience. I came to understand that, in some neighborhoods, school is the safest and most nurturing environment many children experience. School should therefore be a place of education and enrichment as well as a safe haven and a source of emotional strength, reassurance, and, in many cases, much-needed healing. It is critical that law enforcement and the justice system work with schools to keep students in them. This does not mean turning a blind eye to bad behavior. But the police and the justice system need to encourage schools to develop acceptable alternatives to suspension, let alone expulsion. Diversion, counseling, working with the child's family—all these are appropriate alternatives. The cutting edge may be programs in "restorative justice," an approach aimed at delivering consequences for bad behavior that focus on the needs of victims and offenders as well as the community (in this case, primarily the school itself). The core idea of restorative justice is to allow the offender to take responsibility for what he or she has done and to make appropriate "restorative" amends—apologizing, perhaps performing community service, returning stolen money or property, whatever it takes. The idea is to empower the offender to take positive action to correct his or her own behavior and to reaffirm the shared values of the community.

I am in significant measure the product of Sheriff Raymond Hamlin. I am a law and order guy. Law *and* order. Policing is about both. It's about enforcing the law, yes. But it is also about supporting the *order* that is a civilized, free, creative, and nurturing community. This requires enforcement that is proportional, that deescalates dangerous situations rather than aggravates them, that treats everyone with respect, that protects human and constitutional rights, that strives never to do more harm than good, and that, whenever possible, empowers and enables people to do the right thing—not by means of coercion (though sometimes with persuasion) but ultimately of their own free will, because it is what they, as members of the community, *want* to do.

CHAPTER 10

Do (Cyber) Community Policing

I don't want to give the impression that community policing and policing that borrows from the military model are irreconcilable and cannot possibly exist within the same police department. This is far from true. To oppose the one to the other in a zero-sum contest, in which there must be either military-style policing or community-oriented policing but never both, is a false and destructive opposition. The fact is that, done well, twenty-first-century policing is a profession and, like most professions, it is a combination of art and of science. Practiced on this level of professionalism, policing requires, among other things, knowing what approaches, tactics, and policies to apply in a particular situation. The choice of a community-oriented approach versus a SWAT-style approach depends on the situation at a specific time and place and on law enforcement leaders' judgment of that situation.

Under most conditions most of the time, the best baseline approach, the "normal," default approach, is the community-oriented approach. For policing to be sustainable in a community, police officers and the law enforcement agencies they represent must share in the community's values. They need to be a part of the community, and, what is equally important, the members of the community need to perceive the police as partners and part of the community, in sync with it, rooted in the same values. Among other things, this means that SWAT tactics and equipment—military-grade vehicles, weapons, tactical uniforms and gear—are not appropriate for routine patrol and service calls. The First Amendment to the Constitution, which every officer is sworn to uphold, protects free speech, including the right "peaceably to assemble, and to petition the Government for a redress of grievances." That means the military model is also wrong in situations of peaceful demonstration, protest, and even civil disobedience. The sight of a SWAT van, Lenco BearCat, or an M113 armored personnel carrier is more likely to incite violence than it is to preemptively deter it. It tells the people in the street as well as everyone watching 24-hour cable or broadcast news or looking at a YouTube video that the police think of themselves as being at war with the community. It tells everyone that they see their mission as one of conquest, occupation, and pacification—by intimidation certainly, by force probably. When I, like millions of others, watched the television images of a militarized police presence in Ferguson, Missouri, during the unrest of August 2014, I Googled the "Birmingham campaign" of April-May 1963 during the Civil Rights movement. To me, the images from 2014 and 1963 were more similar than different.

Because the police are sworn to uphold the Constitution, they are sworn to protect free speech and peaceable protest. These are among the most important values Americans share, whether they happen to be civilians or police officers. Because these values are shared values, the police protecting them need to take a community approach. But, yes, in the "real world," our world, today's world, peaceable assemblies sometimes have a way of turning violent. Prudence concerning public safety may dictate having that SWAT van or BearCat or M113 or all three and more nearby—parked around the corner, not in the same visual frame as the protestors, not trailing them, not confronting them, but out of sight and ready, if needed. Parked around the corner, this equipment can *respond* quickly, but will not *incite, inspire,* or *exacerbate.*

It is also the case, unfortunately, that SWAT training, tactics, and technology are absolutely necessary in today's threat environment, which includes terrorism, whether instigated or inspired from abroad, as happened in Paris on November 13, 2015, or homegrown, as when a heavily armed man stormed the Planned Parenthood clinic in Colorado Springs on November 29 that same year or a shooter ran amuck in Washington Naval Yard on September 16, 2013.

During the last two decades of the twentieth century and then in the wake of 9/11/2001, police departments across the country have embraced high-tech military hardware. It is indispensable—in situations that make it indispensable. It is, however, provocative, dangerous, and destructive—both immediately and in the long term—when used or even displayed in neighborhood policing, in neighborhood patrol, and in the case of peaceful, constitutionally protected assembly, demonstration, and protest.

Policing and the Technology of Interconnectivity

The twenty-first-century police agency requires proficiency in SWAT as well as in community policing. Both ends of the policing spectrum benefit from technology—although both, first and foremost, rely on the talent, commitment, courage, good sense, and humanity of well-trained officers. Military-grade equipment, weapons, and vehicles are worse than useless in the hands of people lacking the military-grade training to use them. And by "worse than useless," I mean dangerous, both immediately dangerous and dangerous in the long term because of the damage done to the image of law enforcement and to the relationship between law enforcement and the community.

But police officers and police agencies can, in all circumstances, learn much about leadership, discipline, courage, and working productively with civilians from the modern American military. Indeed, engaging a community without a show of military-style intimidation requires military-grade courage and discipline. It is easy to rely on uniforms, badges, and firearms to *project* authority. It is far more difficult to use humanity, common sense, and sound training to *earn* authority and legitimacy by acting in ways that demonstrate a solidarity with the community. As technology is an important adjunct to the professional and human factor in the military aspects of policing, so technology provides valuable leverage for community policing. In fact, for most police work most of the time, military-grade technology is less important than the high technology of social media.

How do we know this?

As discussed in chapter 7, the lessons of the Arab Spring, aspects of which have been called the "Internet Revolution" or the "Twitter Revolution," speak eloquently of the power of digital interconnectivity and social media to create, propagate, and facilitate popular movements for change. The exploitation of websites and social media by the likes of al-Qaeda and ISIS provides even more urgent examples of social media's power to instigate, motivate, organize, and mobilize. Today's police organizations have a lot of catching up to do online.

Social media provides a platform for broadcasting information, for soliciting and receiving feedback, for real-time interactivity, and for making police departments and their initiatives more transparent. Because the Internet yields to few political, physical, or economic boundaries, it is an extraordinary means of overlaying cyber-communities atop existing real-world neighborhoods. It is a highly effective means of reaching out to the community and of inviting the community to reach back in return. Established video technologies, such as dashcams (dashboard-mounted video cameras in police cruisers), and emerging technologies, such as bodycams (body-worn cameras, BWCs), may be used with and without the Internet to create maximum transparency concerning police operations within a community while also enhancing officer safety. If there is a golden key to unlocking a community's trust in law enforcement, it is transparency deployed boldly in every possible way.

I am a believer in technology. With regard to technology, twenty-first century law enforcement has a great deal in common with other fields and professions. Virtually every trade, every enterprise, every business, everything most of us do has been influenced by the technology of digital connectivity and will be influenced by it even more in the years, months, and even weeks to come. There was a time when patrol officers had nothing more than a whistle to blow when they needed help—we've all seen those Jack the Ripper movies! But it is also true that, in 1877, just a year after Bell patented his telephone, the world's first *police telephone* was installed in Albany, New York. Two years later, the first street-corner call boxes were installed in Chicago. They were intended to be used by beat cops as well as by certain trusted civilians, who were given keys to access them. Throughout the 1880s, other American cities followed suit and installed call boxes. We still see their thickly painted iron remains on some street corners today.

Communications technology also played a role in international policing. In 1910, U.S.-born Dr. Peter Hawley Harvey Crippen was suspected of having murdered his wife, Cora. Before London police could move to arrest him, Crippen and his secretary, Ethel Clara LeNeve, with whom he was romantically involved, disappeared. Walter Dew, chief inspector of Scotland Yard, launched an international manhunt, publishing photographs of both Crippen and LeNeve in newspapers worldwide. The captain of the SS *Montrose*, bound for Canada, recognized the couple as passengers on his vessel and used the ship's radiotelegraph to alert Scotland Yard. Dew set off on a faster ship and, en route, kept in touch with the skipper of the *Montrose* by ship-to-ship radiotelegraph. He intercepted the *Montrose* at a place called Father Point, off the Canadian coast, boarded it, and arrested Crippen. This was the first time in history that mass media (the press) was combined with state-of-the-art wireless communication to extend the reach of the "long arm of the law." It was a landmark of connectivity in police work.

By 1916, the New York City Harbor Police were using radios to communicate with police boats as well as ships in the harbor, and in 1921, the Detroit police began experimenting with a receiver-equipped police cruiser. The system was one-way only, allowing headquarters to transmit calls to the car, which had a receiver but no transmitter. Just two years later, the Pennsylvania State Police created a radio-telegraph network to communicate with local police offices statewide. And in 1929, a commercial radio station in Chicago, WGN, began dispatching police alarm calls between its regular entertainment programming; nineteen Chicago squad cars were equipped with receivers. By the 1930s, many American police departments were using one-way radio systems to dispatch police cruisers to service calls, and it was also during the 1930s that two-way radios began to be installed in squad cars and even motorcycles.

In 1937, all of Britain instituted the 999 system, by which anyone with a telephone could use 999 to dial the police directly in an emergency. It was not until 1968 that the 911 system, equivalent to the British 999 system, was introduced in the United States.

Well, better late than never. Fortunately, police agencies have been faster in adopting Internet technology to police investigative work, with systems that provide access to nationwide (and, to some degree, international) databases of fingerprints, criminal records, DNA records, and other means of identification. Agencies have been slower, however, to tap into the power of the Internet for community outreach via social media. It is easy to criticize this, but, in fact, there are legitimate reasons for thoughtful deliberation.

Beyond doubt, police departments can use social media to build trust and legitimacy within the communities they serve by engaging with citizens and opening dialogues about transparency and accountability. Nevertheless, it is important that agencies formulate policies and strategies to guide the use of this communications channel. Goals must be unambiguously set and understood by all. For one thing, Internet-related technology is subject to rapid change. Today's must-have app quickly becomes tomorrow's 8-track cassette player. Police agencies need access to experts and expertise that will enable them to identify and evaluate the best new technologies. The objective is to improve efficiency and community relationships, not simply to acquire the latest gadgetry.

Most important, it seems that each new advance in Internet technology, especially in the realm of social media, poses new challenges to concepts of privacy and, especially in a policing context, to individual rights. Police departments need to assess the effects of adopting new technologies with respect to cost versus benefit as well as the potential for unintended consequences, especially those impacting privacy, constitutional rights, and—in particular—safety. For instance, social media-enabled interactive communication can be a great platform for soliciting and receiving Crime Stoppers and similar tips and investigative information from citizens. This, in turn, is a promising means of leveraging members of the community in the investigation of crime and the apprehension of suspects. But if such systems are hackable, they can pose a dangerous risk to civic-minded citizens whose safety depends on the ability to report information to the police anonymously and securely. And, of course, there is the unintended consequence of too much of a good thing. If investigators rely too heavily on Internet platforms to acquire information from the public, they may neglect the kind of traditional shoe-leather police work that brings them face-to-face with victims, informants, and perpetrators. Too much information can be as bad as insufficient information, maybe even worse.

Yet police adoption of social media has been encouraging. The Boston Police Department, for instance, engaged the city's communities extensively through social media during the investigation of the April 2013 bomb attacks at the finish line of the Boston Marathon. The department used Twitter to keep the public updated on the investigation—and also to provide reassurance about public safety and to correct mistaken information reported by print, broadcast, and cable news media. Through Twitter, the Boston police also asked those who monitored police scanners to refrain from tweeting information they gleaned from those scanners, explaining that the suspects were very likely on Twitter and could use the tweeted information to evade police investigative efforts.[102]

Apart from engaging citizens in the investigation of crime, social media can be used to engage with the community on issues of importance to police and community alike. For years now, businesses, especially consumer businesses—the makers and purveyors of products and services—have been using social media to gauge consumer sentiment about their products, services, and brands and to build customer loyalty. Police agencies can learn much from such social media marketing initiatives by using websites to solicit feedback concerning how the police operate in their community.

Social Media Strategies to Foster Community Trust and Access

The International Association of Chiefs of Police published the results of a 2015 survey of police agencies' use of social media. An impressive 96.4 percent of agencies responding to the survey reported that they use social media "in some capacity," and 73.9 percent not currently using social media said that they were considering its adoption. Facebook is the popular social media platform with police agencies (94.2 percent), with Twitter (71.2 percent) and YouTube (40.0 percent) coming in second and third.[103]

Many agencies use some or all of these online platforms not only to share information with the public, educate the public, and promote the agency's "brand," but the most common use of social media (88.7 percent) is for criminal investigations.[104] Social media, including public departmental websites, also are used as portals to make public records easily available. These days, such records may include video captured via dashcam and bodycam, which suggests that public record laws at federal and state levels need to be reviewed and updated with an eye toward balancing public access with the privacy rights of the subjects of interrogation or arrest as well as victims and bystanders. This balance should be defined by law and not left to individual departments to determine, since conflict between those seeking access and those whose privacy is at stake may easily result in accusations of cover-up on the one hand and insensitive or unlawful violation of privacy on the other.

Beyond revising and updating existing privacy law, the members of the President's Task Force on 21st Century Policing also recommended that law enforcement agencies should collaborate on developing best-practices guidelines for "technology-based community engagement that increases community trust and access."[105] What we can all agree on right now, however, is that social media should—

- Increase transparency
- Maximize public accessibility to police services as well as public records
- Provide frictionless access to such information as crime statistics, data on calls for service, and other dynamic data
- Provide a platform for the public posting of police policy and procedures
- Provide a platform for citizen response to police policy, procedures, programs, and initiatives
- Enhance access to services for persons with disabilities

A police agency's social media presence should not be considered the exclusive property of the agency. Instead, websites and other online platforms should invite public response concerning how the agency uses social media. Ideally, police websites and other online platforms should be a digital community in which the law enforcement agency and people it serves have an equal voice. It should be a virtual extension of community policing and the police-community relationships created by the community policing approach. In addition, law enforcement platforms should invite members of the community to interact with one another, not just with the police department. In short, digital platforms should not be mere PR stages controlled by the police. They should be true online communities with the shared goal of building better, more responsive, more effective, and more equitable enforcement of laws for the security and welfare of the community.

Achieving this level community feeling and function requires police agencies to commit to keeping their online presence current and responsive—often in real time or as close to real time as possible, Not only is fresh and relevant content required to keep the members of the community interested and engaged, but, during an incident, a developing emergency situation, or a criminal investigation, a department's website, its Twitter presence, and its presence on other social media can be invaluable for providing potentially life-saving instructions, for communicating the department's point of view, for disseminating accurate information, for countering rumors and false information, and for correcting rumors and false information. Social media may be used to counter and correct false, misleading, or mistaken information delivered by print, broadcast, and cable outlets. But it is also important that social media be monitored, as the Internet itself is a prodigious producer of both fact and fiction. Finally, law enforcement should monitor social media not merely to counter or correct bad information, but also to persuade the producers of such information that careless reporting and careless posting can be very destructive and can result in serious harm.

BWCs

Bodycams, BWCs, are being adopted by more and more departments nationwide. They are seen as technological aids to improving evidence collection, strengthening officer performance, increasing officer accountability, and generally enhancing public transparency. They are often valuable in investigating as well as resolving complaints about police interaction with members of the public, including officer-involved shootings. BWCs document the behavior and actions of both officers and civilians during an encounter.

Jim Bueermann, retired chief of the Redlands (California) Police Department and President of the Police Foundation, testified to the President's Task Force on 21st-Century Policing about a twelve-month research project that persuasively demonstrates the positive impact of BWCs. The results suggest that wearing bodycams tends to reduce officers' use of force and also to reduce the volume of complaints against officers. The research numbers are impressive. Officers equipped with BWCs had 87.5 percent fewer incidents of use of force than a control group who did not wear the cameras. They also had 59 percent fewer complaints.[106]

Interestingly, BWCs not only tend to increase the self-awareness of officers, they do the same for civilians. "When police officers are acutely aware that their behavior is being monitored (because they turn on the cameras) and when officers tell citizens that the cameras are recording their behavior, everyone behaves better."[107] Better behavior translates into safer and generally more positive outcomes in police interaction with citizens.

Some thirty years of living in a digitally interconnected world has proved Internet technology to be the proverbial double-edged sword. For every advance and advantage of access, connectivity, opportunity, and convenience, there are new threats to security and privacy. Police use of the technology is no different. A 2014 Police Executive Research Forum (PERF) report on implementing BWC programs observed that BWCs offer many benefits but "also raise serious questions about how technology is changing the relationship between police and the community. Body-worn cameras not only create concerns about the public's privacy rights but also can affect how officers relate to people in the community, the community's perception of the police, and expectations about how police agencies should share information with the public."[108] In some jurisdictions, police officers are required to obtain consent from the subject before recording an interaction. Even where this is not required, most police executives believe that it is good policy to inform subjects that they are being recorded. One objective of BWCs is to enhance transparency, not increase opacity—and certainly not to create the impression among the public that the police are covertly surveilling or monitoring them, playing a game of incrimination through "gotcha" technology.

Yet the fact is that many police officers feel that *they* are operating in a tech-enabled gotcha environment, in which anyone with a smartphone—and, increasingly, that means practically everyone—can record video of any police encounter. Such bystander video can be important evidence, but it tells the story from one perspective only. The BWC record provides the officer's perspective and can be used to enhance or challenge bystander video.

We Need to Test More and to Learn More

The National Institute of Justice is the research and development arm of the U.S. Department of Justice.[109] It gets less public attention than it deserves, since it conducts and evaluates valuable research into all aspects of law enforcement, including the effectiveness of equipment, tactics, and policy. The President's Task Force recommended broadening the Institute's R & D efforts to the area of Internet and related digital technologies and to establish national standards for them, with an emphasis on "compatibility and interoperability" not only within the law enforcement community but "across agencies and jurisdictions." We need to remember that police-community relationships must also encompass relationships with other government agencies at the national, state, and local levels. The greater and stronger their interconnection with networks beyond law enforcement, the more effective police agencies can be. The Task Force recommended that the National Institute of Justice also focus on research and development of digital technologies that "maintain civil and human rights protections."[110]

If individual jurisdictions and departments are isolated in their development of technologies whose very purpose is to create connections that transcend all silos and borders, there is a danger that police-related information systems will become fractured and isolated. Data produced by one police department that is unknown or unavailable to other departments does not, for all practical purposes, exist for those other departments. For this reason, shared standards among law enforcement cyber communities are key. The current environment of domestic and global terrorism threats makes such standardization more urgent than ever. At the same time, it is critically important that national standards not be simply imposed on local jurisdictions. The standards need to be designed to accommodate local needs, which vary widely from one region, state, city, community, or neighborhood to the next. While technologies will benefit from broad standardization, their implementation must finally be the product of local decisions. This is the same principle that applies in community policing. While national agencies and organizations can and should provide guidelines, standards, and best practices for community policing policy and procedures, the implementation of these must be uniquely suited to each community. Whether the issue is policy for a physical, geographical community or a cyber community, it cannot be simply imposed. It must be the product of police-community collaboration.

In the private sector, marketers working for consumer businesses of all kinds—from Amazon to the corner mom-and-pop shop—have learned to exploit the unique power of Internet platforms to transform mass marketing into individualized marketing on a mass scale. Before the Internet, consumer businesses tended to take a one-size-fits-all approach. Thanks to the millions of individual consumer relationships that Internet connectivity enables, those businesses now take what we might call the-one-size-that-fits-*you* approach. Anyone who surfs the Web is familiar with pop-up ads. These are very different from billboards or TV commercials. *You* see them on *your* computer or other device because *you* somehow expressed an interest in the product or service advertised. You bought something like it in the past, or you looked at websites offering it or merchandise related to it. Marketers track your Web activity, and they use it to send you ads that appeal uniquely to you.

Police agencies can learn from private sector marketing. They can create websites and use social media in ways that specifically target the unique needs, values, and concerns of each community they serve. Global in scope, the Internet nevertheless makes possible highly customized approaches to community relations. Terrorist organizations with roots that are geographically and even culturally distant from our neighborhoods already realize this. They target communities. They target individuals. By crafting messages uniquely suited to both, they develop intimate relationships with communities as well as individuals. The 2015 IACP survey on police department adoption of Web platforms is encouraging, but, when it comes to social media, we in the law enforcement community still have a lot of catching up to do. With tragic consequences, ISIS and others have repeatedly demonstrated the compelling power of virtual "communities" created via the Internet. Our job is to find ways to use that power even more compellingly to strengthen the social fabric of our own communities, neighborhoods, and nation.

CHAPTER 11

Learn More and Better

Most of the time, military-grade equipment—weapons, uniforms, and vehicles—sends the wrong message about the right relationship between police and the communities they serve. We don't want to be an occupying force, an invader, a hostile presence. We don't want to broadcast to the neighborhood that we believe we are at war with it.

That said, two things are also true.

First, "most of the time" is not "all of the time." From time to time, the police really do need SWAT and its military arsenal and paramilitary vehicle fleet to protect the community. Those who perpetrate mass shootings almost always come armed with a lot more than a handgun. Assault weapons and improvised explosive devices (IEDs) are standard equipment for terrorists, self-styled militia members, disgruntled employees, and psychopaths. No one except the perpetrator will benefit from leaving law enforcement outgunned in encounters with such killers. And while peaceful assembly is a Constitutional right that police officers must not only respect but vigorously defend, mobs happen, and demonstrations that start out as peaceful have been known to escalate into riots, while some riots simply start out that way—no escalation necessary. Given the grave danger to life and property, heavy equipment can be indispensable.

Second, I don't want to give the impression that everything military is tainted, even when it comes to non-emergency, non-violent, so-called routine police work. Police agencies actually have a lot they can learn from the military. The American military has trained some of the best leaders in the world. It has inculcated in generations of soldiers, sailors, marines, and airmen the values of courage, innovative initiative, loyalty, fidelity, self-sacrifice, and a general I-got-your-back orientation that has much to teach any high-stakes organization, including police agencies. In the military, discipline isn't just for show. It is for effectiveness and safety. Any professional entrusted with the means of delivering deadly force needs military-grade discipline.

But perhaps the most profound lesson the American military has to teach the law enforcement community is the value of education, training, and experience. It used to be that a "good soldier" was pretty much somebody who was very good at killing people and breaking things. Today, it takes much more than the efficient delivery of brute kinetic force to be a good soldier. The top American commanders—general officers such as Dwight Eisenhower, Omar Bradley, and George C. Marshall—took away from their experience of fighting in World War II the conviction that, in the modern world, it was no longer sufficient for military leaders to be "good soldiers." They also needed to be able politicians, consummate diplomats, well-informed economists, masters of the management of human assets, and sophisticated technologists while simultaneously embracing a generally humanitarian outlook. Think about it. During World War II, General Marshall was the army's chief of staff, its top soldier. After that war, he went on to become U.S. secretary of state—a consummate diplomat—and the architect of the so-called Marshall Plan, which was crucial in getting the devastated peoples of Europe back on their feet (and, not incidentally, out of the hands of the Soviet communists). Or take Dwight Eisenhower. The army was his schooling (West Point) and his first job, which was also the job he held longest. As World War II Supreme Allied Commander, Europe, he had the responsibility for holding together a difficult alliance among the United States, England, the Soviet Union, and the Free French forces. Even while in uniform he was obliged to be a politician and statesman.

No wonder the nation elected him its thirty-fourth president. In fact, modern military leaders also need sufficient education, training, and experience to understand key aspects of very specialized technologies as well as something of the sciences behind them. General Leslie R. Groves was the military engineer who built the Pentagon beginning at the outbreak of World War II. It was the biggest building in the world when it was built, and yet he built it in just eighteen months. Then he went on to lead the Manhattan Project, working closely with the greatest scientists who ever walked the planet to transform cutting-edge theories of nuclear physics into a working "atomic bomb." He did it in under three years—even though they did not teach nuclear physics at West Point. (They do now.)

A high-level combination of skills and attitudes, more than weaponry and field manuals, is what makes a successful military leader today. Likewise, today's police—from policy makers to line officers—are called on daily to solve problems and manage situations entirely unknown to previous generations of law enforcement professionals. Today's policing takes place in environments that often involve—

- People with mental health issues
- People from widely differing ethnic, religious, and cultural backgrounds and sexual orientations
- Rapidly changing laws, and
- Rapidly evolving technologies

The patrol officer committed to good community policing may encounter a wide array of people and languages and clothing and customs in the space of a city block. She needs to be on a first-name basis with community influencers and community leaders. She needs to know the territory—intimately. At the same time, she also needs to be aware of the influence of gangs—local street gangs as well as terrorist gangs such as al-Qaeda and ISIS, who, based far away, use digital social media to create relationships that can be far more powerful than relationships within the physical confines of the neighborhood or even the family.

On December 2, 2015, ISIS-inspired Syed Rizwan Farook and Tashfeen Malik, husband and wife, drove their six-month-old daughter to the house of Farook's mother and asked her to watch the baby while they went to a doctor's appointment. At 10:59 a.m. (PST), the couple, now arrayed in black tactical clothing and heavily armed with assault weapons, opened fire on Farook's coworkers gathered at a holiday party at a facility providing services and programs to people with developmental disabilities, the Inland Regional Center (IRC) in San Bernardino, California. After a four-minute fusillade, fourteen people lay dead and twenty-three wounded.[111]

Farook had been born and raised in the United States and was a natural-born U.S. citizen. He had a good job and an important one as a county health inspector. He had neighbors who found him pleasant, congenial, soft-spoken, and perfectly normal. He paid his rent, he paid his taxes, and, with his wife, cared for their new baby. They also, however, built pipe bombs in the garage adjacent to their apartment in the suburban community of Redlands, California. In addition to their infant daughter and all the personal belongings, photographs, mementos, medicines, foods, and cosmetics even a modest American family lives with, they owned two .223-caliber variants of the popular AR-15 assault rifle and two 9-mm semiautomatic handguns. They laid in thousands of rounds of ammunition for both, taking with them to the IRC 1,400 rifle rounds and 400 9-mm rounds, along with a remotely detonated bomb made of three pipe bombs tied together.

Farook was a U.S. citizen married to a citizen of Pakistan. Both seemed to embrace their American community, and their neighbors accepted them. Yet the true allegiance of both lay elsewhere. Today, community policing has to accept that such hidden allegiances exist. Today's county sheriff's deputies and city patrol officers have to understand that the block they cruise or walk may be connected to powerful forces with distant roots giving rise to local fruit that can be deadly.

Like the military leaders of the era of Marshall and Eisenhower, and like the "ordinary" soldiers, sailors, airmen, and marines of today, police executives and police officers have to master areas of knowledge wholly unknown to "local" law enforcement just few years ago. It was my combination of experience in policing and clinical psychology that influenced my appointment in 2002 as deputy chief and subsequently chief of the Rochester (New York) Police Department. City and department officials recognized that a large number of calls for service involved dealing with disturbed and mentally ill individuals, something for which few Rochester officers had received any training. I quickly instituted a training program in Rochester such as are now found in departments nationwide.

Training officers to deal with disturbed persons in emergency situations is important, but we also need to enlarge training at every level even beyond the emergency basics. Today's law enforcement professionals, from executives, to dispatchers, to investigators, to patrol officers must have a sound background in evolving technologies, in the Internet and social media, in issues related to terrorism (international and domestic as well as internationally directed or foreign-inspired terrorism in a domestic context), in immigration (including basic bilingual or multilingual facility), in the new understanding of diversity, in our often rapidly changing laws, and—even more today than in 2002—in the crisis of the mentally ill in our communities.

Police agencies all across the nation are responding to the complex demands of a still-new century. The most important general trend is the overall increase in *minimum* education requirements for incoming police recruits. A 2014 Police Executive Research Forum (PERF) survey is revealing. In 2014, 69% of responding departments required a high school diploma, 10.3% some college, 16.8% a 2-year degree, and 3.8% a 4-year degree. Asked what they expected in five years, only 38.6% of departments responded that a high school diploma would remain an adequate minimum requirement; 26.1% responded that they would expect some college, 24.2% would require a 2-year degree, and 11% would require recruits to have a 4-year degree. Clearly, in 2014, police leaders expected a future in which significantly more education would be required for members of the force. The jump from the actual minimum requirements in 2014 to the anticipated requirements in 2019 was markedly greater than that between 2009 and 2014. In 2009, 66.4% of departments required recruits with high school diplomas (compared to 69% in 2014), 13.1% required some college (10.3% in 2014), 16.8% required a 2-year degree (16.8% in 2014), and 3.6% required a 4-year degree (3.8% in 2014).[112]

To a casual reader, the trend toward higher minimum educational requirements for police officers may not seem extraordinarily impressive. But look at it in the context of what Professor William J. Woska of Golden Gate University (Carmel, California) called in 2006 a "public-sector crisis," the decline, since the 1990s, in applicants for jobs in law enforcement.[113] Today, according to ABC News, "the number of applicants [is] down more than 90 percent in some cities." Departments both large and small are having trouble recruiting. Many recruiters report that "scandals and negative publicity ... in recent years" have discouraged applicants, but, mostly, the decline is attributable to a perceived imbalance of risk versus reward. As a Seattle police recruiter put it, "You can get shot at for $40,000, or be home with your family for $60,000." Others in law enforcement see departments hopelessly competing for the best recruits against the technology private sector, "the IBMs, the Microsofts, the Intels."[114]

The truth is that, as a Chicago PD recruiter told ABC, "money has never been the primary reason people want to join the force."[115] Some want the adrenalin rush, of course, but even more want to be in a position to make a difference, to help people, to protect communities, even to save lives. A lot of us want a bit of both. *Nobody*, however, goes into law enforcement to be continually frustrated by a lack of adequate education and training to do what continues to become an increasingly challenging and complex job. As a helping profession—a guardian profession—law enforcement is inherently rewarding for the right people, the people who want to help, to serve, to protect, to make a difference. But, increasingly, reaping these inherent rewards requires knowing more. When I zigged from the law enforcement track to clinical psychology back in the 1990s, I was admittedly something of an oddity. These days? Not nearly as much. Although many police academies require candidates to have at least a two-year college degree and even more require four years these days (the requirement at the federal level is universally four years of college), administrators in leadership roles often have graduate degrees, up to and including doctorates. In addition, most larger departments recruit and hire highly trained, highly educated specialists in a wide variety of fields. Perhaps even more significantly, collaborative and cooperative programs between law enforcement agencies and institutions of higher learning are becoming increasingly common.

Enhanced education and training are in. On its way out? The kneejerk rejection of "book learning" by old-school "streetwise" sergeants, supervisors, and watch commanders.

Goals of Education and Training for 21st Century Policing

Those of us who served on the President's Task Force on 21st Century Policing agreed on the need to enhance foundational skills training, especially in the areas of—

- Community policing and problem-solving principles
- Interpersonal and communication skills
- Bias awareness
- Scenario-based, situational decision making
- Crisis intervention
- Procedural justice and impartial policing
- Trauma and victim services
- Mental health issues
- Analytical research and technology
- Languages and cultural responsiveness

We were convinced that acquiring, cultivating, and imparting the necessary levels of knowledge and proficiency in these areas would require police agencies to reach out to law enforcement associations that create, conduct, and sponsor educational and training programs. These include the International Association of Chiefs of Police (IACP), the Major Cities Chiefs Association (MCCA), the National Organization of Black Law Enforcement Executives (NOBLE), and the Police Executive Research Forum (PERF), among others. Equally important, we concluded, was creating partnerships with academic institutions.

Higher Education Enables Higher Performance

Today, police and policing-related educational programs are offered by many universities. Traditional undergraduate criminal justice and criminology programs remain important foundations for a career in law enforcement, but working officers and police leaders also need access to specialized short courses and graduate programs, which, the Task Force concluded, still have a long way to go if they are to begin adequately addressing the needs of 21st-century law enforcement. The gap between what they offer and what is needed can be seen as a problem or as an opportunity—an opportunity for police agencies and departments to collaborate with the academic community. Community policing has been around since the 1970s—and, informally, long before that. The traditional understanding of this approach is all about developing relationships with individuals in the community, especially with community leaders and other influencers. Twenty-first century policing still thrives on this traditional approach, but it also extends it. Colleges, community colleges, universities, and other academic institutions are also part of the larger community we serve, and we need increasingly to partner with them.

We should not, however, seek to transform the universities into law enforcement vocational schools. A college education is not just about training for a job, career, or profession. As John Henry Cardinal Newman wrote in *The Idea of a University*, knowledge is "its own reward." Even if you go to a college or university to study a particular "practical" subject, Newman wrote, you will find yourself in an "assemblage of learned men"—Newman was writing in 1858, when few colleges admitted women—"zealous for their own sciences, and rivals of each other," but who "adjust together the claims and relations of their respective subjects of investigation" and "learn to respect, to consult, to aid each other."[116] Higher education is a concentrated dose of broad experience. It helps anybody—police officers included—to be more tolerant and understanding of diverse peoples and points of view. I've found that the more I learn, the more appreciative I am of my differences with others and, conversely, the less defensive I am about my own points of view.

Unfortunately, some of our candidates for high political office in recent years—and nowhere more than in the election cycle of 2015-2016—fall into the habit of defining an *us* against a *them*. I don't believe this attitude can sustain a successful American democracy, and I know for a certainty that it cannot sustain a successful, productive, and genuinely helpful career in law enforcement—certainly not in the 21st century. Police officers and police leaders alike need to be sensitive to the needs of an increasingly diverse population: recent immigrants of all origins, African Americans, Latinos, Muslims, and those in the LGBTQ community. Politicians and political candidates who dismiss this sensitivity as "political correctness" will likely make poor leaders and would certainly be inadequate and quite possibly dangerous in law enforcement. In addition to upholding and defending the constitutional rights of everyone in the communities they serve, police officers have to demonstrate personal and professional qualities that go beyond the law. They have to demonstrate respect in every interaction with members of the community. Sometimes this is strictly a matter of exercising good interpersonal skills. Sometimes it is knowing when to avoid policing tactics that, intentionally or unintentionally, demonstrate a bias against minorities.

In the early days of community policing, well-meaning law enforcement leaders sought to create better relations between the police and minority communities, especially neighborhoods of color, by assigning a preponderance of minority officers to patrol those neighborhoods. Ideally, some believed, black neighborhoods should be patrolled primarily by black officers, Hispanic neighborhoods by Hispanics, Asian neighborhoods ... well, you get it. The problem with this approach is that it is *not* community policing. It is a policy of ethnic and racial segregation, however well-intended. A well-trained, well-educated officer should be able to do community policing, build positive relationships, in any community of any ethnicity, racial makeup, and socioeconomic profile. Advanced education tends to cultivate and amplify the skills and attitudes that enable an officer to serve with excellence anywhere.

Among the qualities a good college or university education develops is curiosity, which is very important in policing, from investigating a crime to taking proactive steps to avoid or prevent crime. Advanced study also teaches us to add discipline to curiosity, to satisfy our curiosity in analytical ways, to think about relationships between people and between events, to look beyond and beneath the surface of things. Again, these are the approaches of a good police officer. And today, having an analytical orientation 24/7 has never been more critically important. Today, a good officer must be both local and global in focus. The fight against local crime is, in the broadest sense, part of the fight against terrorism. For instance, to the degree that law and order and other community values appeal to a neighborhood youth, that youngster is in danger of becoming alienated and marginalized. It is from among the ranks of such young people that international terrorism recruits. Moreover, so-called normal or routine criminal activity may be linked to terrorism. We saw this in the Paris attacks of November 13, 2015. The two principal suspects, Abdelhamid Abaaoud and Salah Abdeslam, were not professional ideologues, jihadists, or soldiers, but common criminals—local thugs turned agents of global terrorism. It takes an educated, curious, disciplined imagination to see such links between "common" criminality and terrorism. I couldn't agree more with my fellow members of the President's Task Force on 21st Century Policing in concluding that government at all levels "should encourage and incentivize higher education for law enforcement officers."[117] The diversity and interconnectivity of today's world demand broad minds.

Training to Take Point

Anybody who has served in the military—and, let's face it, just about anybody who has watched more than a few movies on military themes—knows what it means to "take point." It is to get out in front of the main body of troops, to assume the first and most nakedly exposed position in a combat formation. When Detective Jorge Lozano led terrified workers out of the Inland Regional Center in San Bernardino, California, on December 2, 2015, there was no way of knowing whether the terrorist attack that killed fourteen and wounded twenty-three was over or not. One of those workers recorded the evacuation using a smartphone, the very device that has too often recorded incidents of officer misjudgment or misconduct. This time, however, it recorded the very finest in officer performance. As we watch, we hear the officer gently but firmly ask for calm, telling everyone that they will be all right. "I'll take a bullet before you do," he calmly promises them. "That's for damn sure." And then he leads them to safety.[118]

That is what it means to "take point." Now, I don't intend to minimize in any way the bravery and outright heroism of that individual's performance when I say that it is not unusual or extraordinary for a police officer. As a director of public safety, that level of conduct is what I *expect* from my officers. They have volunteered to be the point people of our communities. That's the job they've signed up for. The patrol officer alone in his squad car at three in the morning cruising some dark street or remote country lane could justifiably say the same thing to the people she serves: "I'll take a bullet before you do. That's for damn sure."

I expect boldness and bravery from my officers. The community has a right to expect the same. I do not expect—and I do not want—reckless behavior that will benefit no one. The person who takes point needs to be self-reliant, self-confident, smart, innovative, and resourceful. He or she must be physically and mentally well-equipped to think, decide, and operate independently and, often, alone. But operating independently does not mean making everything up as you go along and hoping for the best. I can assure you that behind what that officer did in San Bernardino, leading a lot of frightened people safely through dangers unknown, was solid education and training.

To ensure that the highest level of training is available to officers throughout the nation, it is important for the central government, the federal government, to support training facilities nationwide that promote consistent standards for training and that encourage continual innovation of standards, so that they will always be well-suited to changing environments and evolving technologies. What we don't want is rigid standards that produce cookie-cutter cops. As point people, officers have to be individually innovative, willing to take initiative, capable of taking action informed by training but also linked to the instincts and wits of someone who is in the moment and on the spot. The objective is to standardize excellence in the kind of training that will produce officers capable of taking point bravely, imaginatively, and effectively every single day or night they are on patrol. This means creating training programs that are less like regimented boot camps and more like adult education. It means opening up to each officer troves of information that reflect actual police experience and best practices. It means showing them how to do aspects of their jobs not "by the book" or because "that's the way it is done," but because the empirical evidence of experience shows that it is the best, most effective way.

We don't have a national police force in the United States. Our democratic traditions have led us away from that. Instead, individual cities, counties, and states have their own police forces. These traditions of local policing have been operative at least since the nation was born in 1776, and they are traditions whose value has been borne out by more than two centuries of experience. Community policing is based on the assumption that intensively local policing is the best and most effective policing. To paraphrase President Abraham Lincoln, it is policing of the community, by the community, and for the community—or at least in good faith attempts to be. If anything, today's technologies of interconnection have actually increased the importance and influence of the local community. Before the rise of these technologies, we lived in an era of mass communication, mass production, and mass marketing. Today, mass communication, which is the one-way communication of we-speak-you-listen, has given way to interactive communication, dialogue, feedback, and innovation often based not in some corporate headquarters or government agency but in the community. That is what crowdsourcing is all about.

Nevertheless, high-stakes enterprises such as law enforcement benefit from a combination of individual and community input on the one hand and, on the other, national standardization based on best practices. Although we don't have a national police force, we do have the FBI National Academy at Quantico, Virginia, which offers education and training to law enforcement personnel from all across the United States as well as the international community. Those of us on the President's Task Force are eager to ensure that the National Academy curriculum benefits from the latest in community policing, including the input of the Office of Community Oriented Policing (COPS Office) and the Office of Justice Programs (OJP) of the U.S. Department of Justice. We also believe that the research projects and initiatives of such organizations as the Police Executive Research Forum (PERF) and the Police Executive Leadership Institute (which is managed by the Major Cities Chiefs Association) should also figure in the National Academy curriculum. This is the most effective way to "surface" the best practices for 21st-century policing rather than simply *impose* these practices from above. In the 21st century, this most interactive of eras, it is important to ensure that no mass market, one-size-fits-all formula stifles approaches that grow out of and respond to local needs and priorities. But it is just as important that local law enforcement have access to *practices* that have truly proven themselves *best* across different and varied jurisdictions.

Law enforcement establishments all across the nation should not only learn from one another, they should also plug into the remarkable network that America's many institutions of higher education represent. The days of the university as an "ivory tower" remote from the realities of the real world are long gone. Higher education today *is* real-world education—but at the highest level. It would be a good move for the U.S. Department of Justice to partner with some of our universities to create a national postgraduate institute of policing for senior executives. The President's Task Force has recommended that such an institute be modeled on the excellent Naval Postgraduate School in Monterey, California, which is a fully accredited masters-level university that offers programs traditionally associated with civilian graduate schools but custom-tailored to naval applications. A national postgraduate institute of policing would bring together curricula from the worlds of civilian technology and management and tailor them to law enforcement application.

Task force members also concluded that standards and programs were needed at every level of leadership, not just at the very top. Successful enterprises in the private sector have long understood that their most valuable assets are not their products or patents, but their people. Accordingly, they devote time, attention, and resources to developing leaders from within their own pool of personnel. Law enforcement can learn from this private sector example. The International Association of Chiefs of Police (IACP) developed a program called Leading Police Organizations, which is modeled on the West Point Leadership Program. Both the IACP program and its U.S. Military Academy model use the insights of behavioral science to craft approaches to leading groups, organizations, and change. The objective at the heart of both programs is to make "every officer a leader," which I take to mean ensuring that every officer is equipped and motivated to take point in whatever situations and contexts a point person is needed.

As we must instill leadership at all levels of our police agencies, we should always reach out beyond the department hierarchy and into the community. Repeatedly in this book, I have emphasized the importance of transparency in building a relationship of mutual confidence and trust between the community and the police. Nowhere is that transparency more important than in police training. To the extent possible, communities should be engaged in creating training programs that reflect the needs and character of the community. This requires departments to take initiative by informing interested members of the community about their training practices. Wherever possible, community leaders and influencers should be given an opportunity to evaluate police training, and they should also be invited, based on their observations, to make comments and suggestions. I can report from personal experience that inviting interested community members, especially the local leaders and influencers, to actually see officers in training, to hear their instructors explain the rationale behind what they do, and even to invite willing folks to participate in some of that training side-by-side with recruits is remarkably valuable. I conduct such outreach programs regularly these days, and I find that they win hearts and minds by opening both.

Actionable Reform

For me, it was a thrill to meet and work with other police leaders on the President's Task Force. Anyone who has ever been part of a team committed to creating something important has some idea of the exhilaration I felt and the enthusiasm I continue to feel about the work. Of course, it is easy to become cynical about the fate of projects of innovation and reform in the labyrinth of government. But I am optimistic in this case. We did not make our recommendations into a vacuum. Throughout the nation, states and regions formulate what we call POSTs, Peace Officer Standards and Training. These are the minimum educational requirements set for law enforcement officers in that region. Thanks to the existence of POSTs, there are administrative bodies nationwide dedicated to evaluating and reevaluating education and training requirements. This means that there is a ready and receptive audience for innovation and reform. In addition to the broad educational initiatives the Task Force recommended, we also specifically addressed the POSTs in establishing specific subject areas as new training priorities. These include:

- Crisis intervention training (CIT), which was originally developed in 1988 in Memphis, Tennessee, to "improve police ability to recognize symptoms of a mental health crisis, enhance their confidence in addressing such an emergency, and reduce inaccurate beliefs about mental illness."[119] Among the situations in which police officers frequently find themselves having to "take point" are encounters with disturbed mentally ill persons. Without training, officers are often at a loss as to how to proceed in managing these often frightening and potentially dangerous encounters. CIT gives them competence and confidence, which enhances their safety, the safety of the subject, and public safety. It is a critical step toward upping the odds in favor of a good outcome in law enforcement engagement with the mentally ill. POSTs need to make CIT a part of recruit training and in-service training.

- Police agencies across the nation do a thorough job of providing *tactical training* for their recruits, but too many of them devote too little attention to improving *social interaction*. Behavioral science has much to offer in the areas of "critical thinking, social intelligence, implicit bias, fair and impartial policing, historical trauma, and other topics that address capacity to build trust and legitimacy in diverse communities and offer better skills for gaining compliance without the use of physical force."[120] POSTs need to link this communications training to tactical and operations training on use of force (lethal and non-lethal) and on de-escalation and tactical retreat.

- Traditionally, the role of police in the enforcement of drug laws has been strictly to enforce the law. Issues relating to the causes of drug use were of no concern to the police. It is now clear that education and training in *addiction as a disease* is as important in dealing with subjects who are under the influence of drugs as CIT is to engaging with mentally ill persons in emergency situations. Officers who understand addiction as a disease rather than as a moral failing tend to treat subjects with more empathy. While understanding addiction as a disease does not absolve the officer from enforcing applicable laws, the adequately trained officer can manage drug offenders in ways less likely to endanger them, the officer, or the public. Equally important, the officer's empathetic engagement with the suspect can do much to help put him or her on a course that will secure effective treatment rather than incarceration. Treatment is more effective than incarceration as a deterrent to additional offenses.

- Educating recruits and in-service officers on mental illness and addiction reduces officer biases against mentally ill persons and addicts. We believe it is also important that POSTs address the broader issue of bias. Officer bias can cause constitutional violations, particularly of the Fourteenth Amendment right to "equal protection of the laws." Beyond the potential for constitutional violation, however, bias also reduces an officer's effectiveness, erodes police-community relations, and increases the risk of an engagement ending badly, due to unwarranted escalation of force. Given the increased diversity of our communities, bias-awareness training has never been more important than it is today. Yet we live in a climate of often heated political rhetoric in which it has become fashionable not only to denounce "political correctness," but to dismiss bias, stereotyping, profiling, and various instances of denigration as violations not of dignity, respect, and, quite possibly, law, but as the excusable and even laudable defiance of political correctness. In this climate, which threatens to reinforce bias, bias education is all the more necessary.

- Related to bias-awareness training, POSTs, we believe, should include training that specifically and explicitly addresses policing in a democratic society. One aspect of this training is to ensure that police conduct protects rather than threatens or even violates constitutional rights. Constitutional and other legal issues are important, of course, but so are issues of legitimacy and procedural justice. As society's point people, police officers are given considerable authority and power by law. As point people in a *democratic* society, however, they near a heavy responsibility to exercise that authority and power not simply to the limits of the law, but with both prudence and empathy.

CHAPTER 12

Restore Trust, Earn Legitimacy

I n the Old West, lawmen wore a star. Most police officers today call their badge a shield. Typically, it looks like one—although it is far too small to offer any real protection or even to confer actual authority. Whatever the uniform, insignia, or symbol of office—Sheriff Raymond Hamlin chomped a cigar and carried a cane—an officer's legitimacy and the trust that legitimacy engenders are not broadcast by a badge or brandished by a baton. Trust and legitimacy are conferred by the people. More specifically, they are conferred by a population that believes police officers in general, as well as the particular police officer with whom they are dealing at the moment, are competent, able, empathetic, and committed to procedural justice. Such officers earn legitimacy by treating everyone with dignity and respect, listening more than talking (let alone shouting), demonstrating an absence of bias, acting with transparency, and generally proving themselves trustworthy.

People confer legitimacy on those they perceive to be their neighbors, at least in spirit and intention: agents of government who also have a stake in their community and prize its values at least as highly as they honor laws, regulations, and rules.

Police officers like this are *guardians*.

It's a word I've already used in this book, and for pretty much anyone with a basic command of English, "guardian" has a readily comprehensible meaning. You can look up the word in any dictionary, and it will tell you most of what you need to know.

But when leaders in law enforcement and related disciplines gathered to together in 2014-2015 at the behest of President Barack Obama to serve on the President's Task Force on 21st Century Policing, that word was used in a very specific historical context. I don't know what you are likely to find more remarkable—the fact that a group of law enforcement types got to together in Washington and talked about Plato's *Republic* or the fact that a task force assigned to provide guidance on *21st-century* policing turned to a book written in about *380 BC*. But this is, in fact, what happened.

Among the foundational recommendations we members of the task force made was this: "Law enforcement culture should embrace a guardian—rather than a warrior—mindset to build trust and legitimacy both within agencies and with the public." As we saw it, this meant that "law enforcement agencies should adopt procedural justice as the guiding principle for internal and external policies" and that they "should also establish a culture of transparency and accountability to build public trust and legitimacy."[121]

This recommendation, that law enforcement officers think of themselves not as warriors but as guardians, was written about by one of our task force members, Sue Rahr, former sheriff of King County, Washington, and now head of the Washington State Criminal Justice Training Commission. Distinguishing between soldiers, "who come into communities as an outside, occupying force," and guardians, who "are members of the community, protecting from within," Rahr specifically cited Plato.

Best Practice, 380 BC

And why not? The task force was seeking "best practices," and what better place to look than in the greatest book by the greatest philosopher who ever lived? In his *Republic*, Plato created a plan for the ideal society, a "republic that honors the core of democracy." In such a republic, he assigned "the greatest amount of power ... to those called Guardians."[122] Speaking through the character of his mentor Socrates, Plato gave the "guardians" a leadership role, entrusting them with the greatest authority in the republic because their character was worthy to "bear the responsibility of protecting the democracy." It was a "character" built on the physical attributes of speed and strength as well as the intellectual qualities of "a spirited philosopher." Indeed, of the three main classes forming Plato's ideal republic—Producers (artisans, craftspeople, farmers, and so on), Auxiliaries (soldiers), and guardians—it was the guardians who had need for the deepest and most diverse education. As spirited philosophers, they both commanded and dispensed understanding and respect.

Plato thought hard about the nature and role of the guardians because, in designing his ideal society, he started from scratch. He asked why it was that people create societies in the first place. His answer was that individual human beings, living in isolation, are not self-sufficient. Working alone, nobody can acquire all of life's necessities. To survive, let alone prosper, people gathered themselves together into communities for the good of all. Key to ensuring this common good, Plato reasoned, was division of labor, with each member of the society specializing in a specific craft or field. Some farmed, some made shoes, some built houses, and so on.

Division and specialization of labor, Plato decided, was *necessary* to building a community, but not *sufficient* for the task. More than food growers and shoemakers were required. Even among people working together for the common good, disputes were inevitable. A class of people was needed to resolve them wisely, justly, and productively. Some disputes, whether internal or external, could easily get out of hand. Moreover, even in a well-ordered community, aberrant or criminal behavior was a distinct possibility. For these reasons, the class of people empowered to resolve disputes was also given the authority to use force, if necessary. Plato called them guardians, and he assigned to them a central role in the management of society. They enforced laws—laws intended to create justice—and they provided protection.

The position of guardian, as Plato saw it, was the most demanding role in the community. Guardians, he believed, should be selected for their strength, agility, and bravery—essentially the qualities of a soldier—but even more important was a philosophical turn of mind. Plato wanted guardians who excelled at digging into the important questions about human life and who were willing and able to judge, in any given situation, what values and actions were true and best.

To an extent, as Plato saw it, guardians were born. They possessed the physical attributes of the natural athlete, and, from early in life, demonstrated a proclivity for the curiosity and analytical thinking of a philosopher. But the most important qualities of a guardian were not inborn, but developed through excellence in education.

The best—and, by "best," I mean most effective—police officers have always been those who are more guardian than soldier. Some officers of the "old school" exulted brute force above all else. According to them, a cop's best friend was his baton, or nightstick. But the veteran officers I always found myself actually listening to defined the virtues of "old school" law enforcement very differently. They were always full of admiring stories about ordinary "beat cops" who had a special talent for what we today call de-escalation. They knew how to use their nightstick and their gun, all right, but their weapon of choice was a combination of their wits and their words. They had an approach founded on street smarts and emotional intelligence, which prompted them to act with empathy and respect. They would use force if need be, but it wasn't their weapon of first resort. These same officers were also the ones who tended to earn legendary reputations as "born detectives." Their inclination was always to accept nothing at face value and always look beneath the surface of things. They combined empathy and curiosity with an analytical instinct and an ability to learn from experience. In this, they were natural philosophers, which is a quality indispensable to any criminal investigator.

In today's increasingly diverse and complex society, in which many threats are visible and apparent, but many others, just as urgent, are not, law enforcement agencies cannot afford to wait for the instinctively talented patrol officers and born detectives to walk through the doorway. The cultivation of talent through smart training and top-flight education is a high priority in the 21st century. A "guardian mindset" is something that must be developed in individual officers, in the executives who lead them, in the institutional makeup of law enforcement agencies, and in the communities in which the police operate. This mindset is partly a product of doctrine, policy, and tactics, but as the *Report of the President's Task Force* on 21st *Century Policing* observes, there is an old saying: "Organizational culture eats policy for lunch."

> Any law enforcement organization can make great rules and policies that emphasize the guardian role, but if policies conflict with the existing culture, they will not be institutionalized and behavior will not change. In police work, the vast majority of an officer's work is done independently outside the immediate oversight of a supervisor. But consistent enforcement of rules that conflict with a military-style culture, where obedience to the chain of command is the norm, is nearly impossible. Behavior is more likely to conform to culture than rules.[123]

It's the Cover Up That Gets You

Adopting a "guardian mindset" implies certain actions, beginning with a willingness to undertake a frank examination not only of a particular department's record but of its historical context.

Wallowing in a flawed past, getting mired in a department's bad reputation, these are, let's face it, possible outcomes of looking the past in the eye. But they are outcomes neither desirable nor productive. Morale and esprit de corps are important to any police organization. Officers should expect to feel good about the job they do and the men and women they do it with. The objective of examining past practices as well as current practices that are rooted in the past is to improve the department, to learn from past errors, and to use these lessons to grow beyond them. Esprit de corps is a feeling that is earned. It is not the same as simply ignoring or denying historical problems. It is not about heedless self-congratulation. To the degree that a department leader can build esprit de corps on a departmental record of merit, of procedural justice, and earned legitimacy, so much the better. But even an organization with a checkered past can build esprit and morale on the resolve to improve and the confidence that improvement will succeed. In the absence of achievement, it is best to embrace heartfelt aspiration.

Atonement for past sins begins with learning from them in order to avoid repeating them. If learning from past errors and injustices can be painful, taking steps to make them right can hurt even more. Some members of a department can be educated and, as it were, rehabilitated. Others may need to be fired or even prosecuted. However sharp the pain, it is far preferable to the slow agony of practices that corrupt and erode, that alienate police from community and community from police, and that chronically increase the risks to officers and the citizens they serve and protect.

Examining the past openly and non-defensively, using it as a source of lessons learned, is possible only in an institution with a culture of transparency and accountability. President Richard M. Nixon, the only chief executive in American history to resign office, famously remarked, "It's not the crime that gets you. It's the cover up." The fact is that the crime *does* sometime get you, but the cover up compounds whatever consequences the original misdeed may entail. Policing is a profession that constantly faces the public. Especially in an era of smartphone, dashcam, and body-cam videos and open-source news gathering, what can be known will be known. Any officer or police manager who believes otherwise is in deep denial and delusion.

The truth will be told, sooner or later, and since, unlike fine wine and good bourbon, bad news does not improve with age, it is always best to be transparent, to tell the truth, tell it fast, and tell it all. The October 20, 2014 shooting of seventeen-year-old Laquan McDonald on Chicago's South Side happened very fast. Officer Jason Van Dyke emptied his service weapon into McDonald, sixteen rounds in the space of fourteen seconds. But what happened after those sixteen shots happened very slowly, at least as far as the public was concerned. In the immediate aftermath of the incident, the "official" CPD account was that provided by Pat Camden, at the time a spokesman for the Fraternal Order of Police. McDonald, who was being pursued for breaking into vehicles, "punctured one of the squad car's front passenger-side tires and damaged the front windshield," Camden told reporters. "Officers got out of their car and began approaching McDonald, ... telling him to drop the knife." Camden said that the "boy allegedly lunged at police, and one of the officers opened fire."[124]

Despite this clear assertion of self-defense, in April 2015, the Chicago City Council voted a $5 million settlement for Laquan McDonald's family—which had not yet even filed a lawsuit. When they voted, no council member had yet seen any dashcam video of the shooting. City officials told them that it could not be released while the FBI and U.S. Attorney were investigating.

A freelance journalist, in the meantime, sued the city and Cook County state's attorney to secure release of the video under the Freedom of Information Act. For months, Chicago mayor Rahm Emanuel and State's Attorney Anita Alvarez fought the lawsuit—right up to the time a judge definitively ordered the video's release. In November, mere hours before the city and county complied with the order, Prosecutor Alvarez charged Officer Van Dyke with first-degree murder.

As for the video, it directly contradicted Camden's narrative, which had stood publicly as "the truth" for thirteen months. The video shows no confrontation between McDonald and the police. What it shows is the youth walking down the middle of Pulaski Road and then veering to his right to avoid the police vehicles stopped in the middle of the street. Officer Van Dyke exits one of the vehicles, gun drawn, and opens fire as McDonald walks at an oblique angle away from him. The first shot brings McDonald down. The next fifteen are fired in rapid succession into the youth's prostrate and soon motionless body.

By the time the video was released, trust between the CPD and the community was broken. It would only get even more broken as time went on. To begin with, there were *five* CPD Tahoe vehicles at the scene, all of which, according to the department's own regulations, were required to have fully functioning dashcams.[125] Only two were documented as functioning, and we have only one actual video, which, however, includes no intelligible audio, even though every vehicle has a front and a rear microphone and the dashcam automatically records both video and audio.[126] Also, in addition to the dashcams, a nearby Burger King had a security camera, but 86 minutes, including the span of the shooting, are missing from its video recording. The *Chicago Tribune* and NBC News reported that the Burger King manager claimed that "Several detectives barged into the Burger King demanding the password to access surveillance footage that would have captured the crucial minutes before and after Officer

Jason Van Dyke opened fire" and that "police wiped more than an hour of surveillance footage from the [fast food] chain's servers."[127]

Not only was the bad news withheld for months, its release, in the form of a single, silent video, served only to raise more speculations of a cover-up, including possible tampering with and outright destruction of evidence.

All of this was very wrong and very bad—for the victim and his family, for Chicago's poor neighborhoods of color, for every neighborhood in every American city. It was wrong and was bad for the great majority of Chicago police officers, who do a hard and dangerous job that now became even harder and more dangerous. It was—and it remains—wrong and bad for police officers everywhere, who absolutely need the trust of the community. It is wrong, bad, and dangerous for every American community, each of which has the right to feel confident in the police whose duty it is to protect them.

"It's the cover up that gets you." The release of that video and all the questions surrounding it was bad for Chicago Police Superintendent Garry McCarthy, who was fired by the mayor. At the time of this writing, a bill is being introduced in the Illinois legislature to remove Rahm Emanuel from office.[128] Right now, it's anybody's guess as to how many will lose their jobs—or suffer even more serious consequences.

Transparency Begins at Headquarters

Transparency, with regard both to the past and the present, is essential to promoting legitimacy both in the eyes of the community and within the police force itself. When something goes wrong, really wrong, with an arrest or other interaction between the police and the public, those in charge all too often ascribe the wrongdoing to the proverbial and solitary bad apple in the barrel. Time and again, however, we discover that, actually, there is something wrong with the barrel.

How police management interacts with patrol officers directly impacts how those officers interact with citizens. If the internal culture is one of cover-up, corner-cutting, little lies, and big ones, you can bet that the external culture—the relationship between police and the community—will likewise become corrupted. Procedural justice begins within the department. If management levels with officers when it comes to policy and decisions made on the base of policy—better yet, if management includes officers in the creation of policy—those officers are likely to relate in an open and honest manner with civilian members of the community. A shared approach to public safety within the department tends to produce a shared approach to public safety out in the community.

A New Metric

There's an old saying: *If you don't like how the conversation's going, change the subject.* Very few people (outside of law enforcement) get out of bed in the morning with the pleasant thought that, *Yes, today I may actually meet a police officer!* For the vast majority of citizens, encounters with law enforcement are inherently negative. Either you're a victim of a crime—or have been caught running a stop sign.

In challenged neighborhoods, citizen-police encounters are often far less innocuous than a stop for a traffic violation. Sometimes, they are so highly charged that they escalate into an arrest, criminal charges, or even violence. In communities that often see interactions with law enforcement, police commanders should consider deliberately creating interactions that are not based on enforcement or investigation. Police-sponsored neighborhood activities—the Police Athletic League is a long-standing example—are not just "good publicity," they are golden opportunities to change the subject of the all-too-typical police-citizen "conversation." The community needs contexts in which to see the police as people, not enforcers. The police need interactions with people as people, not perpetrators.

It is not always easy to motivate police personnel to devote their own down time to non-enforcement, non-investigative activities in a neighborhood that may actually be remote from where they and their own families live. Police leadership needs to see these opportunities not as mere extracurricular activities, but as essential to building effective relationships between the police and the community. Putting in time at the PAL *is* police work, important police work.

We all need to think about that. Any engagement our officers have with the community, on the clock or off, is police work. By the same token, not all police work is effective in creating positive and productive relations with the community. Sir Robert Peel, as you may recall from chapter 8, said that a reduction in the rate of crime in a community was the only measure of the effectiveness of the presence of the police in that community. As truly forward-looking and perceptive as Peel was, I'm convinced he's mistaken here. Reduction in crime is obviously important, but, as the task force concluded, reduction alone is not "self-justifying. Overly aggressive law enforcement strategies can potentially harm communities and do lasting damage to public trust …"[129]

There is another valid measure of the effectiveness of police in a given community, and that is to devise surveys and polls designed to track a given community's level of trust in the police. When it comes to assessing the state of relations between the police and the community, crime stats alone do not tell the whole story.

Although I believe that it is hard to build positive relations between police and community if every police engagement exclusively concerns investigation or enforcement, I am not suggesting that it is sufficient merely to "change the subject" of the "conversation" between the police and communities that are disproportionately impacted by crime. It is also critically important to open the subject of crime and prevention to the community. Sincerely invite consultation and collaboration with community members to develop policies and strategies aimed at both reducing crime and improving the ongoing relationship between the police and the community. Police agencies need to inform the public. They also need to engage the public interactively. The police *enforce* the law, but they *serve* the public. Within that area of service, there is both room and need for collaborative conversation.

In chapter 2, I told the story of how Doug Hughes, commander of the Central Precinct in Miami-Dade, used community policing to reduce crime in the Scott Projects, the kind of subsidized public housing that became infamous in the 1980s as incubators of gang violence, drugs, and what we would today properly call domestic terror. Places like Scott were places the public had pretty much given up on—and the police, quite frankly, were tempted to give up on as well. Hughes, however, recognized that the great majority of the residents of Scott Projects were law-abiding people who wanted to raise their families in peace and safety. He knew that we could not abandon them. Where others looked on Scott Projects as a brick-and-mortar version of Dante's hell, he insisted that we treat it as what it was, a community. In a typical neighborhood, we officers built relationships in the streets, one corner, one resident at a time. Hughes asked us to do the same in the hallways and passageways of Scott. He wanted us to talk with people, to find out what they wanted, what they feared, what they needed. We met with residents who had stepped up as Scott "community" leaders and influencers. We worked out ways to patrol the facility—not as a means of racking up arrest statistics, but as way to make the place safer and more livable. This is intensely local policing—and by "local" I mean person-to-person, one person at a time—but it is the kind of policing that has an impact on entire cities, on the nation, and, potentially, on the world.

Now, when I talk about getting together with interested members of the community to collaborate on public safety solutions for the community, I am not suggesting that we dump the problems of policing in the public's lap. *We* are the professionals, after all. Before a meaningful collaboration can take place, the police in the community have to do two things and do them well.

First, they need to have in place—or to put in place—crystal-clear policies covering the use of force. These policies must not only be unambiguous, they need to be comprehensive, covering training, investigation, and enforcement. Once policies are in place, police officers and leaders need to make an effort, community by community, to ensure that the public is aware of them, understands them, and understands their limits and alternatives. De-escalation is a key aspect of any viable policy concerning force, and this concept should be presented to community members as the alternative the police themselves want to use. To put it in the simplest and most direct terms, people have to be told—and told in a way they can believe—that the police do not want to bully them, dominate them, or hurt them. They want to serve them and keep them safe. Only within a context of understanding, a context of service, can a meaningful collaboration between police and community take place.

Non-punitive Accountability

It is important for members of the community—ordinary citizens—to feel that they can talk to the officers in their neighborhood, not just to pass the time of day (although I would never underestimate the power of so-called small talk), but also to convey concerns, complaints, compliments, investigative information, and to ask for help. The objective is to demonstrate that you, as a police officer, are accountable to the people you serve.

Of course, police officers are also accountable to other police officers. The police are under continual "review" by the residents of the community. They are also under review by their fellow officers and their supervisors and commanders. In the case of critical incidents, the President's Task Force recommended that peer reviews be formalized as frank but non-punitive reviews conducted apart from any criminal or administrative investigations. The object of the peer reviews is to compile lessons learned and improve individual performance as well as departmental policies and practices.

Ultimately, officers are held accountable both legally and administratively for their actions. Non-punitive peer reviews are not intended to take the place of legal and administrative inquires and investigations. But such reviews do introduce another level of accountability. Call it *professional accountability.* It requires everyone participating to have a commitment to improving the systems within which they work. The outcome of such reviews should not be disciplinary or judicial action, but the creation of policy and procedures that make the job more efficient, safer, and more effective for both the public and the police.

The Blessing of Diversity

I mentioned earlier the well-meaning but misguided notion that police departments should try to match the race or ethnicity of their officers to the race or ethnicity of the neighborhoods they serve. To begin with, this is not always possible or even feasible. More important, it is a policy of segregation rather than diversity. A neighborhood should be a neighborhood, not a "ghetto"—in the original sense of the word: a place in which people of a certain race, ethnicity, or religion are confined within a larger city.

Diversity is a fact of 21st-century life in America. Fortunately for us, diversity has always strengthened the nation by making us, as a people, more versatile, more innovative, more empathetic, and more tolerant. The United States is all the richer, in terms of culture and economics, for the diversity of its people. Law enforcement agencies should make a deliberate effort to recruit a diverse workforce in terms of gender, race, ethnicity, national origin, cultural background, and general life experience. This should be done *not* with the intention of putting more black officers in predominantly black communities or more Hispanic officers in Hispanic communities. On the contrary, it should be done to ensure that officers represent the makeup of the 21st-century nation. Educated and trained adequately in a department with sound diversity policies, any police officer of any background, race, ethnicity, or gender should be able to serve with excellence wherever she or he is assigned.

Police take an oath to enforce the law. Their legal authority and power—up to and including the solemn power of life and death—derives from this oath. Yet the duty of enforcement and the authority it entails—that is, the legally derived legitimacy of the police—represent but a fraction of the potential power of a police *force* in a community. It can either be a force for building and enhancing the community in every aspect. Or it can be a force that contributes to the dangers and decay that threaten it.

Which side of this either/or equation a particular force comes down on depends largely on the extra-legal elements on which its legitimacy in the community is built. If the members of the force think of themselves as guardians of a community in which they themselves have a stake, and if departmental and institutional values and policies uphold this guardian model, the odds are favorable that the community itself will grant those officers the legitimacy they need in order to serve and protect it. If, on the other hand, the police in a particular place at a particular time conceive of themselves as a military force, an army of occupation, invaders in hostile territory, they have little hope of earning any legitimacy. Almost certainly, it will be a hard, dispiriting, desperate, and dangerous life for everyone in such a community, officers and residents alike.

There was a time when neighborhoods that found themselves in this situation, preyed upon by gangs and other criminals, yet distrusting and existing at odds with the police who were supposed to protect them, were tragic but strictly local "problems." Today, in the 21st century, there are no strictly local problems. I write this book in the early stages of a presidential election cycle. Each candidate talks about the threat of ISIS and other terrorists. And they do so with good reason. Violent terrorism has come to the United States more than once. Stories of Americans becoming "radicalized" by foreign influencers and thereby turned into terrorists are increasingly common. There is good reason to feel threatened. When we feel threatened from the outside, it is natural to turn to the military. True to expectation, so far, the candidates have offered vague military solutions, everything from small American forces to recruit and train larger indigenous forces in the Middle East to carpet bombing the desert until the sand glows.

These "solutions" make the mistake of defining terrorism as just another kind of "local" threat—a threat emanating from a particular place, the Middle East, from which it is exported to France or Belgium or the United States. In truth, however, the threat is global, and it emanates from whatever hearts and minds happen to embrace "foreign" values, ideas, and promises that appear more satisfying, more meaningful, more empowering than those available at home. The crisis in our communities is broadly global precisely because it is intensely personal.

It is a crisis of belonging. Feeling themselves kicked to the margins of American society, whose most familiar representatives are members of police departments perceived as uncaring at best and hostile at worst, some of our neighbors look beyond both the neighborhood and the nation in search of a cause with which they can identify, in which they can believe, and through which (they feel) they will be given the power to impact the world. They are looking for a feeling that neither their neighborhood nor their nation gives them. They are looking for active membership in something greater than themselves. They are looking for a "community" that will accept and empower them.

No army, navy, or air force is going to solve this threat produced by estrangement and marginalization. It is a threat lodged in who knows how many hearts and minds. It is a threat that anyone, sufficiently motivated, can readily turn into deadly action.

The diversity of our communities is our greatest strength. In the 21st century, no army is positioned to engage and eliminate the internal and external threats to these diverse communities. Ultimately, defeating ISIS and what ISIS represents will require wise political, educational, economic, and spiritual leadership at every level. Taking point in this campaign are the men and women society customarily asks to take point. No surprise, they are the police.

They are the police. They are not soldiers, and they should not try to be. What today's threats call for is a force of guardians, members of the community pledged to work in common cause with the rest of the community to protect the community. It is a mission that requires great courage and a willingness to sacrifice. Recall Detective Jorge Lozano, as he led workers to safety, out of the besieged Inland Regional Center in San Bernardino, California, on December 2, 2015. He asked them to be calm. He assured them that they would be "all right" because "I'll take a bullet before you do," adding, "That's for damn sure."

Being a guardian is also a role that calls for knowledge, competence, and compassion. The peace officer's oath to enforce the law applies in the 21st century just as it did in the 20th. But today, issues lying outside the narrow boundaries of that oath are just as urgently important. Police officers need a working knowledge of the law, naturally, but they need an even stronger grasp of the values *behind* the law, the social treasure that is to be shared by all equally in a democracy. The guardians of the community are also the guardians of this treasure, these key values in which some, especially in our most vulnerable communities, feel a vanishing stake.

No police force can make up for all of the social injustice and economic ills that beset society even in a great nation like ours, a nation established not in allegiance to some monarch or myth, but to a Constitution, a set of universal laws and unalienable rights. Nevertheless, the police can enter a community, work in that community, and serve that community in ways that proclaim to one and all that each of us deserves justice and opportunity and that each of us matters in the neighborhood, the nation, and the world.

ENDNOTES

1. Evan Perez and Shimon Prokupecz, "FBI Struggling with Surge in Homegrown Terror Cases," CNN Politics (May 30, 2015), http://www.cnn.com/2015/05/28/politics/fbi-isis-local-law-enforcement/.

2. Robert Patrick, "Darren Wilson's Radio Calls Show Fatal Encounter Was Brief," *St. Louis Post-Dispatch* (November 14, 2014), http://www.stltoday.com/news/multimedia/special/darren-wilson-s-radio-calls-show-fatal-encounter-was-brief/html_79c17aed-0dbe-514d-ba32-bad908056790.html.

3. United States Department of Justice, *Department of Justice Report Regarding the Criminal Investigation into the Shooting Death of Michael Brown by Ferguson, Missouri Police Officer Darren Wilson,* March 4, 2015, http://www.justice.gov/sites/default/files/opa/press-releases/attachments/2015/03/04/doj_report_on_shooting_of_michael_brown_1.pdf.

4. Amanda Terkel, "Police Officer Caught on Video Calling Michael Brown Protesters 'F***ing Animals," *Huffington Post* August 13, 2014), http://www.huffingtonpost.com/2014/08/12/michael-brown-protests_n_5672163.html.

5. National Organization of Black Law Enforcement Officers, http://www.noblenational.org/home.aspx.

6. Matt Meltzer, "The Arthur McDuffie Riots of 1980," *Miami Beach 411* (August 12, 2007), http://www.miamibeach411.com/news/mcduffie-riots; Patrice Gaines-Carter, "McDuffie: The Case Behind Miami's Riots," *Southern Changes: The Journal of the Southern Regional Council, 1978-2003,* vol. 2, no. 7 (1980), 20-23, http://beck.library.emory.edu/southernchanges/article.php?id=sc02-7_009; David Smiley, "McDuffie Riots: Revisiting, Retelling Story—35 Years Later," *Miami Herald* (May 16, 2015), http://www.miamiherald.com/news/local/community/miami-dade/article21178995.html.

7. "Deadly tide of violence recedes after worst riot in Dade history," *The Miami News* (May 19, 1980), http://miamiarchives.blogspot.com/2010/04/mcduffie-riots-may-1980.html.

8. David Card, "The Impact of the Mariel Boatlift on the Miami Labor Market," *Industrial and Labor Relations Review,* vol. 43, no. 2 (January 1990), 245-257; "Mariel Boatlift," GlobalSecurity.org, http://www.globalsecurity.org/military/ops/mariel-boatlift.htm.

9. Mike Clary and Tamara Jones, "Germany Warns Travelers Who Plan to Visit Florida," *The Los Angeles Times* (April 7, 1993), http://articles.latimes.com/1993-04-07/news/mn-20203_1_florida-tourism.

10. Michelle York, "Mean Streets of New York? Increasingly, They're Found in Rochester," *New York Times* (October 24, 2003), http://www.nytimes.com/2003/12/24/nyregion/mean-streets-of-new-york-increasingly-they-re-found-in-rochester.html.

11. York, http://www.nytimes.com/2003/12/24/nyregion/mean-streets-of-new-york-increasingly-they-re-found-in-rochester.html.

12. E. Fuller Torrey, M.D., and others, *The Treatment of Persons with Mental Illness in Prisons and Jails: A State Survey,* Treatment Advocacy Center (April 8, 2014), http://www.tacreports.org/storage/documents/treatment-behind-bars/treatment-behind-bars.pdf.

13. "New DeKalb County Police Chief Dr. Cedric Alexander Accepts Oath of Office," https://www.youtube.com/watch?v=yJqf5Ue-llA.

14. Reagan Wilson, "Detective Pistol Whipped Unconscious. Bystanders Just Take Photos and Make Negative Facebook Posts," *Controversial Times* (August 9, 2015), http://controversialtimes.com/news/detective-pistol-whipped-unconscious-bystanders-just-take-photos-and-make-negative-facebook-posts/.

15. Nick Valencia, "Pistol-Whipped Detective Says He Didn't Shoot Attacker Because of Headlines," CNN (August 14, 2015), http://www.cnn.com/2015/08/13/us/alabama-birmingham-police-detective-pistol-whipped.

16. Ibid.

17. Ibid.

18. Angelique Chrisafis, "France Train Attack: Americans Overpower Gunman on Paris Express," *The Guardian* (August 22, 2015), http://www.theguard-ian.com/world/2015/aug/21/amsterdam-paris-train-gunman-france.

19. Valencia, http://www.cnn.com/2015/08/13/us/alabama-birmingham-police-detective-pistol-whipped.

20. Carol Robinson, "Man Charged in Birmingham Detective's Beating; Outrage Follows Support of Attack on Social Media," Alabama.com (August 8, 2015), http://www.al.com/news/birmingham/index.ssf/2015/08/suspect_with_violent_past_char.html.

21. United States Department of Justice, Civil Rights Division, *Investigation of the Ferguson Police Department* (March 4, 2015), https://www.justice.gov/sites/default/files/opa/press-releases/attach-ments/2015/03/04/ferguson_police_department_report.pdf.

22. Bill Hudson, "Black Lives Matter Chant Called 'Disgusting' by Police Leader," CBS Minnesota (August 30, 2015), http://minnesota.cbslocal.com/2015/08/30/black-lives-matter-chant-called-disgusting-by-police-leader/.

23. Alex Swoyer, "Ted Cruz Reacts to Vilification of Police: 'Coming from the Top—All the Way to the President of the United States,'" Breitbart (August 31, 2015), http://www.breitbart.com/

big-government/2015/08/31/ted-cruz-reacts-to-vilification-of-police-coming-from-the-top-all-the-way-to-the-president-of-the-united-states/.

24. John Adams quoted in David McCullough, *John Adams* (New York: Simon & Schuster, 2001), 373-374.

25. President's Task Force on 21st Century Policing, *Final Report of the President's Task Force on 21st Century Policing* (Washington, DC: Office of Community Oriented Policing Services, 2015),

26. Larry Diamond, "Liberation Technology," *Journal of Democracy*, 21:3 (July 2010), 70.

27. Diamond, 70.

28. Diamond, 69-70.

29. Sophie Beach, "Rise of Rights?" *China Digital Times* (May 27, 2005), http://chinadigitaltimes.net/2005/05/rise-of-rights/.

30. Mario Machado, "The Revolution Will Be Tweeted," *The World Post* (July 3, 2013), http://www.huffingtonpost.com/mario-machado/the-revolution-will-be-tw_1_b_3530075.html.

31. Colin Delany, "How Social Media Accelerated Tunisia's Revolution: An Inside View," epolitics.com (February 10, 2011), http://www.epolitics.com/2011/02/10/how-social-media-accelerated-tunisias-revolution-an-inside-view/. The narrative of the Tunisia Revolution that follows draws extensively on the Delany article.

32. NBCNews, "McCaskill: Police 'Militarization' Escalated Unrest in Ferguson," http://www.nbcnews.com/video/nbc-news/55867114#55866941.

33. Thomas Johnson and Gail Sullivan, "Thousands Donated to Crowdfunding Campaign for Darren Wilson, the Officer Who Shot Michael Brown," *The Washington Post* (August 22, 2014), https://www.washingtonpost.com/news/morning-mix/wp/2014/08/22/thousands-donated-to-crowdfunding-campaign-for-darren-wilson-the-officer-who-shot-michael-brown/.

34. Rubina Madan Fillion, "How Ferguson Protesters Use Social Media to Organize," *The Wall Street Journal* (November 24, 2014), http://blogs.wsj.com/dispatch/2014/11/24/how-ferguson-protesters-use-social-media-to-organize/.

35. Joshua Tucker, "Tweeting Ferguson: How Social Media Can (and Cannot) Facilitate Protest, *The Washington Post* (November 25, 2014), https://www.washingtonpost.com/blogs/monkey-cage/wp/2014/11/25/tweeting-ferguson-how-social-media-can-and-can-not-facilitate-protest/.

36. Clay Shirky, "The Political Power of Social Media," *Foreign Affairs* 90, no. 1 (January/February 2011), 29.

37. George Holliday, "Rodney King Beating Video Full Length Footage Screener," https://www.youtube.com/watch?v=sb1WywIpUtY.

38. For complete narratives of the Rodney King case, see Stacey Koon, *Presumed Guilty: The Tragedy of the Rodney King Affair* (Chicago: Regnery, 1992) and Rodney King, *The Riot Within: My Journey from Rebellion to Redemption* (New York: HarperOne, 2012).

39. See Margaret Hartmann, Jamie Fuller, and Chas Danner, "Everything We Know about the New York Prison Break," *New York Magazine* (June 29, 2015), http://nymag.com/daily/intelligencer/2015/06/; and "2015 Clinton Correctional Facility Escape," Wikipedia, https://en.wikipedia.org/wiki/2015_Clinton_Correctional_Facility_escape.

40. Mark Mazzetti and Michael R. Gordon, "ISIS Is Winning the Social Media War, U.S. Concludes," *New York Times* (June 12, 2015), http://www.nytimes.com/2015/06/13/world/middleeast/isis-is-winning-message-war-us-concludes.html?_r=0.

41. Natalie Johnson, "How ISIS Is Waging a 'War of Ideas' Through Social Media," *The Daily Signal* (June8, 2015), http://dailysignal.com/2015/06/08/how-isis-is-waging-a-war-of-ideas-through-social-media/.

42. Dr. Oliver Roeder and others, *What Caused the Crime Decline?* (New York: Brennan Center for Justice, 2015), https://www.brennancenter.org/sites/default/files/analysis/What_Caused_The_Crime_Decline.pdf.

43. Jennifer L. Truman and Lynn Langton, "Criminal Victimization, 2013," U.S. Department of Justice (September 2014), http://www.bjs.gov/content/pub/pdf/cv13.pdf.

44. Truman, https://www.brennancenter.org/sites/default/files/analysis/What_Caused_The_Crime_Decline.pdf, p. 7.

45. Lauren-Brooke Eisen and Oliver Roeder, "America's Faulty Perception of Crime Rates," *Huffington Post* (May 16, 2015), http://www.huffingtonpost.com/laurenbrooke-eisen/americas-faulty-perceptio_b_6878520.html.

46. Craig Fischer, ed., *Legitimacy and Procedural Justice: A New Element of Police Leadership,*" Police Executive Research Forum (PERF), March 2014, http://www.policeforum.org/assets/docs/Free_Online_Documents/Leadership/legitimacy%20and%20procedural%20justice%20-%20a%20new%20element%20of%20police%20leadership.pdf, p. 2.

47. Fischer, http://www.policeforum.org/assets/docs/Free_Online_Documents/Leadership/legitimacy%20and%20procedural%20justice%20

-%20a%20new%20element%20of%20police%20leadership.pdf, p. 2; President's Task Force, 9.

48. President's Task Force, 11

49. Radley Balko, *Rise of the Warrior Cop: The Militarization of America's Police Forces* (New York: Public Affairs, 2013).

50. Radley Balko, "Guardians, Not Warriors," *The Washington Post* (July 28, 2015), https://www.washingtonpost.com/news/the-watch/wp/2015/07/28/guardians-not-warriors/.

51. Kate Mather, "LAPD Urges Officer to Be Community Guardians, Not Warriors on Crime," *Los Angeles Times* (August 21, 2015), http://www.latimes.com/local/crime/la-me-warrior-guardians-20150821-story.html.

52. Monica Davey and Mitch Smith, "Murder Rates Rising Sharply in Many U.S. Cities," *New York Times* (August 31, 2015), http://www.nytimes.com/2015/09/01/us/murder-rates-rising-sharply-in-many-us-cities.html?_r=1.

53. Max Ehrenfreund, "I Went Looking for the Uptick in Murders in U.S. Cities. Here's What I Found," *The Washington Post* (September 4, 2015), http://www.washingtonpost.com/news/wonkblog/wp/2015/09/04/the-crime-wave-in-u-s-cities-doesnt-show-up-in-the-data/.

54. Ehrenfreund, http://www.washingtonpost.com/news/wonkblog/wp/2015/09/04/the-crime-wave-in-u-s-cities-doesnt-show-up-in-the-data.

55. Mather, http://www.latimes.com/local/crime/la-me-warrior-guardians-20150821-story.html.

56. Ibid.

57. Ibid.

58. Jane Morice, "Baby Shot, Killed on Cleveland's East Side, Police Still Searching for Suspect," Cleveland.com (October 2, 2015), http://www.cleveland.com/metro/index.ssf/2015/10/baby_shot_on_clevelands_east_s.html.

59. See *The Guardian* articles collected at http://www.theguardian.com/world/charlie-hebdo-attack.

60. Holly Bailey, "The Mystery of Tamerlan Tsarnaev's Widow," Yahoo News (April 14, 2014), http://news.yahoo.com/katherine-russell-tsarnaev-boston-marathon-bombing-210147523.html.

61. Adam Chandler, "Boston Bomber Suspected in Triple Homicide, *The Scroll* (April 22, 2013), http://www.tabletmag.com/scroll/130396/boston-bomber-suspected-in-triple-homicide. http://abcnews.go.com/Blotter/boston-bomb-suspect-eyed-connection-2011-triple-murder/story?id=19015628#.UXWWj4JAvlV

62. Tim Lister and Paul Cruickshank, "Dead Boston Bomb Suspect Posted Video of Jihadist, Analysis Shows," CNN (April 22, 2013), http://edition.cnn.com/2013/04/20/us/brother-religious-language.

63. Richard Fausset, "Young Mississippi Couple Linked to ISIS, Perplexing All," *New York Times* (August 14, 2015), http://nyti.ms/1lOgQlk.

64. Chris Thies, "Timeline of Events Leading to the Arrest of Alleged ISIS Recruits," FIX Carolina (August 13, 2015), http://www.foxcarolina.com/story/29784129/timeline-of-events-leading-to-the-arrest-of-alleged-isis-recruits.

65. Globe Editorial, "The Nine Commandments of Policing—which Ferguson Police Forgot," *The Globe and Mail* (August 15, 2014), http://www.theglobeandmail.com/opinion/editorials/the-nine-

commandments-of-policing-and-how-ferguson-police-forgot-them/article20076106/.

66. "Sir Robert Peel's Nine Principles of Policing," *New York Times* (April 15, 2014), http://www.nytimes.com/2014/04/16/nyregion/sir-robert-peels-nine-principles-of-policing.html.

67. NBC New, "Video Shows NYPD Cop Tackle Former Tennis Star James Blake," NBC News (September 11, 2015), http://www.nbcnews.com/news/us-news/video-shows-nypd-cop-tackle-former-tennis-star-james-blake-n426031.

68. Ilya Somin, "Federal Court Rejects Third Amendment Claim against Police Officers," *The Washington Post* (March 23, 2015), https://www.washingtonpost.com/news/volokh-conspiracy/wp/2015/03/23/federal-court-rejects-third-amendment-claim-against-police-officers/.

69. Radley Balko, *Rise of the Warrior Capo: The militarization of America's Police Forces* (New York: Public Affairs, 2013), 280-281.

70. Law Enforcement Working Group, "Recommendations Pursuant to Executive Order 13688 Federal Support for Local Law Enforcement Equipment Acquisition" (May 2015), https://www.whitehouse.gov/sites/default/files/docs/le_equipment_wg_final_report_final.pdf.

71. Darryl Gates, *Chief: My Life in the LAPD* (New York: Bantam, 1992), 104.

72. Michael S. Schmidt and Matt Apuzzo, "F.B.I. Chief Links Scrutiny of Police With Rise in Violent Crime," *New York Times*, October 23, 2015.

73. Ibid.

74. President's Task Force.

75. George L. Kelling and James Q. Wilson, "Broken Windows: The Police and Neighborhood Safety," *The Atlantic* (March 1992), http://www.the-atlantic.com/magazine/archive/1982/03/broken-windows/304465/.

76. Ibid.

77. Ibid.

78. Ibid.

79. Ibid.

80. Ibid.

81. Kelling and Wilson, http://www.theatlantic.com/magazine/ar-chive/1982/03/broken-windows/304465/.

82. Ibid.

83. Ibid.

84. Justin Glawe, "America's Mass-Shooting Capital Is Chicago," *The Daily Beast* (October 8, 2015), http://www.thedailybeast.com/arti-cles/2015/10/08/america-s-mass-shooting-capital-is-chicago.html.

85. Dana Ford, "Chicago Police: 9-Year-Old Tyshawn Lee Lured into Alley, Shot to Death," CNN (November 6, 2015), http://www.cnn.com/2015/11/06/us/chicago-tyshawn-lee-shooting/.

86. Ford, http://www.cnn.com/2015/11/06/us/chicago-tyshawn-lee-shoot-ing/.

87. Jeremy Gorner, "McCarthy Sats 9-Year-Old Boy Targeted, Lured into Alley and Executed, *Chicago Tribune* (November 5, 2015), http://www.chicagotribune.com/news/local/breaking/ct-child-fatally-shot-briefing-met-20151105-story.html.

88. Mary Wisniewski, "Chicago Boy Shot Dead Was Targeted in Gang Rivalry: Police," *Tornto Sun* (November 5, 2015), http://www.toronto-sun.com/2015/11/05/chicago-boy-shot-dead-was-targeted-in-gang-rivalry-police.

89. Gorner, http://www.chicagotribune.com/news/local/breaking/ct-child-fatally-shot-briefing-met-20151105-story.html.

90. President's Task Force, 41.

91. Ibid, 43

92. Michael S. Schmidt and Matt Apuzzo, "South Carolina Officer Is Charged with Murder of Walter Scott," *New York Times* (April 7, 2015), http://www.nytimes.com/2015/04/08/us/south-carolina-officer-is-charged-with-murder-in-black-mans-death.html; Catherine E. Soichet and Chandler Friedman, "Walter Scott Case: Michael Slager Released from Jail After Posting Bond," CNN (January 5, 2016), http://www.cnn.com/2016/01/04/us/south-carolina-michael-slager-bail/.

93. David Montgomery, "New Details Released in Sandra Bland's Death in Texas Jail," *New York Times* (July 20, 2015), http://www.nytimes.com/2015/07/21/us/new-details-released-in-sandra-blands-death-in-texas-jail.html?mtrref=undefined&gwh=C498825151728A7408FC02ADA501E4EE&gwt=pay&assetType=nyt_now; K. K. Rebecca Lai, Haeyoun Park, Larry Buchanan, and Wilson Andres, "Assessing the Legality of Sandra Bland's Arrest," *New York Times* (July 22, 2015), http://www.nytimes.com/interactive/2015/07/20/us/sandra-bland-arrest-death-videos-maps.html.

94. Lai, Park, Buchanan, and Andres, http://www.nytimes.com/interactive/2015/07/20/us/sandra-bland-arrest-death-videos-maps.html.

95. Although a grand jury failed to indict anyone in Sandra Bland's death, Trooper Encinia was indicted on charges of perjury in connection with the incident; Dana Ford and Ed Payne, "Grand Jury Decides against

Indictments in Sandra Bland's Death," CNN (December 23, 2015), http://www.cnn.com/2015/12/21/us/sandra-bland-no-indictments/; Steve Almasy and Chandler Friedman, "Trooper Who Arrested Sandra Bland Indicted on Perjury Charge," CNN (January 6, 2016), http://www.cnn.com/2016/01/06/us/sandra-bland-trooper-brian-encinia-indicted/.

96. Michael Smith, "Video: Ray Tensing's Bodycam Video as He Shot and Killed Sam DuBose (unedited video), YouTube (July 29, 2015), https://www.youtube.com/watch?v=5iL3lj_thsA.

97. Kevin Williams, Wesley Lowery, and Mark Berman, "University of Cincinnati Police Officer Who Shot Man During Traffic Stop Charged with Murder," The Washington Post (July 29, 2015), https://www.washingtonpost.com/news/post-nation/wp/2015/07/29/prosecutors-to-announce-conclusion-of-probe-into-cincinnati-campus-police-shooting/. As of this writing, Officer Tensing, charged with murder and voluntary manslaughter, is awaiting trial, having been released on bail.

98. Insurance Institute for Highway Safety Highway Loss Data Institute, "General Statistics" (2014), http://www.iihs.org/iihs/topics/t/general-statistics/fatalityfacts/state-by-state-overview.

99. President's Task Force, 47.

100. Dana Ford, Greg Botelho, and Kevin Conlon, "Spring Valley High School Officer Suspended after Violent Classroom Arrest," CNN (October 27, 2015), http://www.cnn.com/2015/10/27/us/south-caro-lina-school-arrest-video/. As of this writing, the FBI and U.S. Justice Department were investigating the case; Glen Luke Flanagan, "FBI, U.S. Justice Department Agree to Investigate Spring Valley Incident," The State (October 27, 2015), http://www.thestate.com/news/local/crime/article41523774.html.

101. President's Task Force, 47.

102. Ibid, 32-33.

103. International Association of Chiefs of Police 2015 Social Media Survey Results, http://www.iacpsocialmedia.org/Portals/1/documents/FULL%202015%20Social%20Media%20Survey%20Results.pdf.

104. International Association of Chiefs of Police 2015 Social Media Survey Results, http://www.iacpsocialmedia.org/Portals/1/documents/FULL%202015%20Social%20Media%20Survey%20Results.pdf.

105. President's Task Force, 26.

106. Ibid, 33.

107. Ibid.

108. Lindsay Miller, Jessica Toliver, and Police Executive Research Forum, Implementing a Body-Worn Camera Program: Recommendations and Lessons Learned (Washington, DC: Office of Community Oriented Policing Services, Police Executive Research Forum, 2014), http://ric-zai-inc.com/Publications/cops-p296-pub.pdf.

109. NIJ, http://www.nij.gov/Pages/welcome.aspx.

110. President's Task Force, 33.

111. The best brief but comprehensive overview of the 2015 San Bernardino attack is found on Wikipedia, https://en.wikipedia.org/wiki/2015_San_Bernardino_attack.

112. Police Executive Research Forum, Future Trends in Policing (Washington, D.C.: Office of Community Oriented Policing Services, 2014), 48.

113. William J. Woska, "Police Officer Recruitment: A Public-Sector Crisis," The Police Chief (February 2016), http://www.policechiefmagazine.org/

magazine/index.cfm?fuseaction=display&article_id=1020&issue_id=102006.

114. Oliver Yates Libaw, "Police Face Severe Shortage of Recruits," ABC News (July 10, 2015), http://abcnews.go.com/US/story?id=96570&page=1.

115. Libaw, http://abcnews.go.com/US/story?id=96570&page=1.

116. John Henry Cardinal Newman, The Idea of a University Defined and Illustrated (1858; London: Longmans, Green, and Co., 1907), 101-103.

117. President's Task Force, 59.

118. Kieran Corcoran, "'I'll Take a Bullet Before You Do—That's for Damn Sure': Moment Brave Cop Reassures Terrified Workers He'll Protect Them from San Bernardino Massacre Couple," Daily Mail (December 3, 2015), http://www.dailymail.co.uk/news/article-3344487/Moment-brave-San-Bernardino-cop-reassures-terrified-workers-ll-protect-massacre.html.

119. Natalie Bonfine, Christian Ritter, and Mark R. Munetz, "Police Officer Perceptions of the Impact of Crisis Intervention Team (CIT) Programs," International Journal of Law and Psychiatry 37, no. 4 (July–August 2014): 341–350, doi:10.1016/j.ijlp.2014.02.004.

120. President's Task Force, 56-57.

121. Ibid, 1.

122. Ibid, 11; Sue Rahr, "Transforming the Culture of Policing from Warriors to Guardians in Washington State," International Association of Directors of Law Enforcement Standards and Training Newsletter 25, no. 4 (2014): 3–4; see also Sue Rahr and Stephen K. Rice, "From Warriors to Guardians: Recommitting American Police Culture to Democratic Ideals," New Perspectives in Policing Bulletin

(Washington, DC: National Institute of Justice, 2015), NCJ 248654, http://www.hks.harvard.edu/ content/download/76023/1708385/version/1/file/ ; WarriorstoGuardians.pdf. For Plato's own discussion of the guardians, see The Republic, Books II, III, and V (in, for example, Scot Buchanan, ed., The Portable Plato [New York: Viking, 1948]).

123. President's Task Force, 11-12.

124. Quinn Ford, "Cops: Boy, 17, Fatally Shot by Officer after Refusing to Drop Knife," Chicago Tribune (October 21, 2014), http://www.chicagotribune.com/news/local/breaking/chi-chicago-shootings-violence-20141021-story.html.

125. Carol Marin and Don Moseley, "Chicago Police Dashboard Cameras Questioned in Death of Teen Shot by Cop," 5 NBC Chicago (November 13, 2015), http://www.nbcchicago.com/investigations/Police-Dashboard-Cameras-Questioned-347836441.html.

126. Marin and Moseley, http://www.nbcchicago.com/investigations/Police-Dashboard-Cameras-Questioned-347836441.html.

127. Carol Marin and Don Moseley, "Missing Minutes from Security Video Raises Questions," 5 NBC Chicago (May 26, 2015),http://www.nbcchicago.com/investigations/laquan-mcdonald-investigation-305105631.html.

128. Gregory Krieg, "Illinois Lawmaker Introduces 'Recall Rahm' Bill as Protests Continue," CNN, December 10, 2015, http://www.cnn.com/2015/12/10/politics/rahm-emanuel-recall-bill-protests/.

129. President's Task Force, 16

Acknowledgements

This book is the product of my life and career, and I want to thank the people who have contributed the most to both. There are, first, my mother, Juanita Scott; my late father, Will Alexander; and my stepfather, Richard Wilson Sr. They were and remain my role models and my support.

My daughter, Adrienne Alexander, has proven to be a wonderful person who, all of her life, has stayed close to the will of God and has devoted herself to helping people through her Christianity.

And there are the people in my professional life. The late Raymond Hamlin, long-time sheriff of Leon County, Florida, opened the door to my four decades in law enforcement. Ken Katsaris, who succeeded Raymond Hamlin as Leon County sheriff, gave me my first job as a deputy. His enlightened leadership guided me through my earliest years as a lawman.

I have not seen Major Doug Hughes in many years, but serving under him in the Miami-Dade Police Department awakened in me a passion for community policing. Major Hughes championed this approach when few had even heard about it and before it even had a name. A visionary, he saw years down the road what modern policing needed to be.

I need as well to acknowledge and thank William "Bill" Johnson, former mayor of Rochester, New York, who recruited me as deputy chief of the Rochester Police Department and gave me the opportunity to apply all that I had learned as a police officer and a practicing clinical psychologist to helping that great department serve a challenged but vibrant community.

And to my dear friend Pastor Kenneth Dean, I offer my thanks and gratitude. He is a Christian whose personal and professional history is that of a man who stood at the door of righteousness and democracy for all people during the Civil Rights movement. His enduring friendship and loyalty have been more precious than gold.

There are those family and friends who have come into this world and have gone on to a better place. No matter how long or short a role you played in my life, I will never forget you in my life's journey. To Denise, you are gone, but, I will never forget you as I feel you still look over me.

Finally, my sincere thanks and deep respect to all the men and women in law enforcement across our nation. Despite the dangers, they put it on the line every day.

Made in the USA
Middletown, DE
14 July 2016